Simpsons Comics
BIG BONANZA

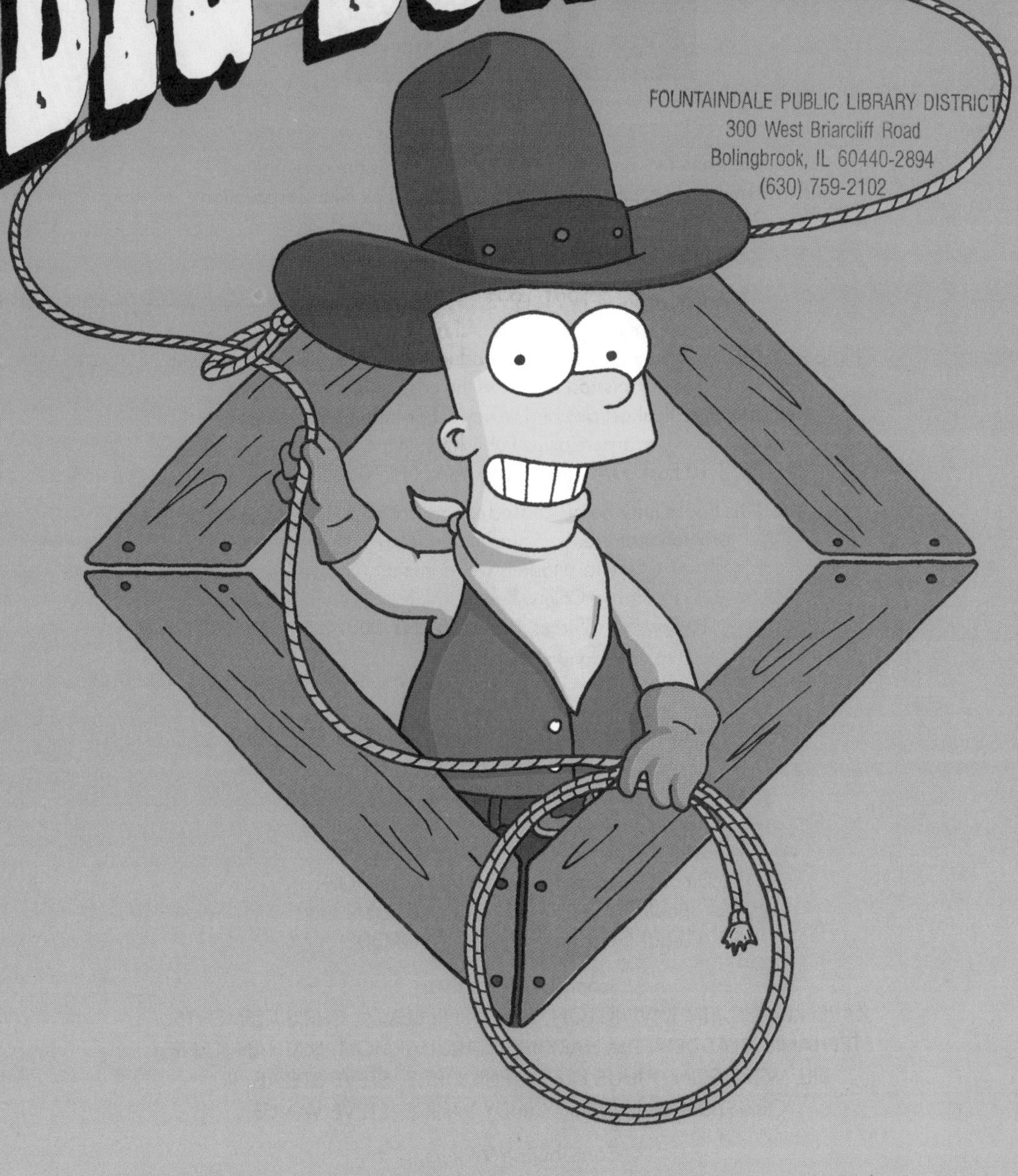

HARPER

NEW YORK • LONDON • TORONTO • SYDNEY

To the loving memory of Snowball I:
You are missed every day because we can't
find your burial marker in the backyard.

SIMPSONS COMICS BIG BONANZA

Copyright ©1991,1993,1997 & 1998 by
Bongo Entertainment, Inc. All rights reserved.
No part of this book may be used or reproduced in any manner whatsoever
without written permission except in the case of brief quotations
embodied in critical articles and reviews. For information address:
HarperCollins Publishers, Inc.
10 East 53rd Street, New York, NY 10022

HarperCollins books may be purchased for educational, business,or sales
promotional use. For information, please write:
Special Markets Department
HarperCollins Publishers, Inc.
10 East 53rd Street, New York, NY 10022

FIRST EDITION

ISBN 978-0-060953-17-1

12 13 14 SCP 10 9 8 7

Publisher: MATT GROENING
Art Director / Editor: BILL MORRISON
Managing Editor: TERRY DELEGEANE
Director of Operations: ROBERT ZAUGH
Book Design: MARILYN FRANDSEN
Legal Guardian: SUSAN A. GRODE

Contributing Artists:
KAREN BATES, TIM BAVINGTON, JEANNINE BLACK, CHRIS CLEMENTS,
STEPHANIE GLADDEN, TIM HARKINS, CARL HARMON, NATHAN KANE,
BILL MORRISON, JULIUS PREITE, PHIL ORTIZ, STEVE STEERE, JR.,
CHRISTOPHER UNGAR, CINDY VANCE, STEVE VANCE

Contributing Writers:
SCOTT M. GIMPLE, GARY GLASBERG, JIM LINCOLN, BILL MORRISON,
JEFF ROSENTHAL, DAN STUDNEY, CINDY VANCE, STEVE VANCE, ROB WALTON

Printed in China

CONTENTS

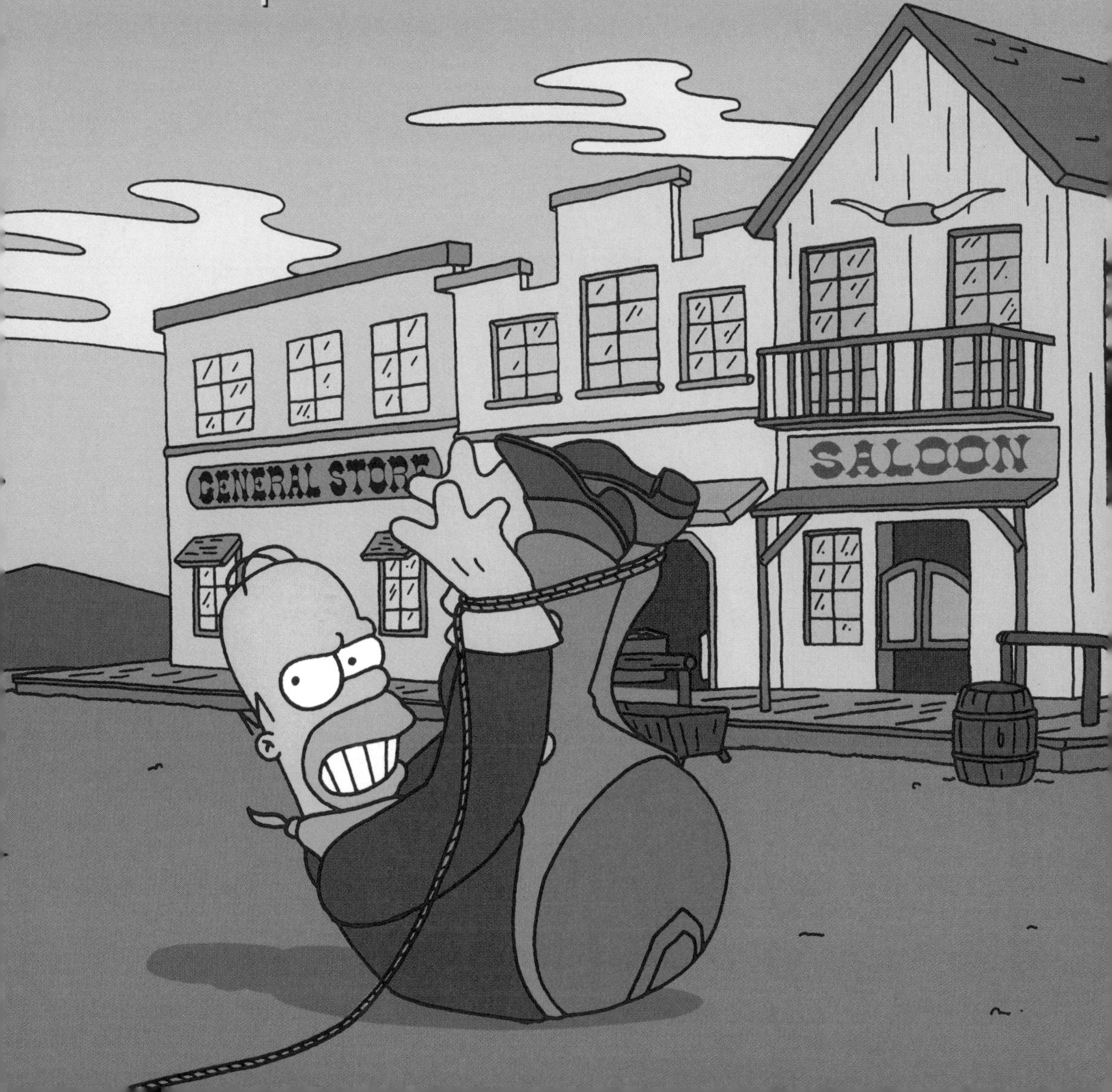

GENERAL STORE
SALOON

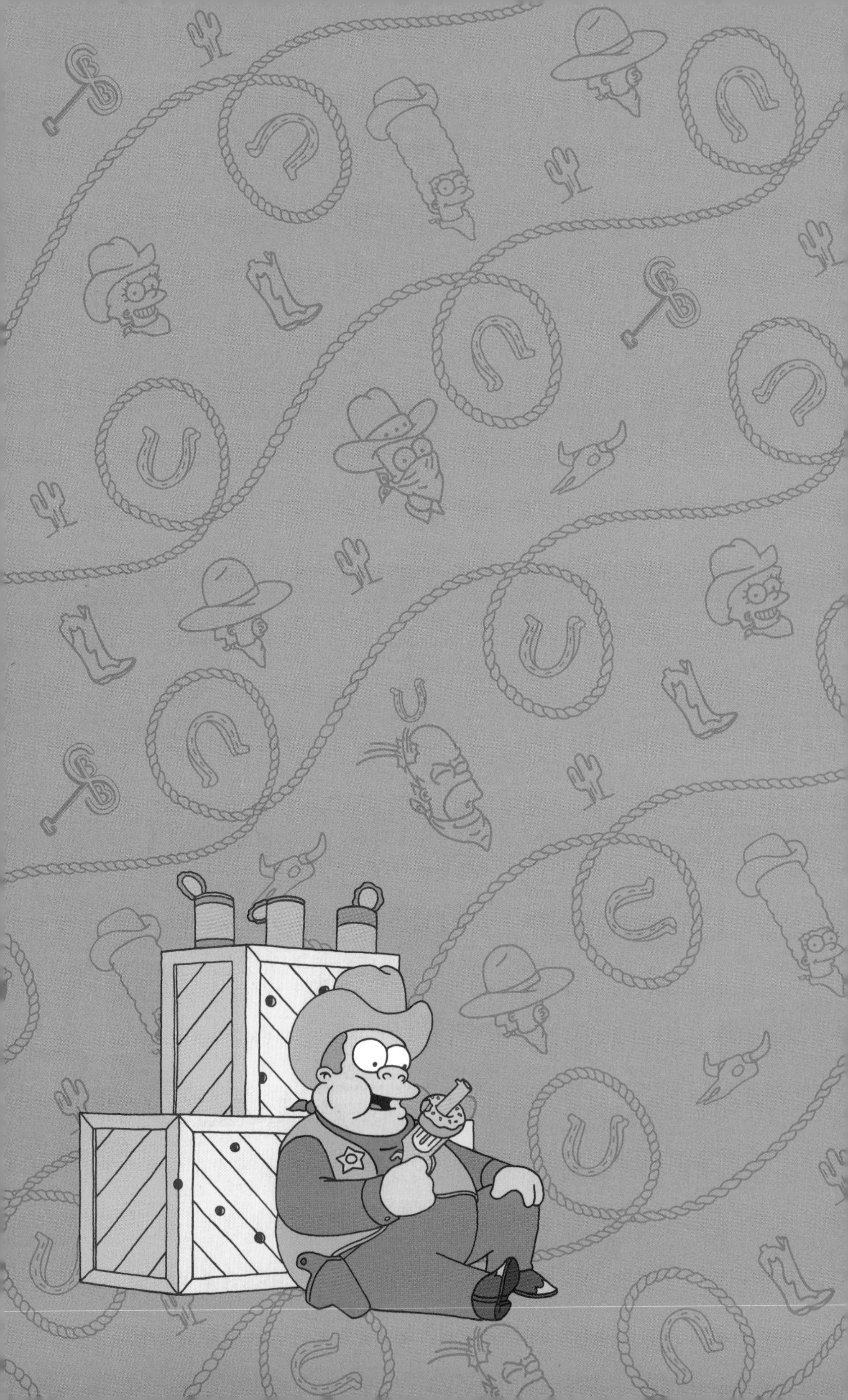

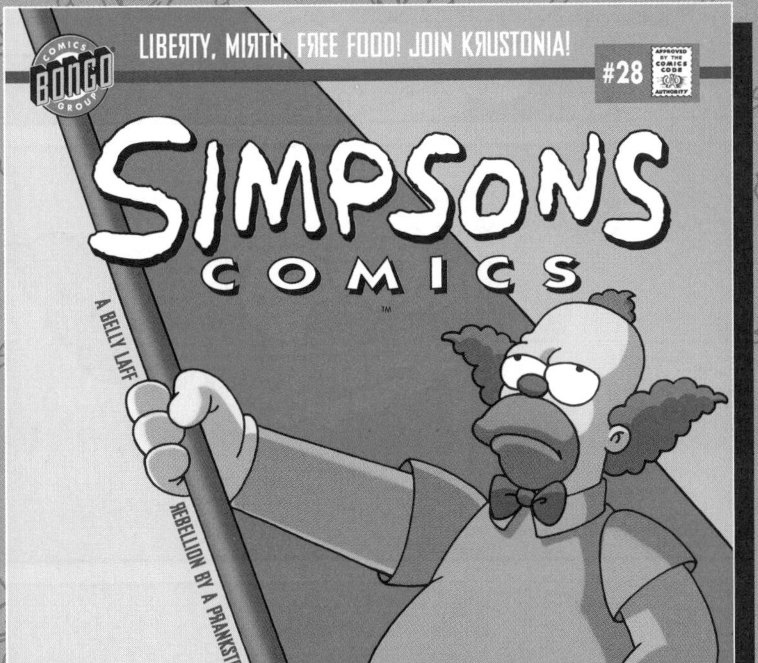

LIBERTY, MIRTH, FREE FOOD! JOIN KRUSTONIA!
BONGO COMICS GROUP
#28
SIMPSONS COMICS
A BELLY LAFF
REBELLION BY A PRANKSTER'S PROLETARIAT!
GROENING

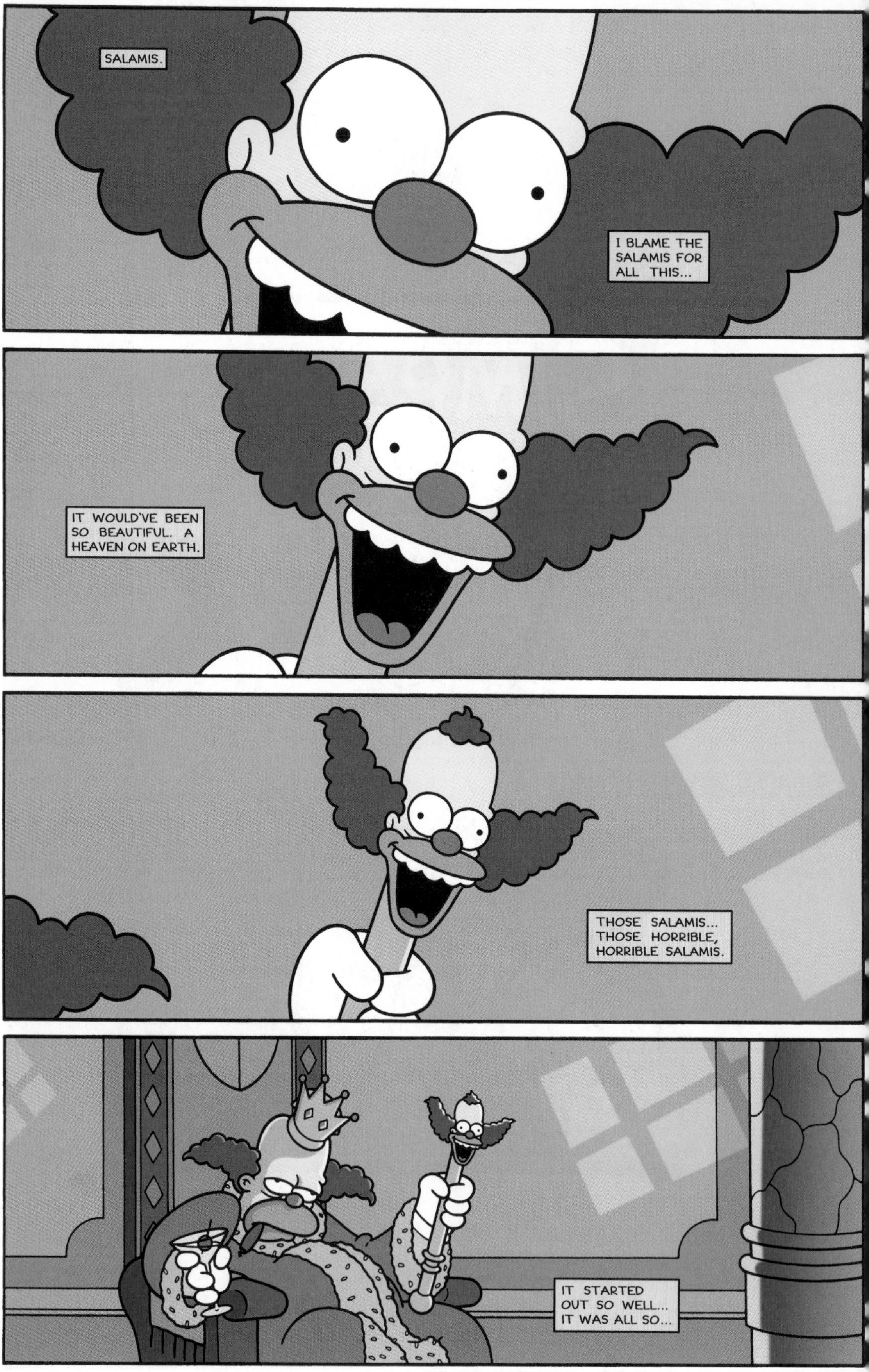
SALAMIS.
I BLAME THE SALAMIS FOR ALL THIS...
IT WOULD'VE BEEN SO BEAUTIFUL. A HEAVEN ON EARTH.
THOSE SALAMIS... THOSE HORRIBLE, HORRIBLE SALAMIS.
IT STARTED OUT SO WELL... IT WAS ALL SO...

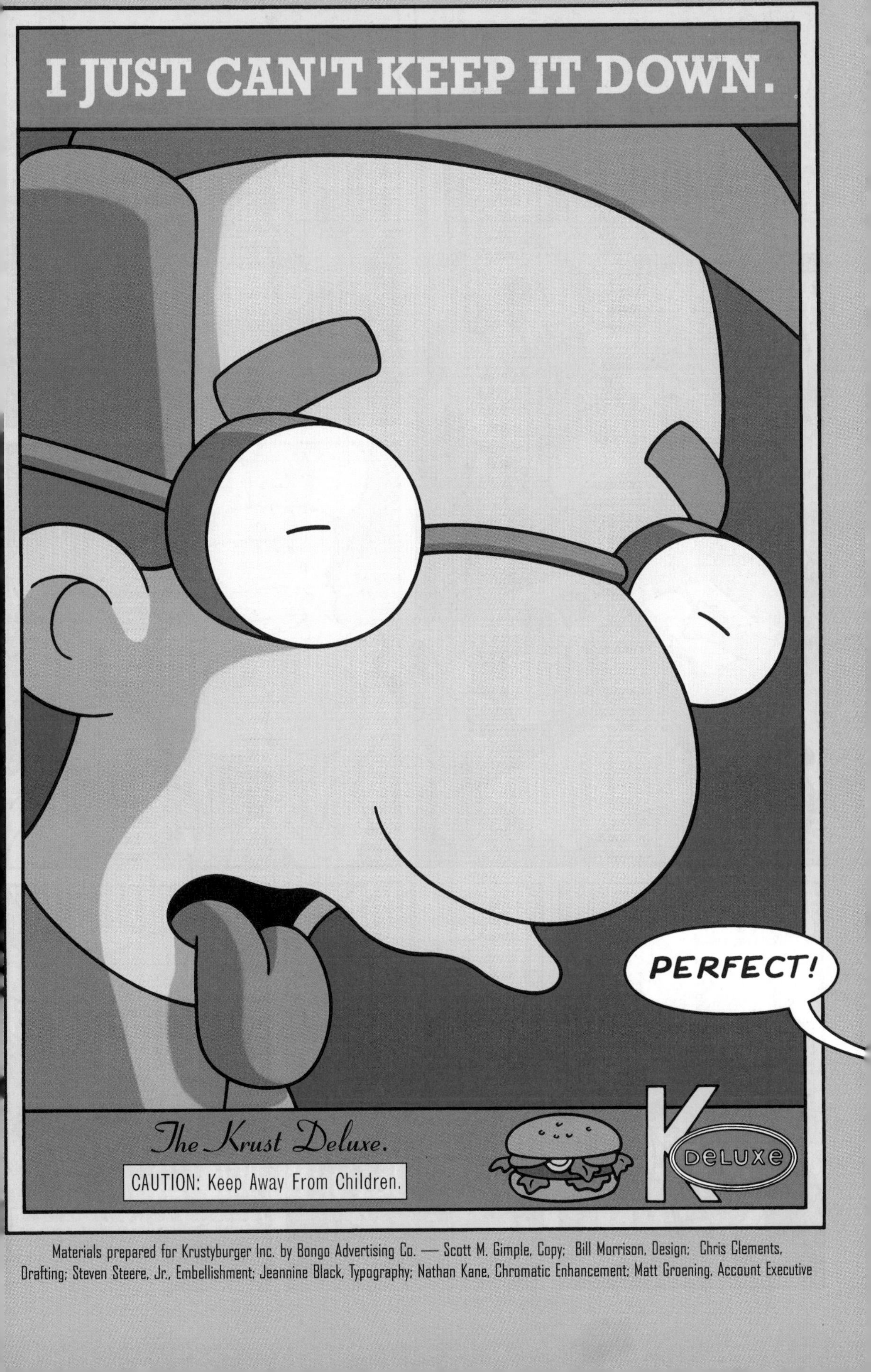
I JUST CAN'T KEEP IT DOWN.
PERFECT!
The Krust Deluxe.
CAUTION: Keep Away From Children.
DELUXE

Materials prepared for Krustyburger Inc. by Bongo Advertising Co. — Scott M. Gimple, Copy; Bill Morrison, Design; Chris Clements, Drafting; Steven Steere, Jr., Embellishment; Jeannine Black, Typography; Nathan Kane, Chromatic Enhancement; Matt Groening, Account Executive

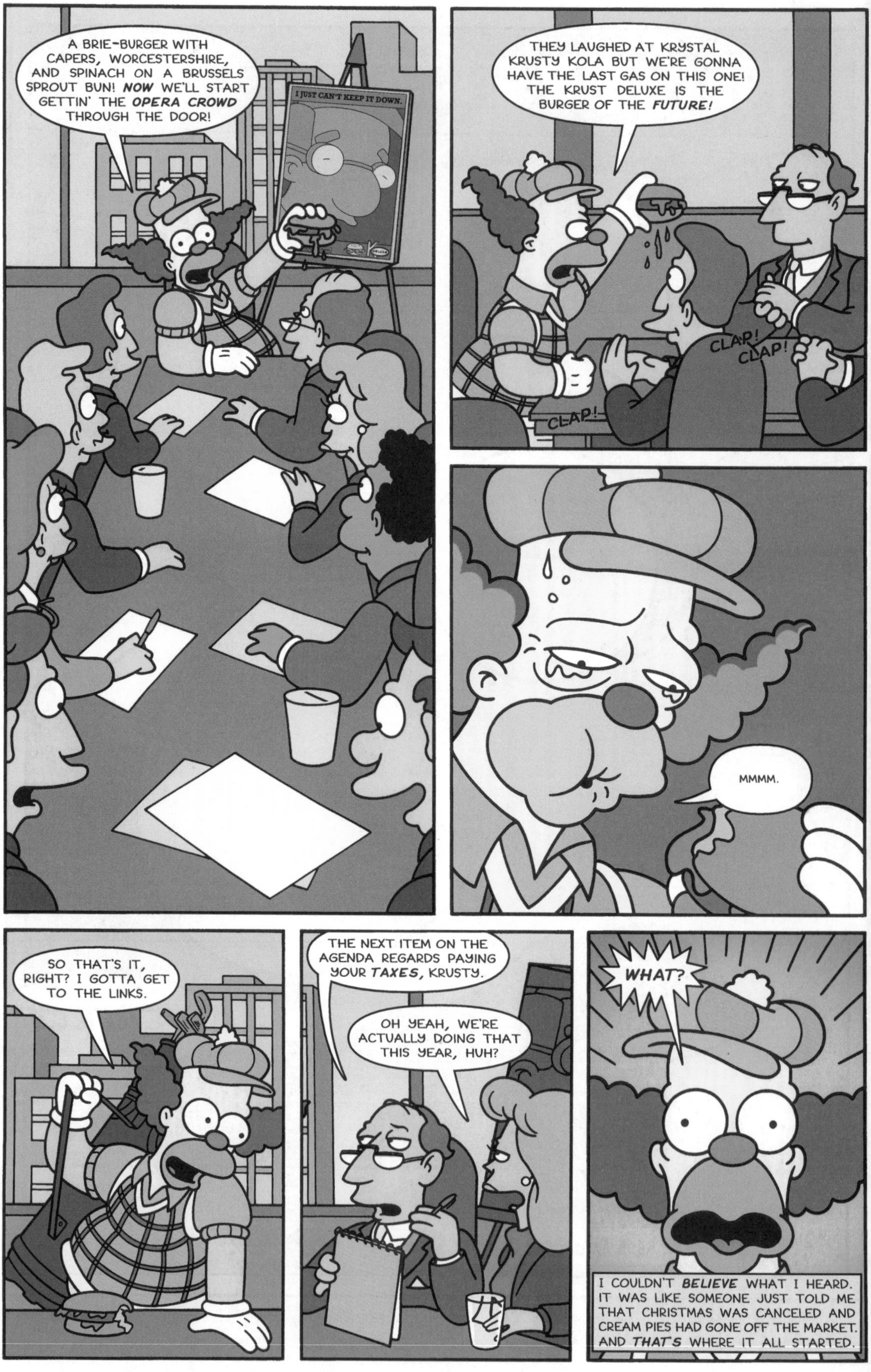
A BRIE-BURGER WITH CAPERS, WORCESTERSHIRE, AND SPINACH ON A BRUSSELS SPROUT BUN! NOW WE'LL START GETTIN' THE OPERA CROWD THROUGH THE DOOR!
I JUST CAN'T KEEP IT DOWN.
THEY LAUGHED AT KRYSTAL KRUSTY KOLA BUT WE'RE GONNA HAVE THE LAST GAS ON THIS ONE! THE KRUST DELUXE IS THE BURGER OF THE FUTURE!
CLAP!
CLAP!
CLAP!
MMMM.
SO THAT'S IT, RIGHT? I GOTTA GET TO THE LINKS.
THE NEXT ITEM ON THE AGENDA REGARDS PAYING YOUR TAXES, KRUSTY.
OH YEAH, WE'RE ACTUALLY DOING THAT THIS YEAR, HUH?
WHAT?
I COULDN'T BELIEVE WHAT I HEARD. IT WAS LIKE SOMEONE JUST TOLD ME THAT CHRISTMAS WAS CANCELED AND CREAM PIES HAD GONE OFF THE MARKET. AND THAT'S WHERE IT ALL STARTED.

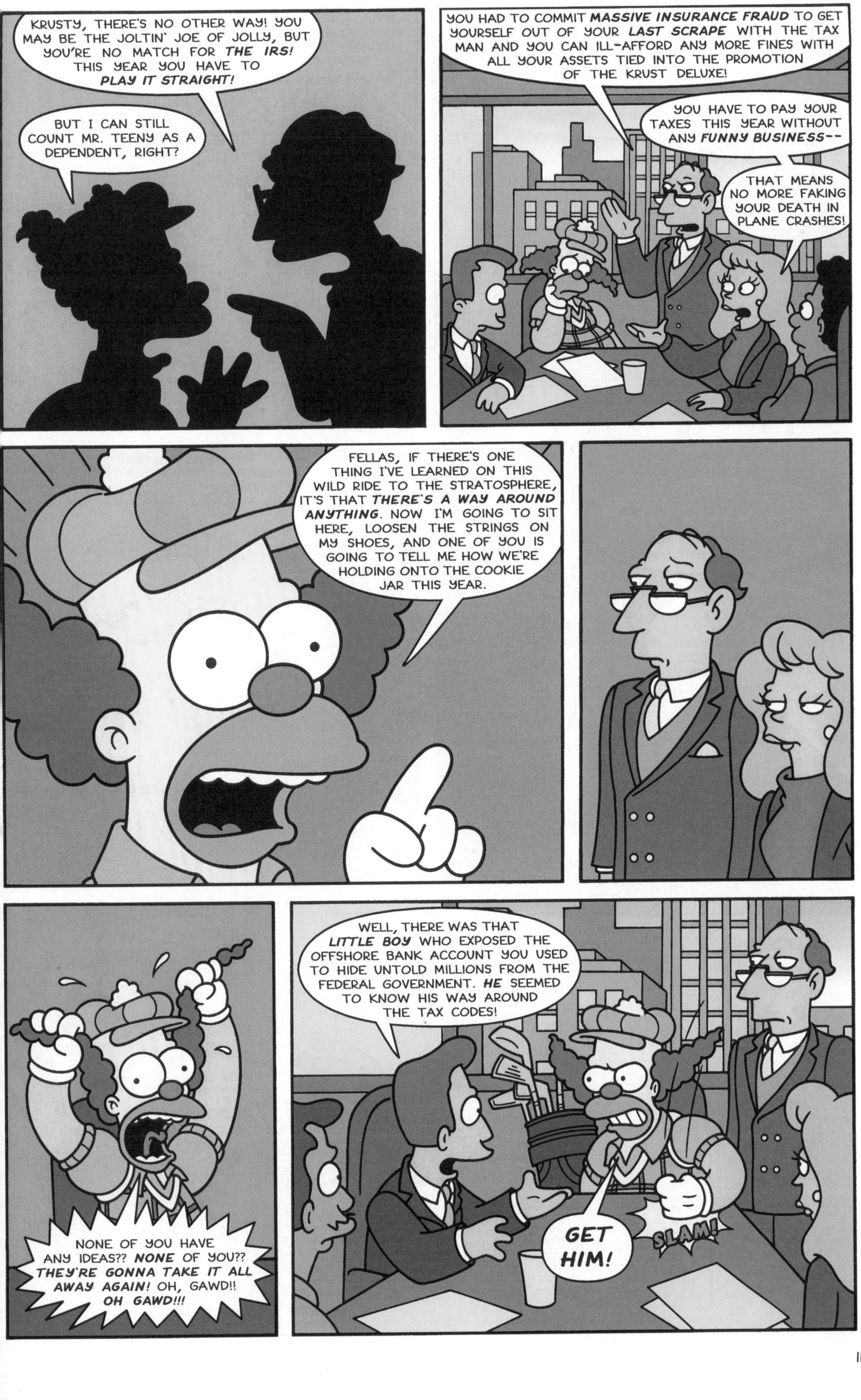
KRUSTY, THERE'S NO OTHER WAY! YOU MAY BE THE JOLTIN' JOE OF JOLLY, BUT YOU'RE NO MATCH FOR THE IRS! THIS YEAR YOU HAVE TO PLAY IT STRAIGHT!
BUT I CAN STILL COUNT MR. TEENY AS A DEPENDENT, RIGHT?
YOU HAD TO COMMIT MASSIVE INSURANCE FRAUD TO GET YOURSELF OUT OF YOUR LAST SCRAPE WITH THE TAX MAN AND YOU CAN ILL-AFFORD ANY MORE FINES WITH ALL YOUR ASSETS TIED INTO THE PROMOTION OF THE KRUST DELUXE!
YOU HAVE TO PAY YOUR TAXES THIS YEAR WITHOUT ANY FUNNY BUSINESS--
THAT MEANS NO MORE FAKING YOUR DEATH IN PLANE CRASHES!
FELLAS, IF THERE'S ONE THING I'VE LEARNED ON THIS WILD RIDE TO THE STRATOSPHERE, IT'S THAT THERE'S A WAY AROUND ANYTHING. NOW I'M GOING TO SIT HERE, LOOSEN THE STRINGS ON MY SHOES, AND ONE OF YOU IS GOING TO TELL ME HOW WE'RE HOLDING ONTO THE COOKIE JAR THIS YEAR.
NONE OF YOU HAVE ANY IDEAS?? NONE OF YOU?? THEY'RE GONNA TAKE IT ALL AWAY AGAIN! OH, GAWD!! OH GAWD!!!
WELL, THERE WAS THAT LITTLE BOY WHO EXPOSED THE OFFSHORE BANK ACCOUNT YOU USED TO HIDE UNTOLD MILLIONS FROM THE FEDERAL GOVERNMENT. HE SEEMED TO KNOW HIS WAY AROUND THE TAX CODES!
GET HIM!
SLAM!

HI, I'M *TROY MCCLURE*. YOU MAY REMEMBER ME FROM *OTHER* CORPORATE-SPONSORED EDUCATIONAL TELEVISION SEGMENTS LIKE "*SHELLRON'S COLONIALISM SHAMOLONIALISM-- WE CALL IT WORK*" AND "*SCHEVITZCO'S 16 MINUTES ON THE MEANING OF MATZOH*."

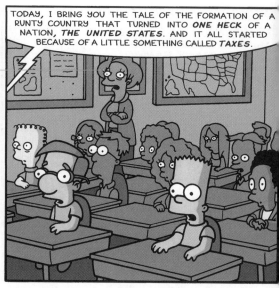

TODAY, I BRING YOU THE TALE OF THE FORMATION OF A RUNTY COUNTRY THAT TURNED INTO *ONE HECK* OF A NATION, *THE UNITED STATES*. AND IT ALL STARTED BECAUSE OF A LITTLE SOMETHING CALLED *TAXES*.

FORTY MINUTES LATER...

HMMM...ALL THAT TALK ABOUT THE *TEA PARTY'S* MADE ME *THIRSTY*. BOY, COULD I GO FOR A NICE, ICY GLASS OF *NESCATEA* RIGHT NOW!

I'LL HAVE TO *PAY* SOME *SALES TAX* ON THAT -- BUT AT LEAST I KNOW I'M *REPRESENTED IN CONGRESS*. I'M TROY MCCLURE. THANKS FOR WATCHING!

ALL RIGHT CHILDREN, TIME FOR RECESS. CANS OF NESCATEA WILL BE AVAILABLE FOR PURCHASE OUT BY THE JUNGLE GYM.

THIS SUCKS. EVERY TIME WE BUY AN ISH OF RADIOACTIVE MAN, *TWENTY CENTS* GOES TO THE GOVERNMENT, AND DO WE SEE ANY OF THOSE *FAT CAT POLITICOS* GIVING A RIP ABOUT *OUR* CONCERNS?

C'MON BART! SHHHH!

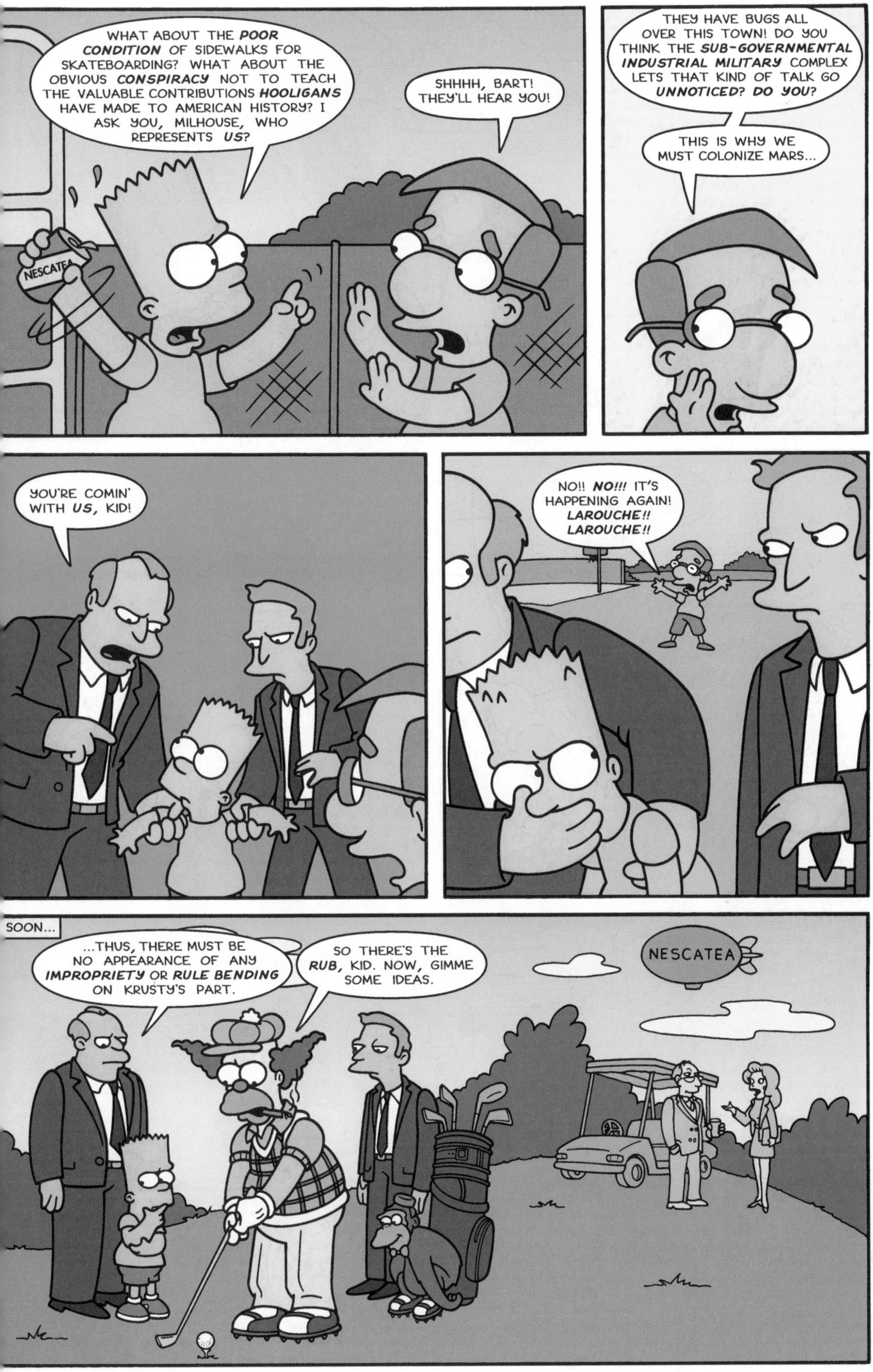
WHAT ABOUT THE POOR CONDITION OF SIDEWALKS FOR SKATEBOARDING? WHAT ABOUT THE OBVIOUS CONSPIRACY NOT TO TEACH THE VALUABLE CONTRIBUTIONS HOOLIGANS HAVE MADE TO AMERICAN HISTORY? I ASK YOU, MILHOUSE, WHO REPRESENTS US?
NESCATEA
SHHHH, BART! THEY'LL HEAR YOU!
THEY HAVE BUGS ALL OVER THIS TOWN! DO YOU THINK THE SUB-GOVERNMENTAL INDUSTRIAL MILITARY COMPLEX LETS THAT KIND OF TALK GO UNNOTICED? DO YOU?
THIS IS WHY WE MUST COLONIZE MARS...
YOU'RE COMIN' WITH US, KID!
NO!! NO!!! IT'S HAPPENING AGAIN! LAROUCHE!! LAROUCHE!!
SOON...
...THUS, THERE MUST BE NO APPEARANCE OF ANY IMPROPRIETY OR RULE BENDING ON KRUSTY'S PART.
SO THERE'S THE RUB, KID. NOW, GIMME SOME IDEAS.
NESCATEA

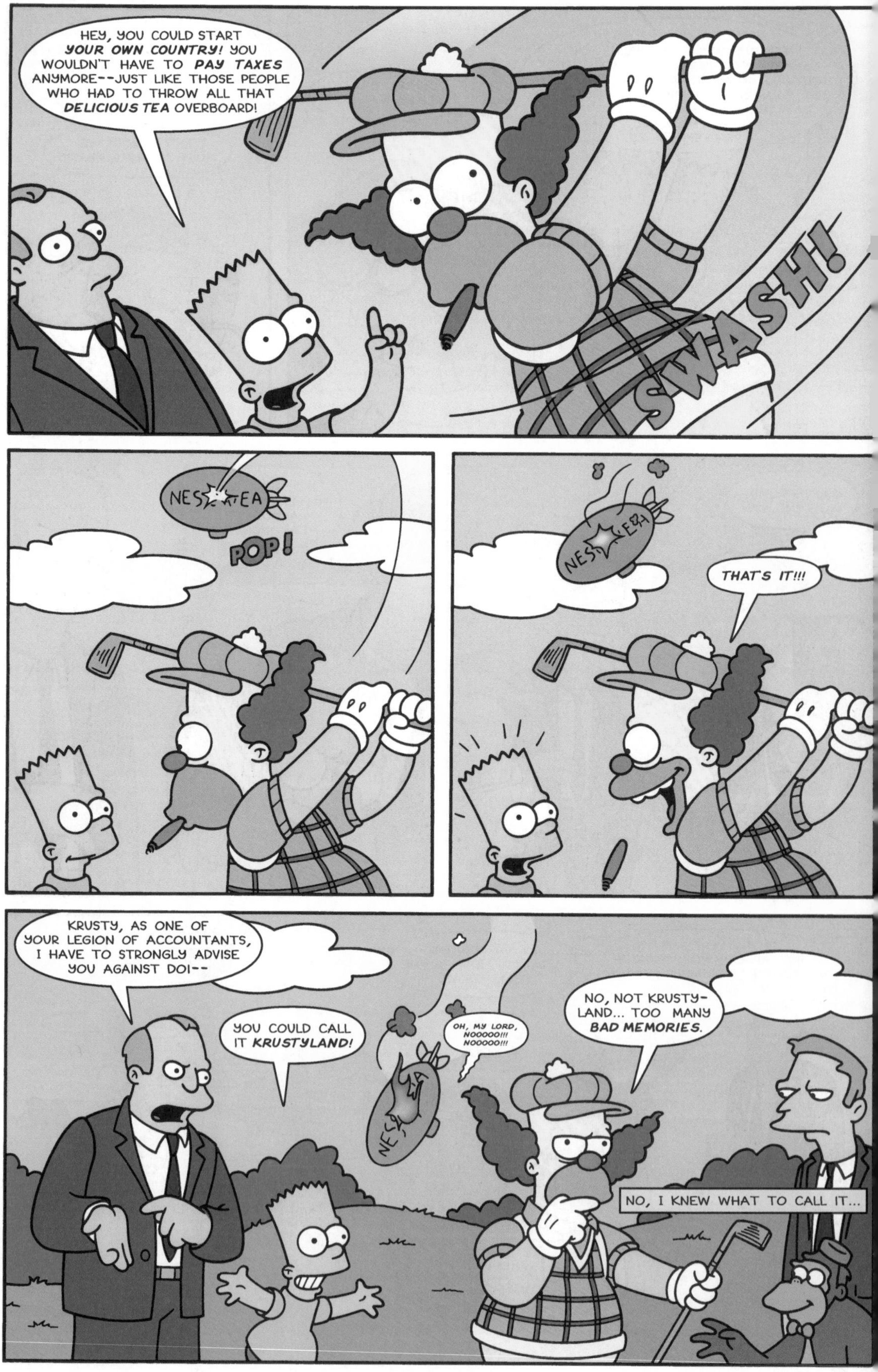
HEY, YOU COULD START YOUR OWN COUNTRY! YOU WOULDN'T HAVE TO PAY TAXES ANYMORE--JUST LIKE THOSE PEOPLE WHO HAD TO THROW ALL THAT DELICIOUS TEA OVERBOARD!
SWASH!
POP!
THAT'S IT!!!
KRUSTY, AS ONE OF YOUR LEGION OF ACCOUNTANTS, I HAVE TO STRONGLY ADVISE YOU AGAINST DOI--
YOU COULD CALL IT KRUSTYLAND!
OH, MY LORD, NOOOOO!!! NOOOOO!!!
NO, NOT KRUSTY-LAND... TOO MANY BAD MEMORIES.
NO, I KNEW WHAT TO CALL IT...

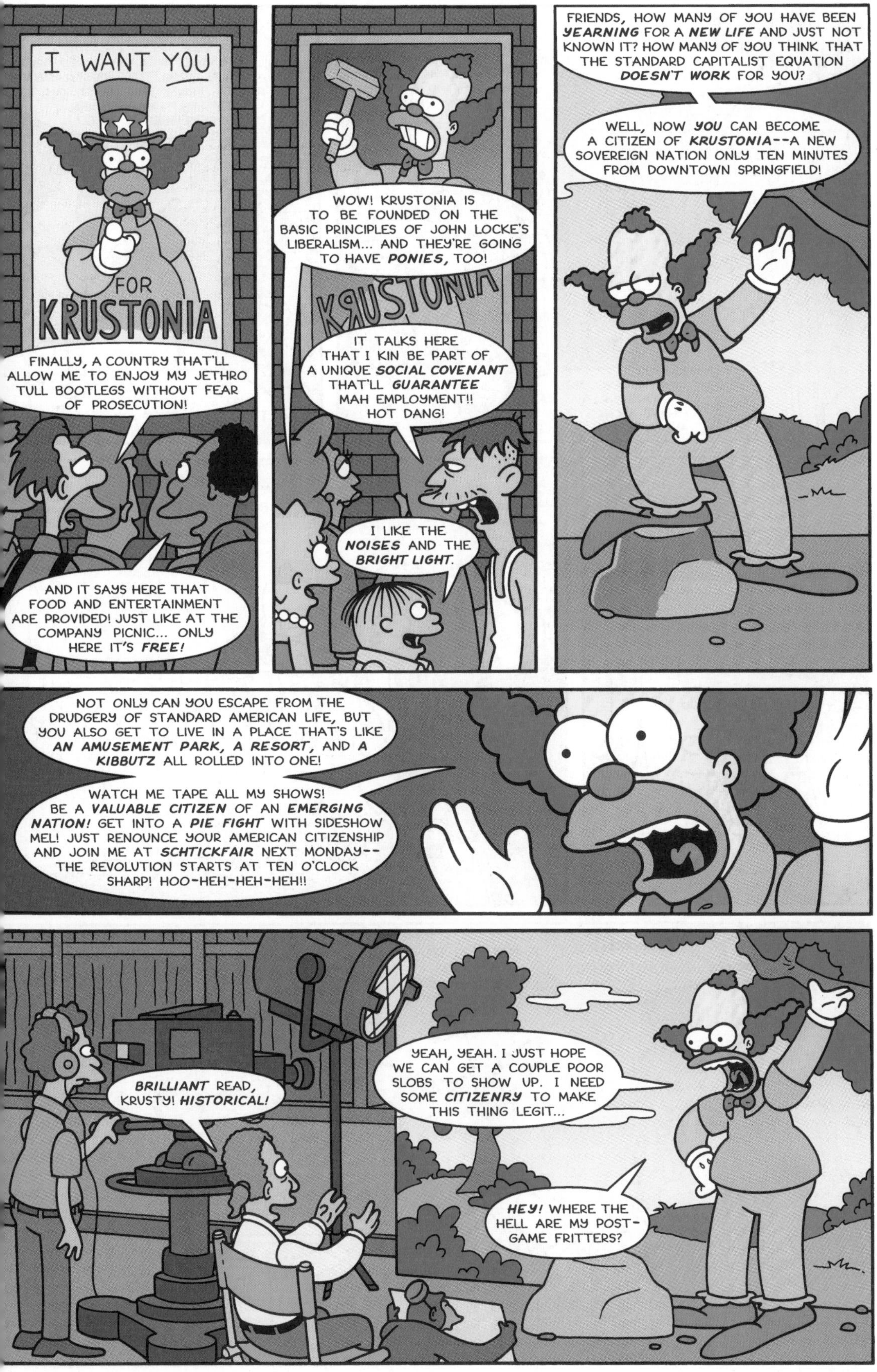
I WANT YOU FOR KRUSTONIA
FINALLY, A COUNTRY THAT'LL ALLOW ME TO ENJOY MY JETHRO TULL BOOTLEGS WITHOUT FEAR OF PROSECUTION!
AND IT SAYS HERE THAT FOOD AND ENTERTAINMENT ARE PROVIDED! JUST LIKE AT THE COMPANY PICNIC... ONLY HERE IT'S FREE!
KRUSTONIA
WOW! KRUSTONIA IS TO BE FOUNDED ON THE BASIC PRINCIPLES OF JOHN LOCKE'S LIBERALISM... AND THEY'RE GOING TO HAVE PONIES, TOO!
IT TALKS HERE THAT I KIN BE PART OF A UNIQUE SOCIAL COVENANT THAT'LL GUARANTEE MAH EMPLOYMENT!! HOT DANG!
I LIKE THE NOISES AND THE BRIGHT LIGHT.
FRIENDS, HOW MANY OF YOU HAVE BEEN YEARNING FOR A NEW LIFE AND JUST NOT KNOWN IT? HOW MANY OF YOU THINK THAT THE STANDARD CAPITALIST EQUATION DOESN'T WORK FOR YOU?
WELL, NOW YOU CAN BECOME A CITIZEN OF KRUSTONIA--A NEW SOVEREIGN NATION ONLY TEN MINUTES FROM DOWNTOWN SPRINGFIELD!
NOT ONLY CAN YOU ESCAPE FROM THE DRUDGERY OF STANDARD AMERICAN LIFE, BUT YOU ALSO GET TO LIVE IN A PLACE THAT'S LIKE AN AMUSEMENT PARK, A RESORT, AND A KIBBUTZ ALL ROLLED INTO ONE!
WATCH ME TAPE ALL MY SHOWS! BE A VALUABLE CITIZEN OF AN EMERGING NATION! GET INTO A PIE FIGHT WITH SIDESHOW MEL! JUST RENOUNCE YOUR AMERICAN CITIZENSHIP AND JOIN ME AT SCHTICKFAIR NEXT MONDAY--THE REVOLUTION STARTS AT TEN O'CLOCK SHARP! HOO-HEH-HEH-HEH!!
BRILLIANT READ, KRUSTY! HISTORICAL!
YEAH, YEAH. I JUST HOPE WE CAN GET A COUPLE POOR SLOBS TO SHOW UP. I NEED SOME CITIZENRY TO MAKE THIS THING LEGIT...
HEY! WHERE THE HELL ARE MY POST-GAME FRITTERS?

I JUST DON'T KNOW ABOUT THIS, HOMEY.

MAAARGE! THAT INFOMERCIAL *SPOKE* TO ME! IT'S BEEN MY LIFELONG DREAM TO LEAVE AMERICA BEHIND TO FIND A *LAND OF OPPORTUNITY*!

I THOUGHT YOUR LIFELONG DREAM WAS TO HAVE A *CHEESE* NAMED AFTER YOU! REMEMBER?

OH, I *REMEMBER!* I REMEMBER SIRENS AND LIGHTS! MILK SPLASHED AGAINST A RED BRICK WALL! THE TRIAL! THE *RESTRAINING ORDER* FROM THE DAIRY! OH, I REMEMBER MARGE! YES, I REMEMBER IT *WELL!*

BESIDES, MOM, *A VOTE IS A VOTE!* THREE FOR, YOU AGAINST, MAGGIE ABSTAINING.

I'M SORRY, BUT THIS COULD BE A CHANCE TO BE A PART OF *HISTORY*-- TO WELCOME A BRAVE, NEW WORLD INTO EXISTENCE!!

I'M GOING TO NAME MY PONY *ALDOUS*.

LET'S SEE HOW MANY CHUMPS SHOWED UP...

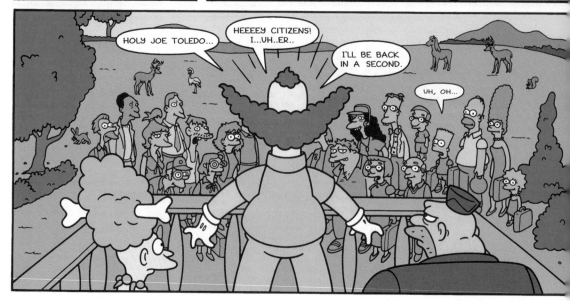

HOLY JOE TOLEDO...

HEEEEY CITIZENS! I...UH..ER..

I'LL BE BACK IN A SECOND.

UH, OH...

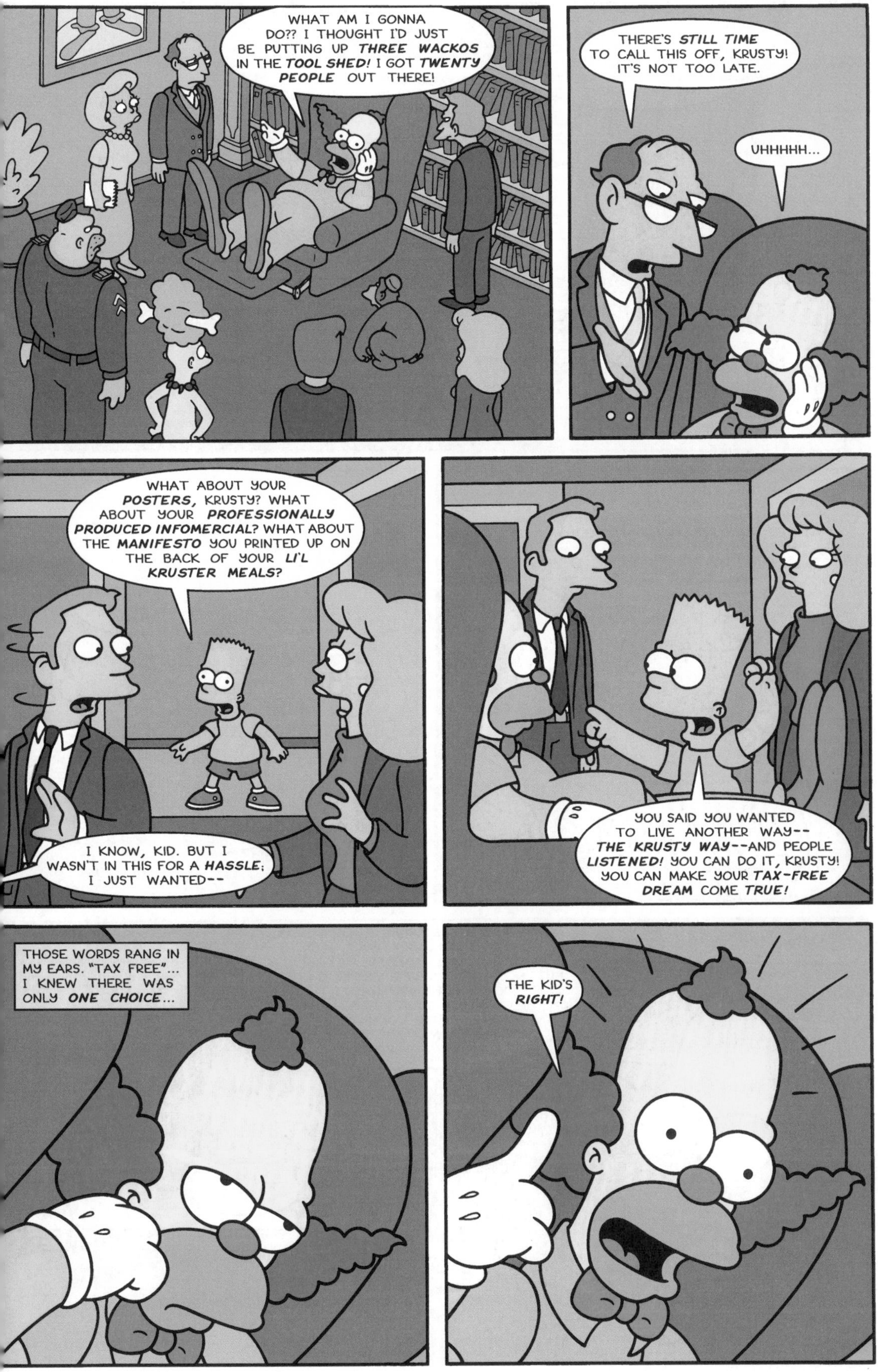
WHAT AM I GONNA DO?? I THOUGHT I'D JUST BE PUTTING UP THREE WACKOS IN THE TOOL SHED! I GOT TWENTY PEOPLE OUT THERE!
THERE'S STILL TIME TO CALL THIS OFF, KRUSTY! IT'S NOT TOO LATE.
UHHHHH...
WHAT ABOUT YOUR POSTERS, KRUSTY? WHAT ABOUT YOUR PROFESSIONALLY PRODUCED INFOMERCIAL? WHAT ABOUT THE MANIFESTO YOU PRINTED UP ON THE BACK OF YOUR LI'L KRUSTER MEALS?
I KNOW, KID. BUT I WASN'T IN THIS FOR A HASSLE; I JUST WANTED--
YOU SAID YOU WANTED TO LIVE ANOTHER WAY-- THE KRUSTY WAY--AND PEOPLE LISTENED! YOU CAN DO IT, KRUSTY! YOU CAN MAKE YOUR TAX-FREE DREAM COME TRUE!
THOSE WORDS RANG IN MY EARS. "TAX FREE"... I KNEW THERE WAS ONLY ONE CHOICE...
THE KID'S RIGHT!

OKAY! *SIDESHOW MEL*, GO WITH MR. TEENY AND PACK UP THE STUDIO--FROM NOW ON, WE'RE SHOOTIN' THE SHOW *HERE!*

CORPORAL PUNISHMENT, GET OUR TRAILERS OUT HERE AND FIX 'EM UP FOR *MY PEOPLE*-- THAT MEANS TAKE OUT THE YOU-KNOW-WHAT-GRAPHY!

MS. PENNYCANDY! GET ME OL' MAN GIBBERSON AT THE DISCOUNT INDUSTRIAL FEED N' SEED WAREHOUSE! I NEED *FOOD* FOR MY PEOPLE!

WHY NOT FEED 'EM KRUSTYBURGERS?

I NEED SOMETHIN' *CHEAP!* I GOT A COUPLE DOZEN PEOPLE OUT THERE!

CHEAPER THAN KRUSTYBURGERS?

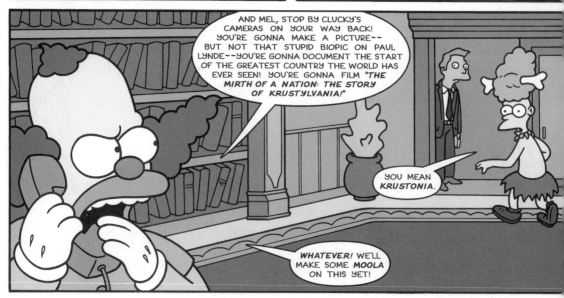

AND MEL, STOP BY CLUCKY'S CAMERAS ON YOUR WAY BACK! YOU'RE GONNA MAKE A PICTURE-- BUT NOT THAT STUPID BIOPIC ON PAUL LYNDE--YOU'RE GONNA DOCUMENT THE START OF THE GREATEST COUNTRY THE WORLD HAS EVER SEEN! YOU'RE GONNA FILM *"THE MIRTH OF A NATION: THE STORY OF KRUSTYLVANIA!"*

YOU MEAN *KRUSTONIA.*

WHATEVER! WE'LL MAKE SOME *MOOLA* ON THIS YET!

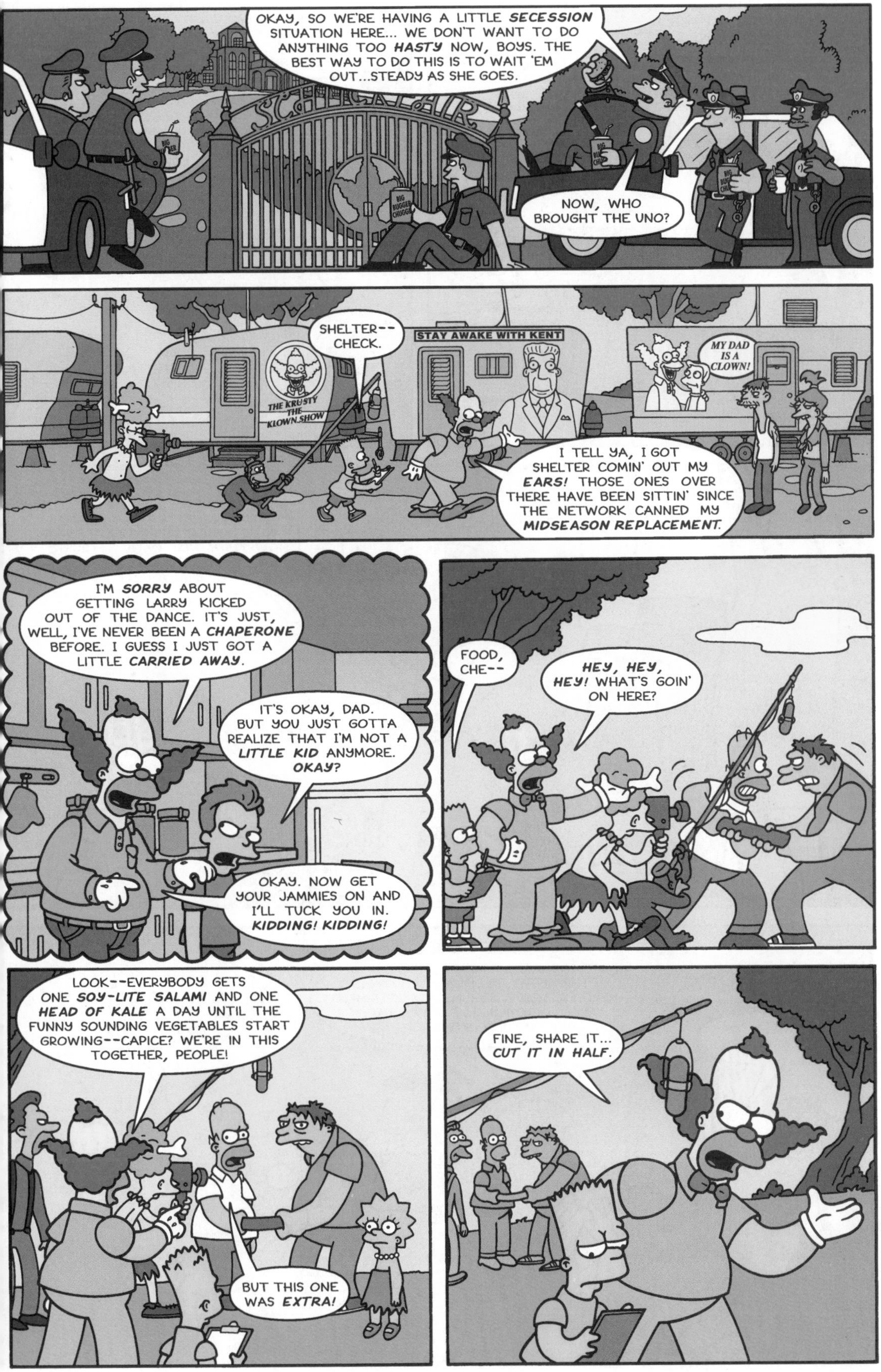

OKAY, SO WE'RE HAVING A LITTLE SECESSION SITUATION HERE... WE DON'T WANT TO DO ANYTHING TOO HASTY NOW, BOYS. THE BEST WAY TO DO THIS IS TO WAIT 'EM OUT...STEADY AS SHE GOES.
NOW, WHO BROUGHT THE UNO?
SHELTER-- CHECK.
STAY AWAKE WITH KENT
MY DAD IS A CLOWN!
THE KRUSTY THE KLOWN SHOW
I TELL YA, I GOT SHELTER COMIN' OUT MY EARS! THOSE ONES OVER THERE HAVE BEEN SITTIN' SINCE THE NETWORK CANNED MY MIDSEASON REPLACEMENT.
I'M SORRY ABOUT GETTING LARRY KICKED OUT OF THE DANCE. IT'S JUST, WELL, I'VE NEVER BEEN A CHAPERONE BEFORE. I GUESS I JUST GOT A LITTLE CARRIED AWAY.
IT'S OKAY, DAD. BUT YOU JUST GOTTA REALIZE THAT I'M NOT A LITTLE KID ANYMORE. OKAY?
OKAY. NOW GET YOUR JAMMIES ON AND I'LL TUCK YOU IN. KIDDING! KIDDING!
FOOD, CHE--
HEY, HEY, HEY! WHAT'S GOIN' ON HERE?
LOOK--EVERYBODY GETS ONE SOY-LITE SALAMI AND ONE HEAD OF KALE A DAY UNTIL THE FUNNY SOUNDING VEGETABLES START GROWING--CAPICE? WE'RE IN THIS TOGETHER, PEOPLE!
BUT THIS ONE WAS EXTRA!
FINE, SHARE IT... CUT IT IN HALF.

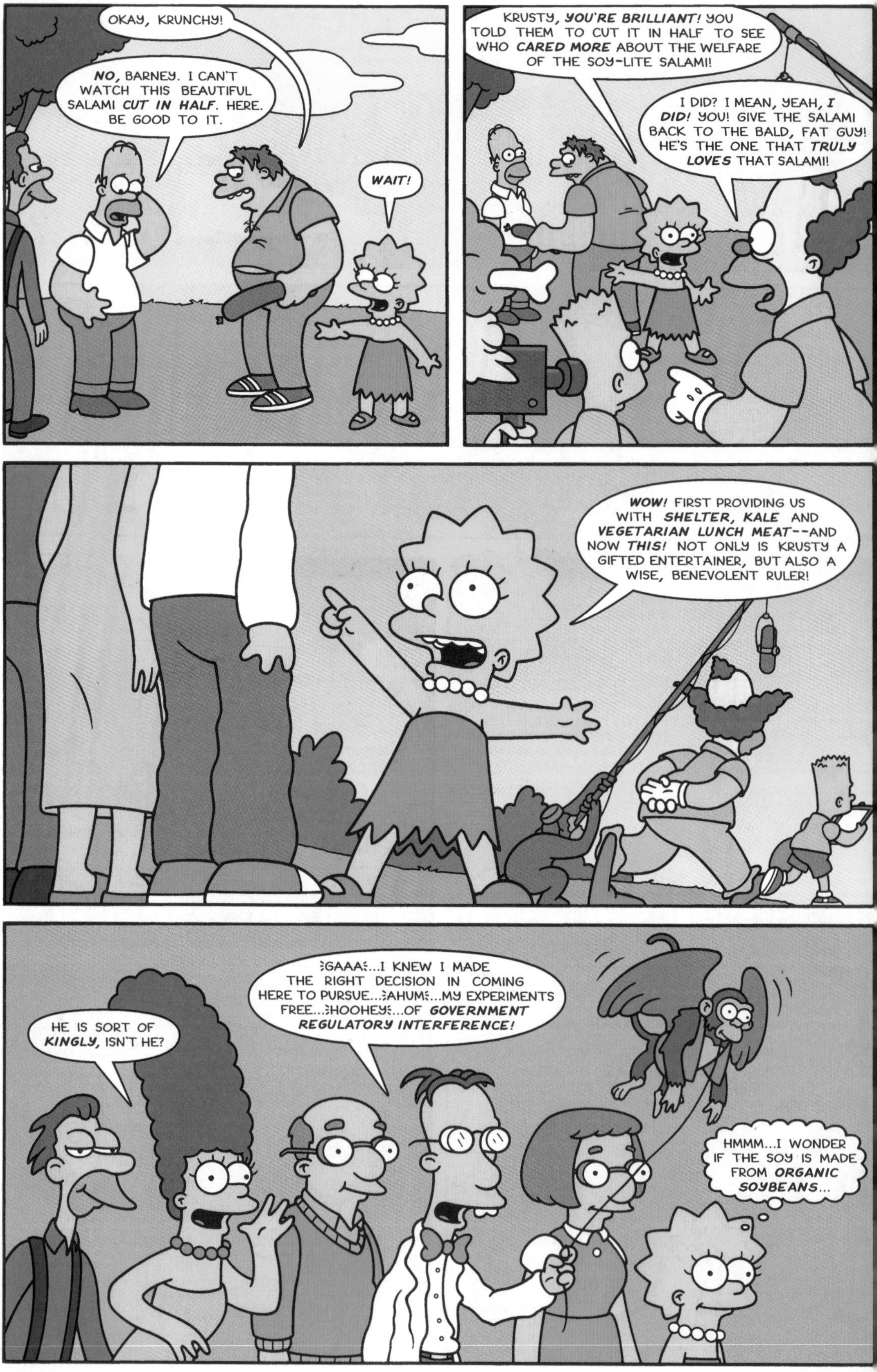
OKAY, KRUNCHY!
NO, BARNEY. I CAN'T WATCH THIS BEAUTIFUL SALAMI CUT IN HALF. HERE. BE GOOD TO IT.
WAIT!
KRUSTY, YOU'RE BRILLIANT! YOU TOLD THEM TO CUT IT IN HALF TO SEE WHO CARED MORE ABOUT THE WELFARE OF THE SOY-LITE SALAMI!
I DID? I MEAN, YEAH, I DID! YOU! GIVE THE SALAMI BACK TO THE BALD, FAT GUY! HE'S THE ONE THAT TRULY LOVES THAT SALAMI!
WOW! FIRST PROVIDING US WITH SHELTER, KALE AND VEGETARIAN LUNCH MEAT--AND NOW THIS! NOT ONLY IS KRUSTY A GIFTED ENTERTAINER, BUT ALSO A WISE, BENEVOLENT RULER!
HE IS SORT OF KINGLY, ISN'T HE?
GAAA...I KNEW I MADE THE RIGHT DECISION IN COMING HERE TO PURSUE...AHUM...MY EXPERIMENTS FREE...HOOHEY...OF GOVERNMENT REGULATORY INTERFERENCE!
HMMM...I WONDER IF THE SOY IS MADE FROM ORGANIC SOYBEANS...

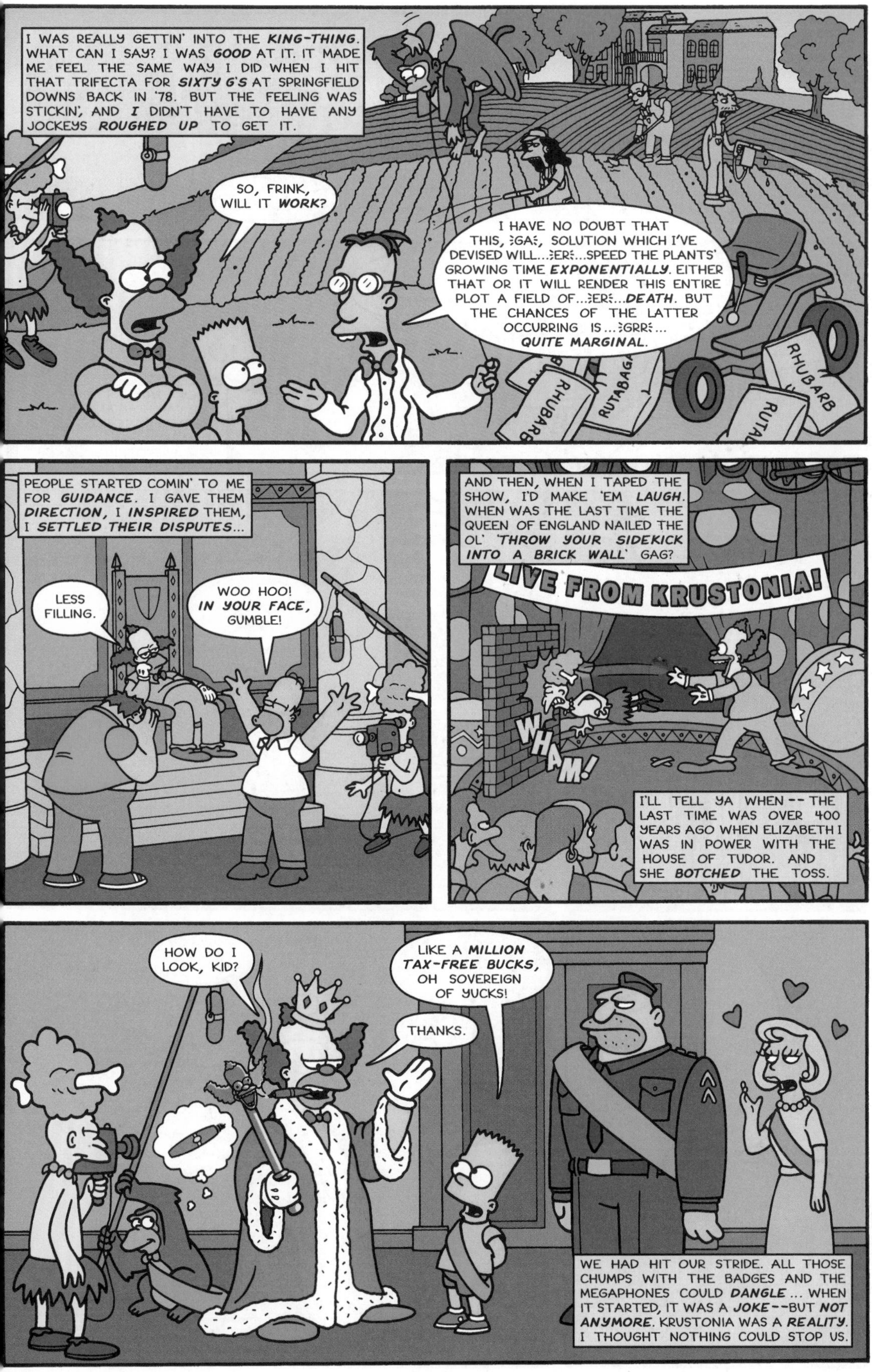
I WAS REALLY GETTIN' INTO THE KING-THING. WHAT CAN I SAY? I WAS GOOD AT IT. IT MADE ME FEEL THE SAME WAY I DID WHEN I HIT THAT TRIFECTA FOR SIXTY G'S AT SPRINGFIELD DOWNS BACK IN '78. BUT THE FEELING WAS STICKIN', AND I DIDN'T HAVE TO HAVE ANY JOCKEYS ROUGHED UP TO GET IT.
SO, FRINK, WILL IT WORK?
I HAVE NO DOUBT THAT THIS, GA, SOLUTION WHICH I'VE DEVISED WILL...ER...SPEED THE PLANTS' GROWING TIME EXPONENTIALLY. EITHER THAT OR IT WILL RENDER THIS ENTIRE PLOT A FIELD OF...ER...DEATH. BUT THE CHANCES OF THE LATTER OCCURRING IS...GRR... QUITE MARGINAL.
RHUBARB
RUTABAGA
RHUBARB
RUTABAGA
PEOPLE STARTED COMIN' TO ME FOR GUIDANCE. I GAVE THEM DIRECTION, I INSPIRED THEM, I SETTLED THEIR DISPUTES...
LESS FILLING.
WOO HOO! IN YOUR FACE, GUMBLE!
AND THEN, WHEN I TAPED THE SHOW, I'D MAKE 'EM LAUGH. WHEN WAS THE LAST TIME THE QUEEN OF ENGLAND NAILED THE OL' 'THROW YOUR SIDEKICK INTO A BRICK WALL' GAG?
LIVE FROM KRUSTONIA!
WHAM!
I'LL TELL YA WHEN -- THE LAST TIME WAS OVER 400 YEARS AGO WHEN ELIZABETH I WAS IN POWER WITH THE HOUSE OF TUDOR. AND SHE BOTCHED THE TOSS.
HOW DO I LOOK, KID?
LIKE A MILLION TAX-FREE BUCKS, OH SOVEREIGN OF YUCKS!
THANKS.
WE HAD HIT OUR STRIDE. ALL THOSE CHUMPS WITH THE BADGES AND THE MEGAPHONES COULD DANGLE ... WHEN IT STARTED, IT WAS A JOKE--BUT NOT ANYMORE. KRUSTONIA WAS A REALITY. I THOUGHT NOTHING COULD STOP US.

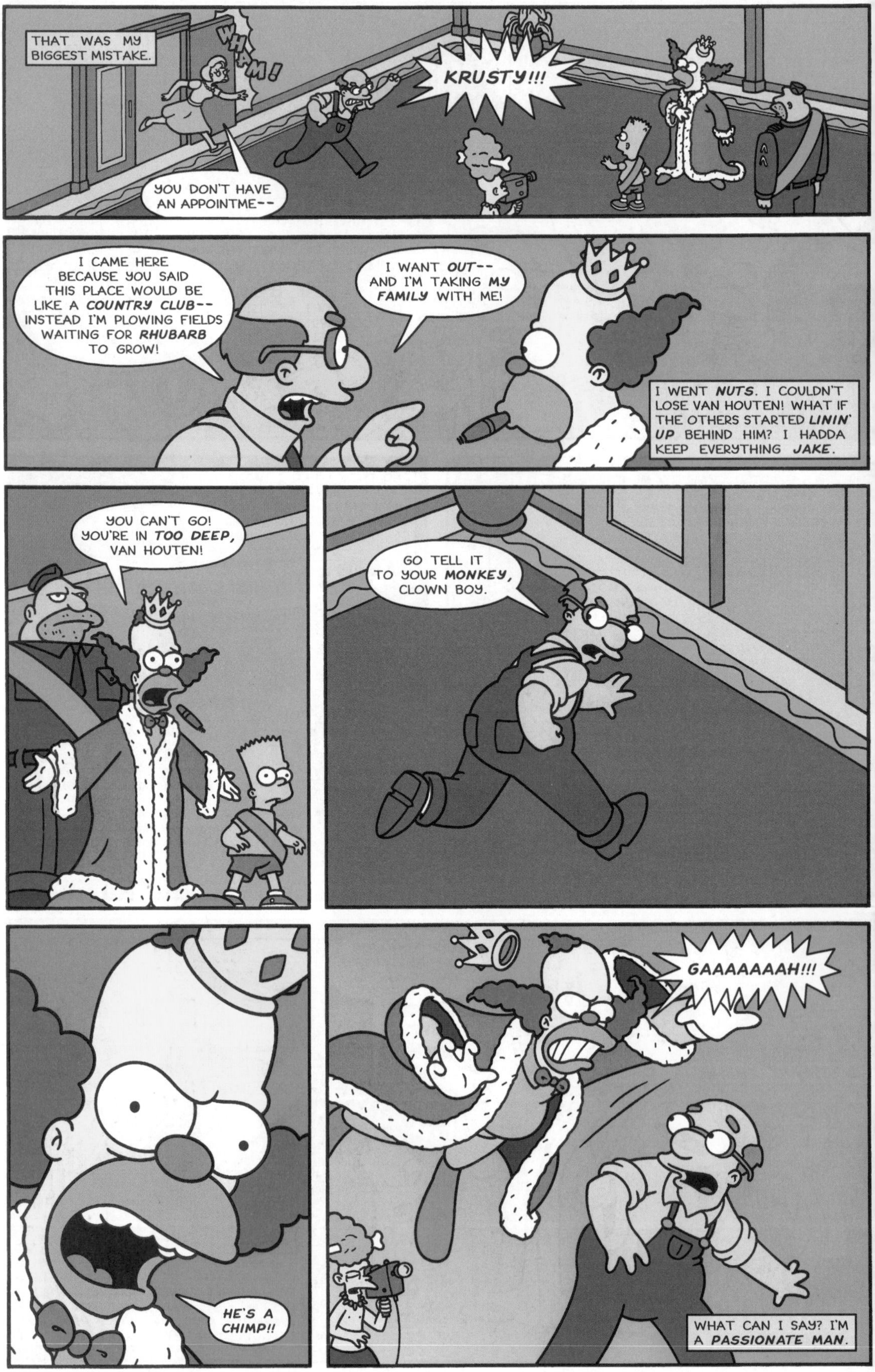
THAT WAS MY BIGGEST MISTAKE.
WHAM!
YOU DON'T HAVE AN APPOINTME--
KRUSTY!!!
I CAME HERE BECAUSE YOU SAID THIS PLACE WOULD BE LIKE A COUNTRY CLUB-- INSTEAD I'M PLOWING FIELDS WAITING FOR RHUBARB TO GROW!
I WANT OUT-- AND I'M TAKING MY FAMILY WITH ME!
I WENT NUTS. I COULDN'T LOSE VAN HOUTEN! WHAT IF THE OTHERS STARTED LININ' UP BEHIND HIM? I HADDA KEEP EVERYTHING JAKE.
YOU CAN'T GO! YOU'RE IN TOO DEEP, VAN HOUTEN!
GO TELL IT TO YOUR MONKEY, CLOWN BOY.
HE'S A CHIMP!!
GAAAAAAAH!!!
WHAT CAN I SAY? I'M A PASSIONATE MAN.

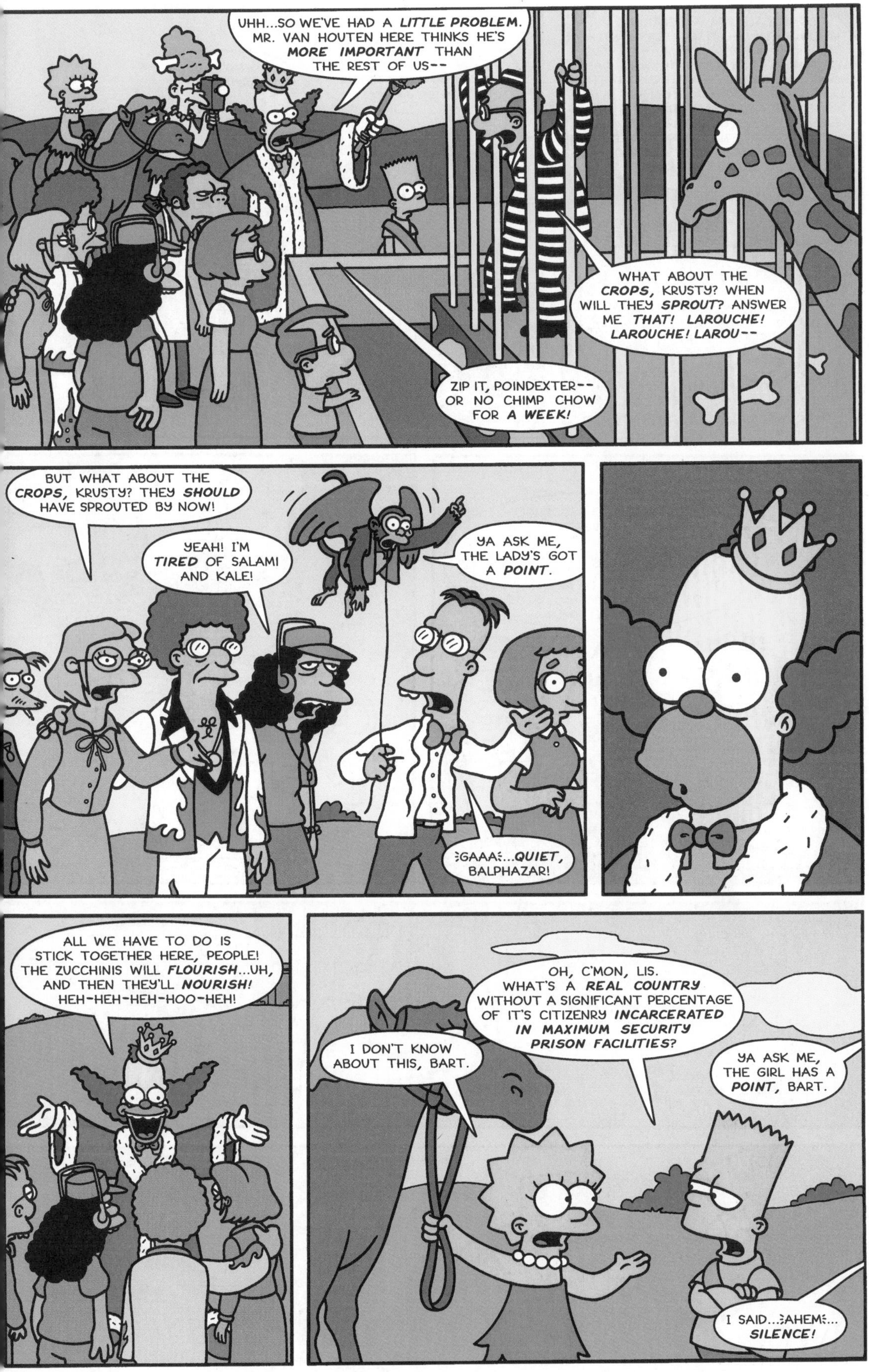
UHH...SO WE'VE HAD A LITTLE PROBLEM. MR. VAN HOUTEN HERE THINKS HE'S MORE IMPORTANT THAN THE REST OF US--
WHAT ABOUT THE CROPS, KRUSTY? WHEN WILL THEY SPROUT? ANSWER ME THAT! LAROUCHE! LAROUCHE! LAROU--
ZIP IT, POINDEXTER--OR NO CHIMP CHOW FOR A WEEK!
BUT WHAT ABOUT THE CROPS, KRUSTY? THEY SHOULD HAVE SPROUTED BY NOW!
YEAH! I'M TIRED OF SALAMI AND KALE!
YA ASK ME, THE LADY'S GOT A POINT.
⁝GAAA⁝...QUIET, BALPHAZAR!
ALL WE HAVE TO DO IS STICK TOGETHER HERE, PEOPLE! THE ZUCCHINIS WILL FLOURISH...UH, AND THEN THEY'LL NOURISH! HEH-HEH-HEH-HOO-HEH!
I DON'T KNOW ABOUT THIS, BART.
OH, C'MON, LIS. WHAT'S A REAL COUNTRY WITHOUT A SIGNIFICANT PERCENTAGE OF IT'S CITIZENRY INCARCERATED IN MAXIMUM SECURITY PRISON FACILITIES?
YA ASK ME, THE GIRL HAS A POINT, BART.
I SAID...⁝AHEM⁝...SILENCE!

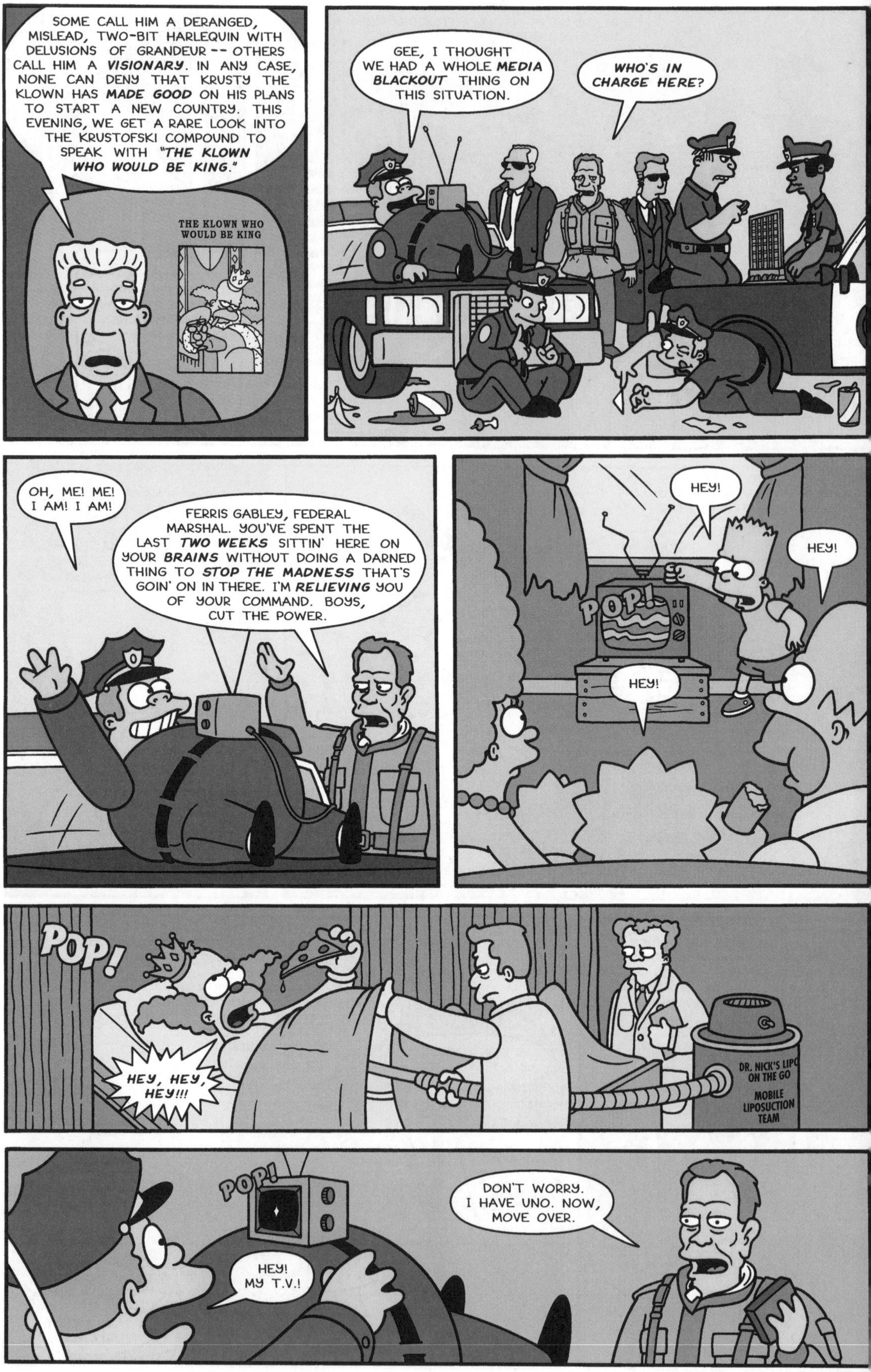

SOME CALL HIM A DERANGED, MISLEAD, TWO-BIT HARLEQUIN WITH DELUSIONS OF GRANDEUR -- OTHERS CALL HIM A VISIONARY. IN ANY CASE, NONE CAN DENY THAT KRUSTY THE KLOWN HAS MADE GOOD ON HIS PLANS TO START A NEW COUNTRY. THIS EVENING, WE GET A RARE LOOK INTO THE KRUSTOFSKI COMPOUND TO SPEAK WITH "THE KLOWN WHO WOULD BE KING."
THE KLOWN WHO WOULD BE KING
GEE, I THOUGHT WE HAD A WHOLE MEDIA BLACKOUT THING ON THIS SITUATION.
WHO'S IN CHARGE HERE?
OH, ME! ME! I AM! I AM!
FERRIS GABLEY, FEDERAL MARSHAL. YOU'VE SPENT THE LAST TWO WEEKS SITTIN' HERE ON YOUR BRAINS WITHOUT DOING A DARNED THING TO STOP THE MADNESS THAT'S GOIN' ON IN THERE. I'M RELIEVING YOU OF YOUR COMMAND. BOYS, CUT THE POWER.
HEY!
HEY!
POP!
HEY!
POP!
HEY, HEY, HEY!!!
DR. NICK'S LIPO ON THE GO
MOBILE LIPOSUCTION TEAM
POP!
DON'T WORRY. I HAVE UNO. NOW, MOVE OVER.
HEY! MY T.V.!

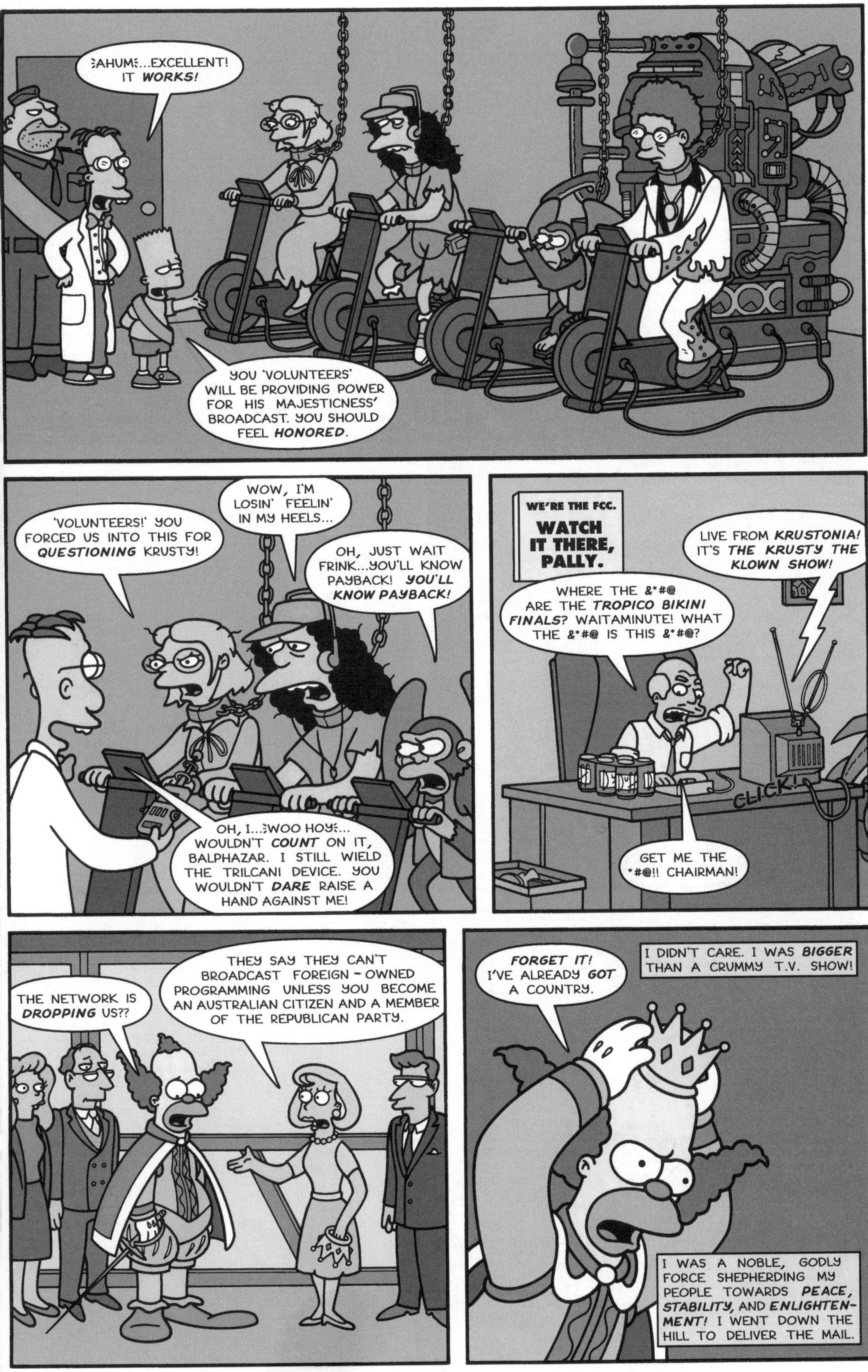

≈AHUM≈...EXCELLENT! IT WORKS!
YOU 'VOLUNTEERS' WILL BE PROVIDING POWER FOR HIS MAJESTICNESS' BROADCAST. YOU SHOULD FEEL HONORED.
'VOLUNTEERS!' YOU FORCED US INTO THIS FOR QUESTIONING KRUSTY!
WOW, I'M LOSIN' FEELIN' IN MY HEELS...
OH, JUST WAIT FRINK...YOU'LL KNOW PAYBACK! YOU'LL KNOW PAYBACK!
OH, I...≈WOO HOY≈... WOULDN'T COUNT ON IT, BALPHAZAR. I STILL WIELD THE TRILCANI DEVICE. YOU WOULDN'T DARE RAISE A HAND AGAINST ME!
WE'RE THE FCC.
WATCH IT THERE, PALLY.
LIVE FROM KRUSTONIA! IT'S THE KRUSTY THE KLOWN SHOW!
WHERE THE &*#@ ARE THE TROPICO BIKINI FINALS? WAITAMINUTE! WHAT THE &*#@ IS THIS &*#@?
CLICK!
GET ME THE *#@!! CHAIRMAN!
THE NETWORK IS DROPPING US??
THEY SAY THEY CAN'T BROADCAST FOREIGN-OWNED PROGRAMMING UNLESS YOU BECOME AN AUSTRALIAN CITIZEN AND A MEMBER OF THE REPUBLICAN PARTY.
FORGET IT! I'VE ALREADY GOT A COUNTRY.
I DIDN'T CARE. I WAS BIGGER THAN A CRUMMY T.V. SHOW!
I WAS A NOBLE, GODLY FORCE SHEPHERDING MY PEOPLE TOWARDS PEACE, STABILITY, AND ENLIGHTENMENT! I WENT DOWN THE HILL TO DELIVER THE MAIL.

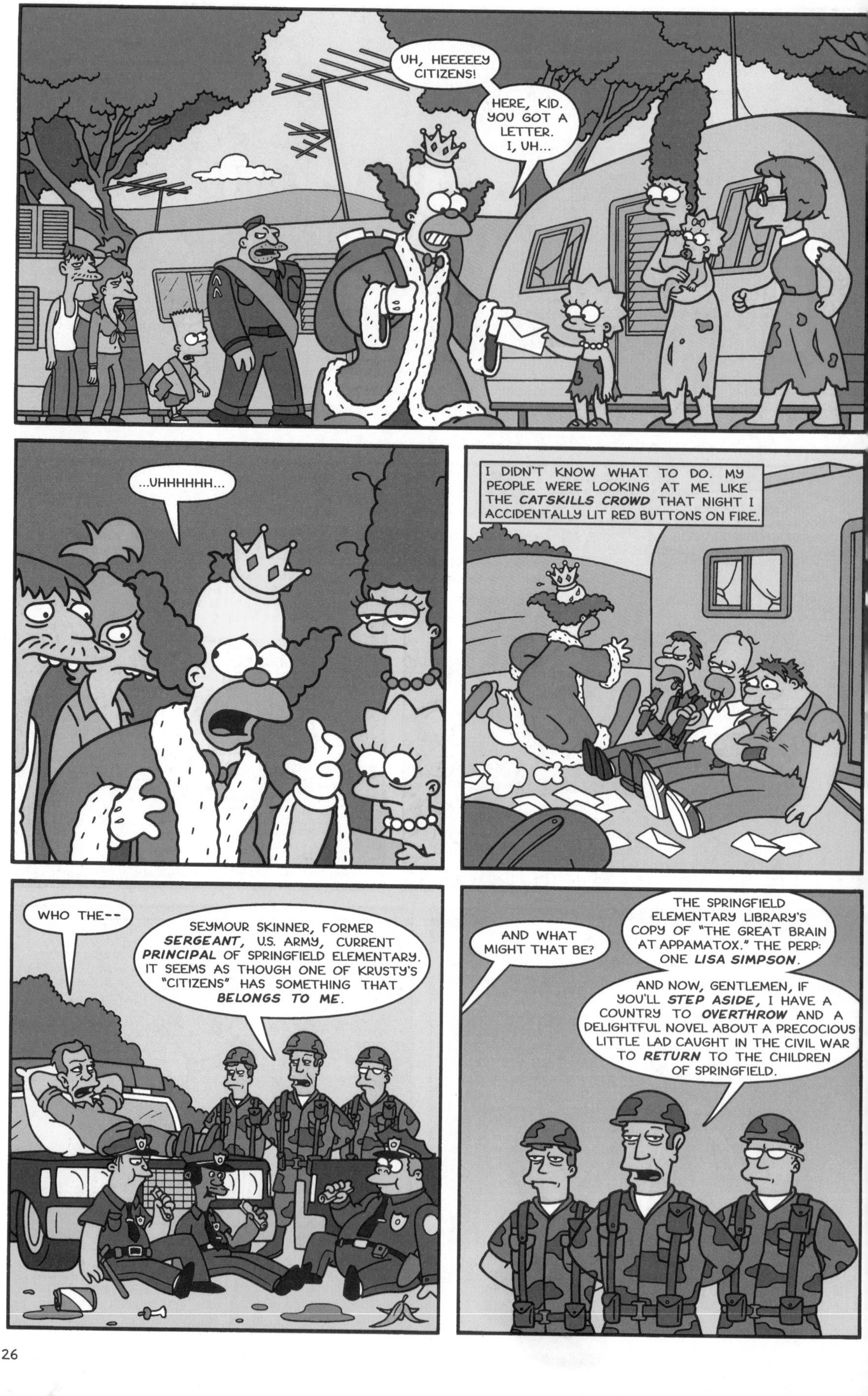
UH, HEEEEEY CITIZENS!
HERE, KID. YOU GOT A LETTER. I, UH...
...UHHHHHHH...
I DIDN'T KNOW WHAT TO DO. MY PEOPLE WERE LOOKING AT ME LIKE THE CATSKILLS CROWD THAT NIGHT I ACCIDENTALLY LIT RED BUTTONS ON FIRE.
WHO THE--
SEYMOUR SKINNER, FORMER SERGEANT, U.S. ARMY, CURRENT PRINCIPAL OF SPRINGFIELD ELEMENTARY. IT SEEMS AS THOUGH ONE OF KRUSTY'S "CITIZENS" HAS SOMETHING THAT BELONGS TO ME.
AND WHAT MIGHT THAT BE?
THE SPRINGFIELD ELEMENTARY LIBRARY'S COPY OF "THE GREAT BRAIN AT APPAMATOX." THE PERP: ONE LISA SIMPSON.
AND NOW, GENTLEMEN, IF YOU'LL STEP ASIDE, I HAVE A COUNTRY TO OVERTHROW AND A DELIGHTFUL NOVEL ABOUT A PRECOCIOUS LITTLE LAD CAUGHT IN THE CIVIL WAR TO RETURN TO THE CHILDREN OF SPRINGFIELD.

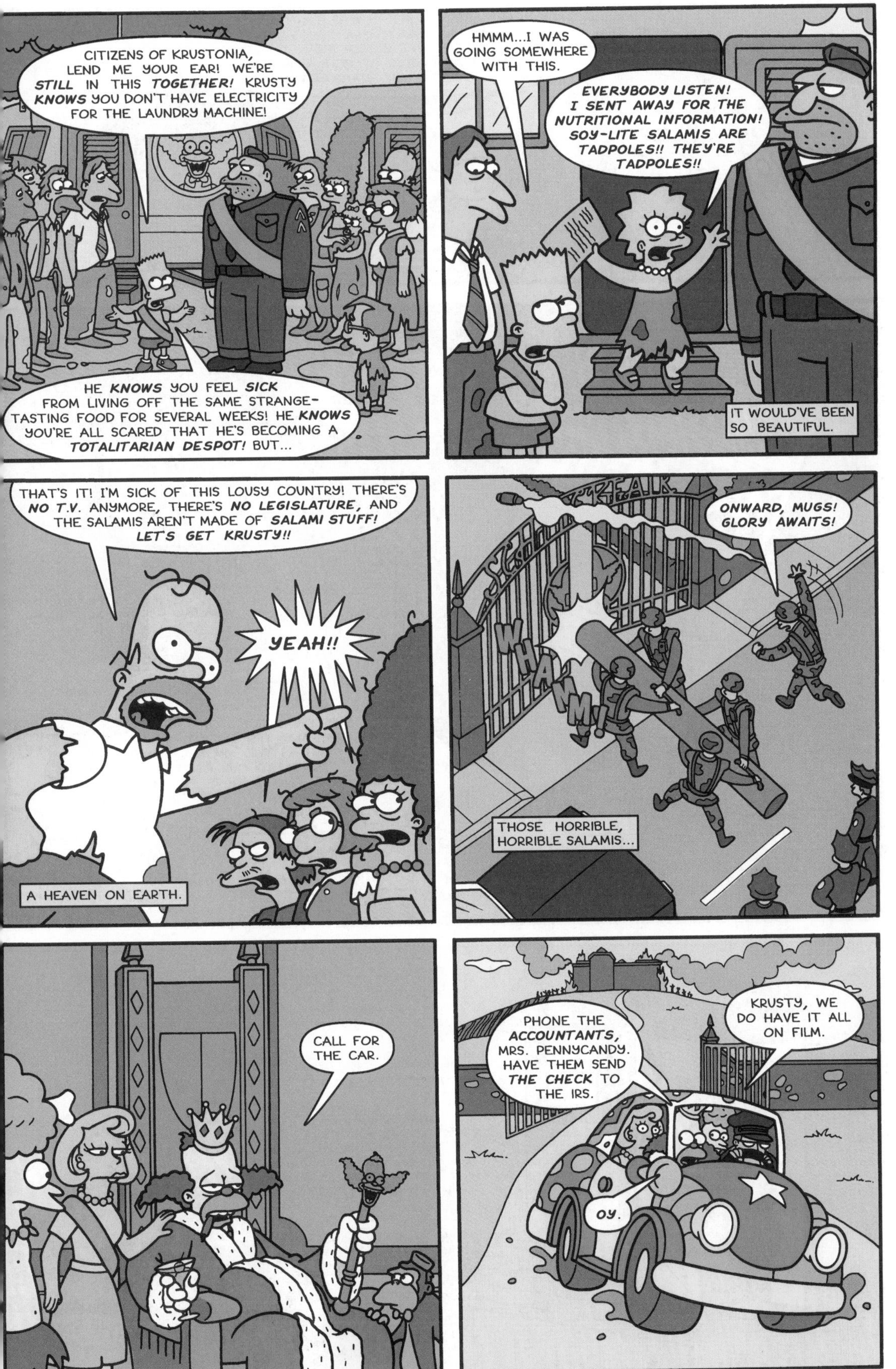
CITIZENS OF KRUSTONIA, LEND ME YOUR EAR! WE'RE STILL IN THIS TOGETHER! KRUSTY KNOWS YOU DON'T HAVE ELECTRICITY FOR THE LAUNDRY MACHINE!
HE KNOWS YOU FEEL SICK FROM LIVING OFF THE SAME STRANGE-TASTING FOOD FOR SEVERAL WEEKS! HE KNOWS YOU'RE ALL SCARED THAT HE'S BECOMING A TOTALITARIAN DESPOT! BUT...
HMMM...I WAS GOING SOMEWHERE WITH THIS.
EVERYBODY LISTEN! I SENT AWAY FOR THE NUTRITIONAL INFORMATION! SOY-LITE SALAMIS ARE TADPOLES!! THEY'RE TADPOLES!!
IT WOULD'VE BEEN SO BEAUTIFUL.
THAT'S IT! I'M SICK OF THIS LOUSY COUNTRY! THERE'S NO T.V. ANYMORE, THERE'S NO LEGISLATURE, AND THE SALAMIS AREN'T MADE OF SALAMI STUFF! LET'S GET KRUSTY!!
YEAH!!
A HEAVEN ON EARTH.
ONWARD, MUGS! GLORY AWAITS!
WHAMM!
THOSE HORRIBLE, HORRIBLE SALAMIS...
CALL FOR THE CAR.
PHONE THE ACCOUNTANTS, MRS. PENNYCANDY. HAVE THEM SEND THE CHECK TO THE IRS.
KRUSTY, WE DO HAVE IT ALL ON FILM.
OY.

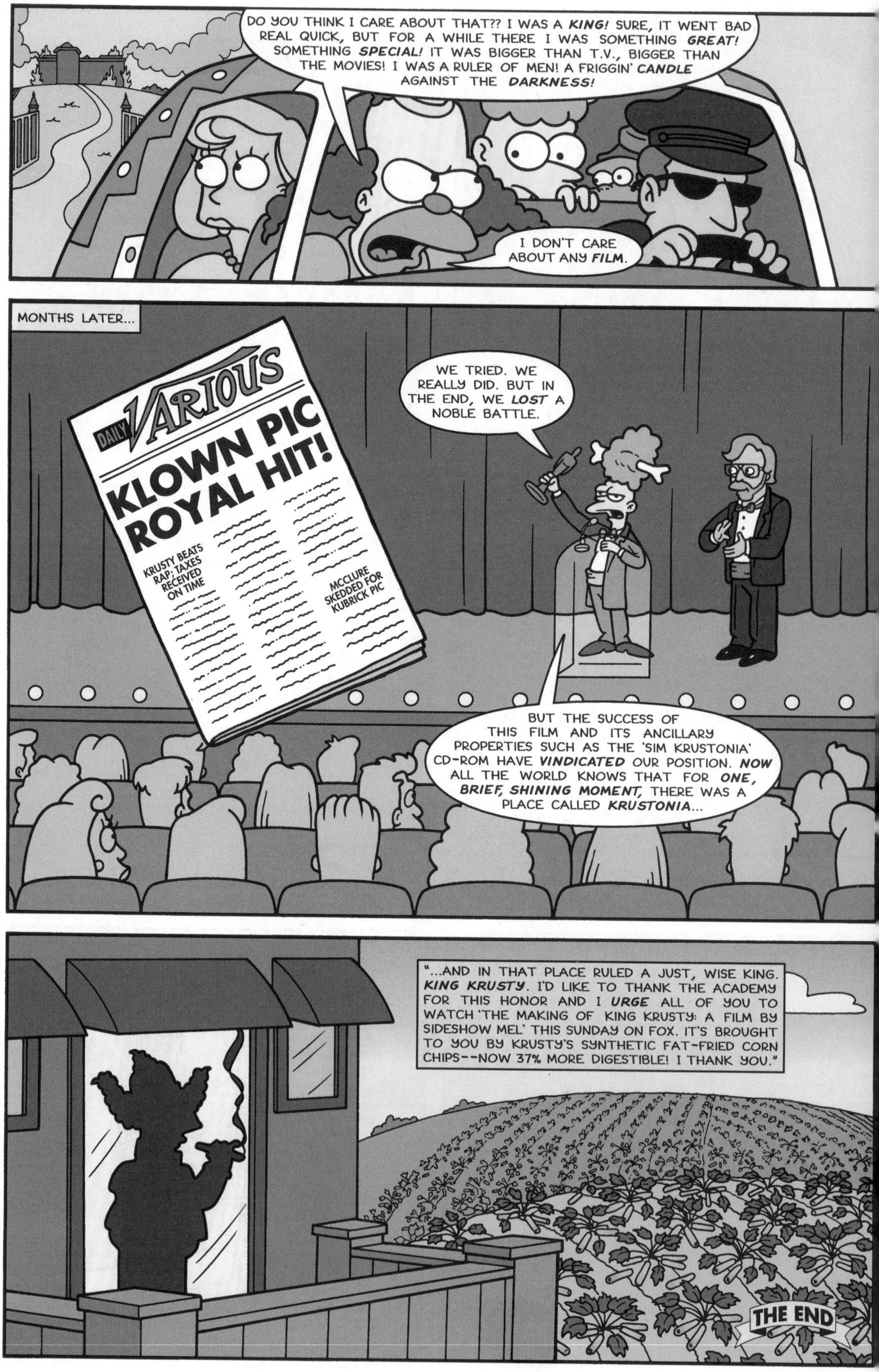
DO YOU THINK I CARE ABOUT THAT?? I WAS A KING! SURE, IT WENT BAD REAL QUICK, BUT FOR A WHILE THERE I WAS SOMETHING GREAT! SOMETHING SPECIAL! IT WAS BIGGER THAN T.V., BIGGER THAN THE MOVIES! I WAS A RULER OF MEN! A FRIGGIN' CANDLE AGAINST THE DARKNESS!
I DON'T CARE ABOUT ANY FILM.
MONTHS LATER...
DAILY VARIOUS
KLOWN PIC ROYAL HIT!
KRUSTY BEATS RAP; TAXES RECEIVED ON TIME
MCCLURE SKEDDED FOR KUBRICK PIC
WE TRIED. WE REALLY DID. BUT IN THE END, WE LOST A NOBLE BATTLE.
BUT THE SUCCESS OF THIS FILM AND ITS ANCILLARY PROPERTIES SUCH AS THE 'SIM KRUSTONIA' CD-ROM HAVE VINDICATED OUR POSITION. NOW ALL THE WORLD KNOWS THAT FOR ONE, BRIEF, SHINING MOMENT, THERE WAS A PLACE CALLED KRUSTONIA...
"...AND IN THAT PLACE RULED A JUST, WISE KING. KING KRUSTY. I'D LIKE TO THANK THE ACADEMY FOR THIS HONOR AND I URGE ALL OF YOU TO WATCH 'THE MAKING OF KING KRUSTY: A FILM BY SIDESHOW MEL' THIS SUNDAY ON FOX. IT'S BROUGHT TO YOU BY KRUSTY'S SYNTHETIC FAT-FRIED CORN CHIPS--NOW 37% MORE DIGESTIBLE! I THANK YOU."
THE END

FLANDERS' BIG SCORE

A NED FLANDERS MYSTERY

HEY-DILLY-HO, *MYSTERY MAVENS!* THE NAME'S *FLANDERS* BUT SOME FOLKS CALL ME *NED!* TO OTHERS I'M KNOWN AS NEDDY, DAD, DA-DIDDLE-ADDY, MR. F., AND FOR SOME STRANGE REASON, THE LOCAL POLICE INSIST ON CALLING ME HUGGY-BEAR! BUT NO MATTER THE HANDLE, I'M ALWAYS READY TO ANSWER WHEN TROUBLE CALLS MY NAME... *ESPECIALLY* THE LORD'S TROUBLE!

THIS PARTICULAR LITTLE PICKLE STARTED ONE AFTERNOON AT THE SPRINGFIELD COMMUNITY CHURCH. I HAD ARRIVED A TEENSY BIT LATE FOR AN IMPORTANT COMMITTEE MEETING. OUR MISSION: PUT THE *'FUN'* BACK IN *FUND-RAISER!*

LISTEN UP, FOLKS. IT'S TIME FOR OUR ANNUAL "I *AM THAT I AMBROSIA"* COOK-OFF! AS USUAL, WE NEED TO LAY IN A TREMENDOUS SUPPLY OF PINK GELATIN, MAYONNAISE, AND TINY MARSHMALLOWS.

MMM...AMBROSIA! SO PINK... SO GOOPY...

THANKS BE TO GOD FOR A *HEALTHY CHURCH TREASURY* AND A *BULKRAGEOUS BIG BUYERS CLUB MEMBER-SHIP CARD!*

GOOD LORD ≋CHOKE≋ WE'VE BEEN ROBBED.

BULK BUYERS
MEMBERSHIP CARD

Jim J.
&
Tammy Fay
Fan Club

LET'S NOT PANIC PEOPLE. IT JUST SO HAPPENS THAT A MEMBER OF OUR OWN FLOCK IS QUALIFIED TO INVESTIGATE THIS HEINOUS CRIME. IT SEEMS LIKE JUST THE OTHER DAY...

"...WHEN I HANDED THAT *DETECTIVE CORRESPONDENCE COURSE* OVER TO NED FLANDERS AT THE CHARITY AUCTION WE HELD TO BUY BARNEY GUMBLE A NEW LIVER..."

WITH *THIS*, I'LL BE ABLE TO FERRET OUT THE RASCAL THAT'S BEEN CLIPPING THE *DOUGHNUT COUPONS* OUT OF OUR *SUNDAY PAPER!*

PRISON PASTELS

HYPNOHEAD'S
MIND CONTROL KIT

DAVE 'MR. SNOOPY' NAGELMAN'S
DETECTIVE CORRESPONDENCE KIT

DUFF HOME BREWERY

"...BEFORE LONG, HE BECAME A TOP-NOTCH PRIVATE RICHARD."

YES INDEEDLY, REVEREND! NED FLANDERS, PRIVATE EYE IS ON THE CASE.

OOH!

WHOA!

AND THE FIRST CLUE TO FINDING THE THIEF IS THIS *UNMARKED KEY* THAT JUST DROPPED OUT OF THE *COLLECTION KITTY.* I'D BETTER DUST THIS LIL' BEAUTY FOR PRINTS!

SCRIPT	*PENCILS*	*INKS*	*LETTERS*	*COLORS*	*USUAL SUSPECT*
GARY GLASBERG	PHIL ORTIZ	TIM HARKINS	JEANNINE BLACK	NATHAN KANE	MATT GROENING

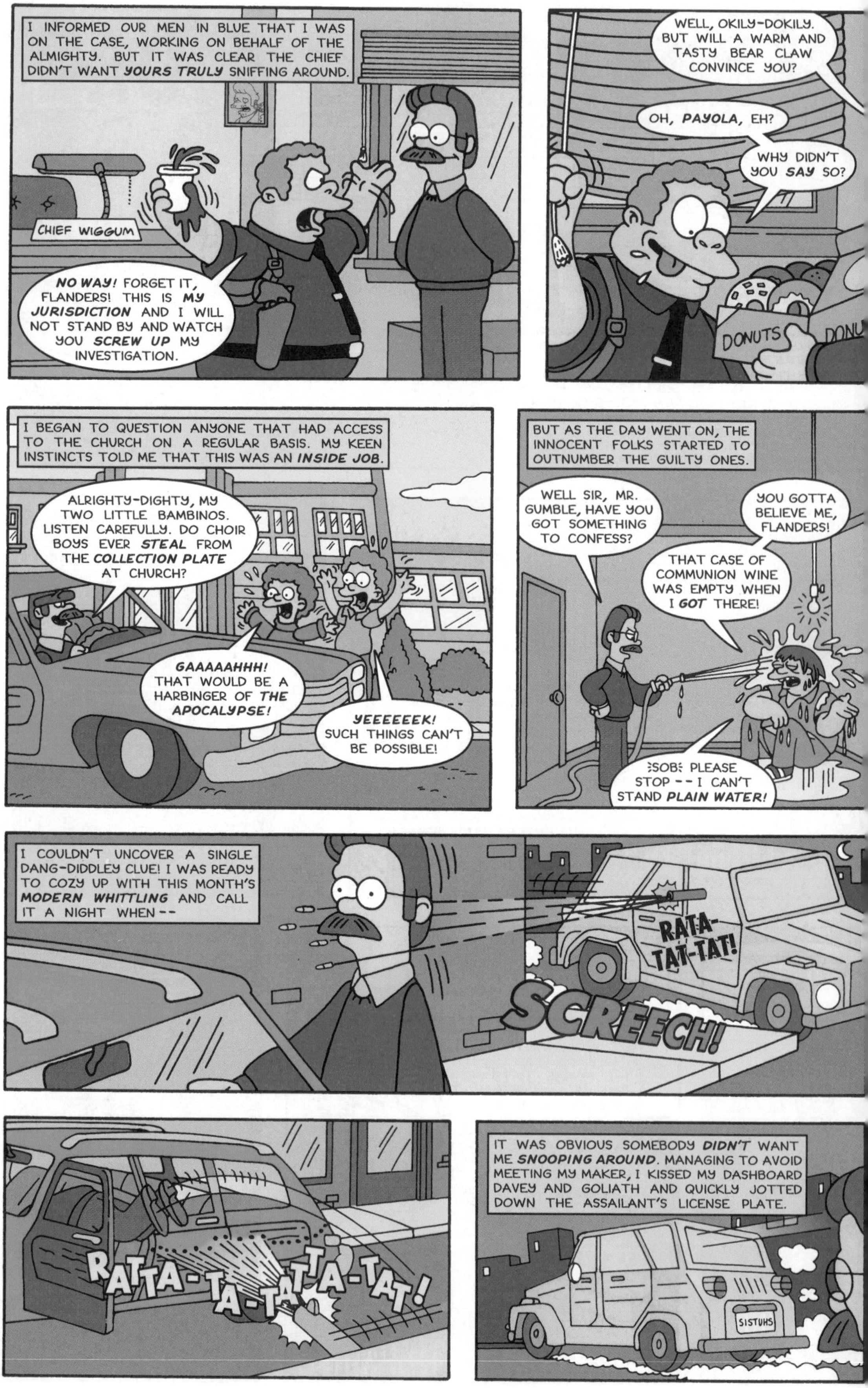

I INFORMED OUR MEN IN BLUE THAT I WAS ON THE CASE, WORKING ON BEHALF OF THE ALMIGHTY. BUT IT WAS CLEAR THE CHIEF DIDN'T WANT ***YOURS TRULY*** SNIFFING AROUND.
CHIEF WIGGUM
NO WAY! FORGET IT, FLANDERS! THIS IS ***MY JURISDICTION*** AND I WILL NOT STAND BY AND WATCH YOU ***SCREW UP*** MY INVESTIGATION.
WELL, OKILY-DOKILY. BUT WILL A WARM AND TASTY BEAR CLAW CONVINCE YOU?
OH, ***PAYOLA,*** EH?
WHY DIDN'T YOU ***SAY*** SO?
DONUTS
I BEGAN TO QUESTION ANYONE THAT HAD ACCESS TO THE CHURCH ON A REGULAR BASIS. MY KEEN INSTINCTS TOLD ME THAT THIS WAS AN ***INSIDE JOB.***
ALRIGHTY-DIGHTY, MY TWO LITTLE BAMBINOS. LISTEN CAREFULLY. DO CHOIR BOYS EVER ***STEAL*** FROM THE ***COLLECTION PLATE*** AT CHURCH?
GAAAAAHHH! THAT WOULD BE A HARBINGER OF ***THE APOCALYPSE!***
YEEEEEEK! SUCH THINGS CAN'T BE POSSIBLE!
BUT AS THE DAY WENT ON, THE INNOCENT FOLKS STARTED TO OUTNUMBER THE GUILTY ONES.
WELL SIR, MR. GUMBLE, HAVE YOU GOT SOMETHING TO CONFESS?
YOU GOTTA BELIEVE ME, FLANDERS!
THAT CASE OF COMMUNION WINE WAS EMPTY WHEN I ***GOT*** THERE!
:SOB: PLEASE STOP -- I CAN'T STAND ***PLAIN WATER!***
I COULDN'T UNCOVER A SINGLE DANG-DIDDLEY CLUE! I WAS READY TO COZY UP WITH THIS MONTH'S ***MODERN WHITTLING*** AND CALL IT A NIGHT WHEN--
RATA-TAT-TAT!
SCREECH!
RATTA-TA-TATTA-TAT!
IT WAS OBVIOUS SOMEBODY ***DIDN'T*** WANT ME ***SNOOPING AROUND.*** MANAGING TO AVOID MEETING MY MAKER, I KISSED MY DASHBOARD DAVEY AND GOLIATH AND QUICKLY JOTTED DOWN THE ASSAILANT'S LICENSE PLATE.
SISTUHS

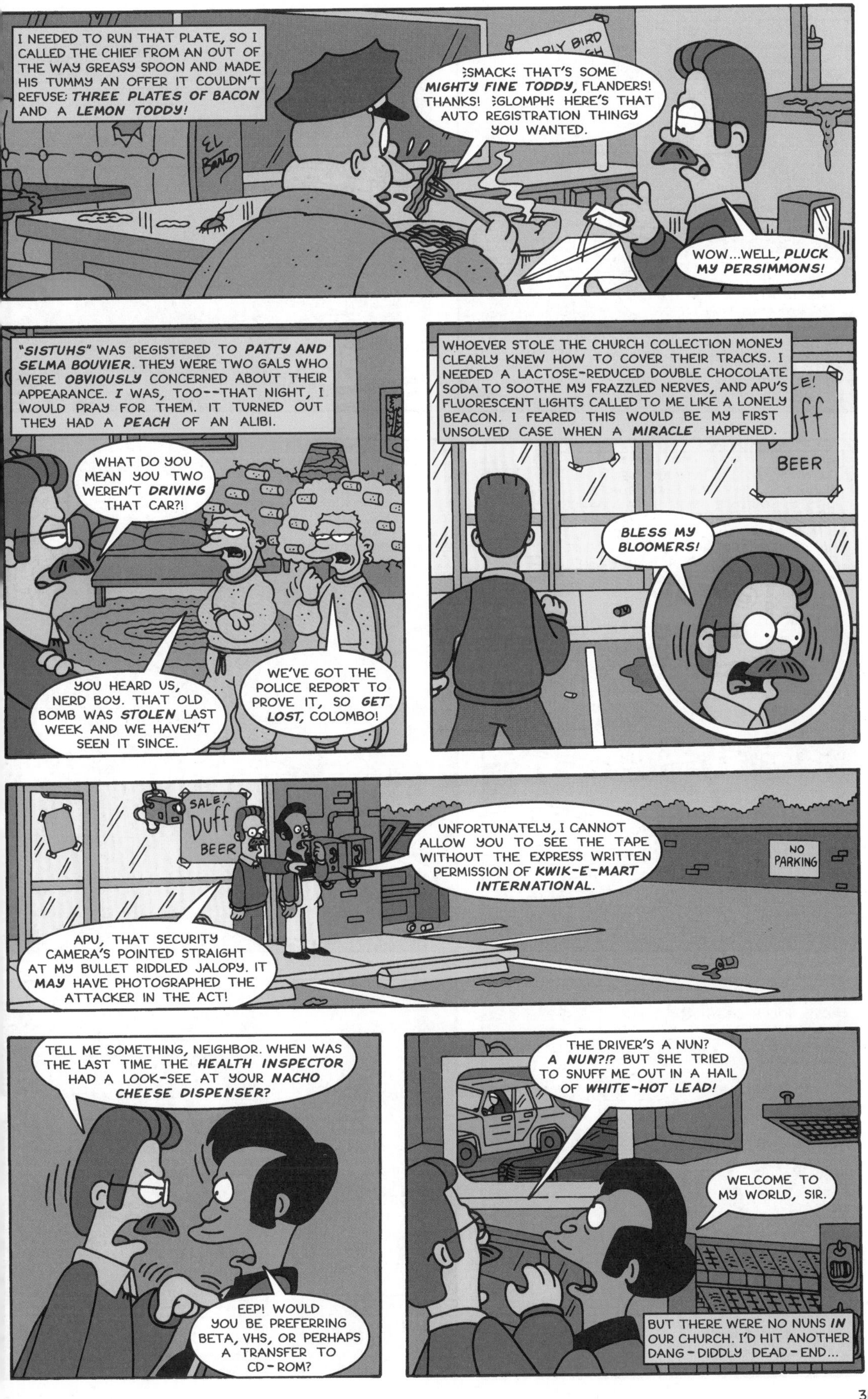
I NEEDED TO RUN THAT PLATE, SO I CALLED THE CHIEF FROM AN OUT OF THE WAY GREASY SPOON AND MADE HIS TUMMY AN OFFER IT COULDN'T REFUSE: THREE PLATES OF BACON AND A LEMON TODDY!
EL Barto
ᗒSMACKᗕ THAT'S SOME MIGHTY FINE TODDY, FLANDERS! THANKS! ᗒGLOMPHᗕ HERE'S THAT AUTO REGISTRATION THINGY YOU WANTED.
WOW...WELL, PLUCK MY PERSIMMONS!
"SISTUHS" WAS REGISTERED TO PATTY AND SELMA BOUVIER. THEY WERE TWO GALS WHO WERE OBVIOUSLY CONCERNED ABOUT THEIR APPEARANCE. I WAS, TOO--THAT NIGHT, I WOULD PRAY FOR THEM. IT TURNED OUT THEY HAD A PEACH OF AN ALIBI.
WHAT DO YOU MEAN YOU TWO WEREN'T DRIVING THAT CAR?!
YOU HEARD US, NERD BOY. THAT OLD BOMB WAS STOLEN LAST WEEK AND WE HAVEN'T SEEN IT SINCE.
WE'VE GOT THE POLICE REPORT TO PROVE IT, SO GET LOST, COLOMBO!
WHOEVER STOLE THE CHURCH COLLECTION MONEY CLEARLY KNEW HOW TO COVER THEIR TRACKS. I NEEDED A LACTOSE-REDUCED DOUBLE CHOCOLATE SODA TO SOOTHE MY FRAZZLED NERVES, AND APU'S FLUORESCENT LIGHTS CALLED TO ME LIKE A LONELY BEACON. I FEARED THIS WOULD BE MY FIRST UNSOLVED CASE WHEN A MIRACLE HAPPENED.
BEER
BLESS MY BLOOMERS!
SALE!
Duff
BEER
UNFORTUNATELY, I CANNOT ALLOW YOU TO SEE THE TAPE WITHOUT THE EXPRESS WRITTEN PERMISSION OF KWIK-E-MART INTERNATIONAL.
NO PARKING
APU, THAT SECURITY CAMERA'S POINTED STRAIGHT AT MY BULLET RIDDLED JALOPY. IT MAY HAVE PHOTOGRAPHED THE ATTACKER IN THE ACT!
TELL ME SOMETHING, NEIGHBOR. WHEN WAS THE LAST TIME THE HEALTH INSPECTOR HAD A LOOK-SEE AT YOUR NACHO CHEESE DISPENSER?
EEP! WOULD YOU BE PREFERRING BETA, VHS, OR PERHAPS A TRANSFER TO CD-ROM?
THE DRIVER'S A NUN? A NUN?!? BUT SHE TRIED TO SNUFF ME OUT IN A HAIL OF WHITE-HOT LEAD!
WELCOME TO MY WORLD, SIR.
BUT THERE WERE NO NUNS IN OUR CHURCH. I'D HIT ANOTHER DANG-DIDDLY DEAD-END...

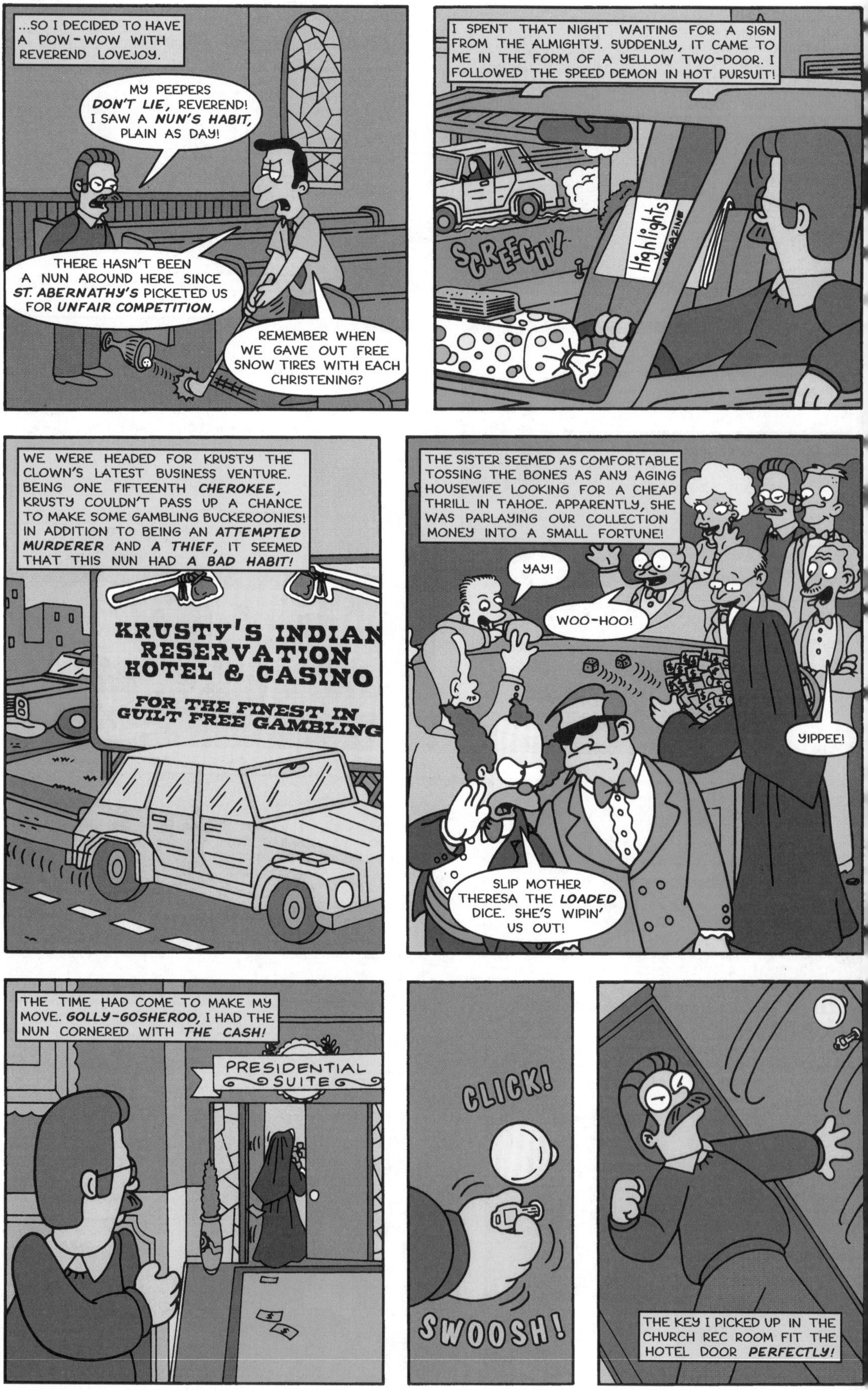

...SO I DECIDED TO HAVE A POW-WOW WITH REVEREND LOVEJOY.
MY PEEPERS DON'T LIE, REVEREND! I SAW A NUN'S HABIT, PLAIN AS DAY!
THERE HASN'T BEEN A NUN AROUND HERE SINCE ST. ABERNATHY'S PICKETED US FOR UNFAIR COMPETITION.
REMEMBER WHEN WE GAVE OUT FREE SNOW TIRES WITH EACH CHRISTENING?
I SPENT THAT NIGHT WAITING FOR A SIGN FROM THE ALMIGHTY. SUDDENLY, IT CAME TO ME IN THE FORM OF A YELLOW TWO-DOOR. I FOLLOWED THE SPEED DEMON IN HOT PURSUIT!
SCREECH!
Highlights MAGAZINE
WE WERE HEADED FOR KRUSTY THE CLOWN'S LATEST BUSINESS VENTURE. BEING ONE FIFTEENTH CHEROKEE, KRUSTY COULDN'T PASS UP A CHANCE TO MAKE SOME GAMBLING BUCKEROONIES! IN ADDITION TO BEING AN ATTEMPTED MURDERER AND A THIEF, IT SEEMED THAT THIS NUN HAD A BAD HABIT!
KRUSTY'S INDIAN RESERVATION HOTEL & CASINO
FOR THE FINEST IN GUILT FREE GAMBLING
THE SISTER SEEMED AS COMFORTABLE TOSSING THE BONES AS ANY AGING HOUSEWIFE LOOKING FOR A CHEAP THRILL IN TAHOE. APPARENTLY, SHE WAS PARLAYING OUR COLLECTION MONEY INTO A SMALL FORTUNE!
YAY!
WOO-HOO!
YIPPEE!
SLIP MOTHER THERESA THE LOADED DICE. SHE'S WIPIN' US OUT!
THE TIME HAD COME TO MAKE MY MOVE. GOLLY-GOSHEROO, I HAD THE NUN CORNERED WITH THE CASH!
PRESIDENTIAL SUITE
CLICK!
SWOOSH!
THE KEY I PICKED UP IN THE CHURCH REC ROOM FIT THE HOTEL DOOR PERFECTLY!

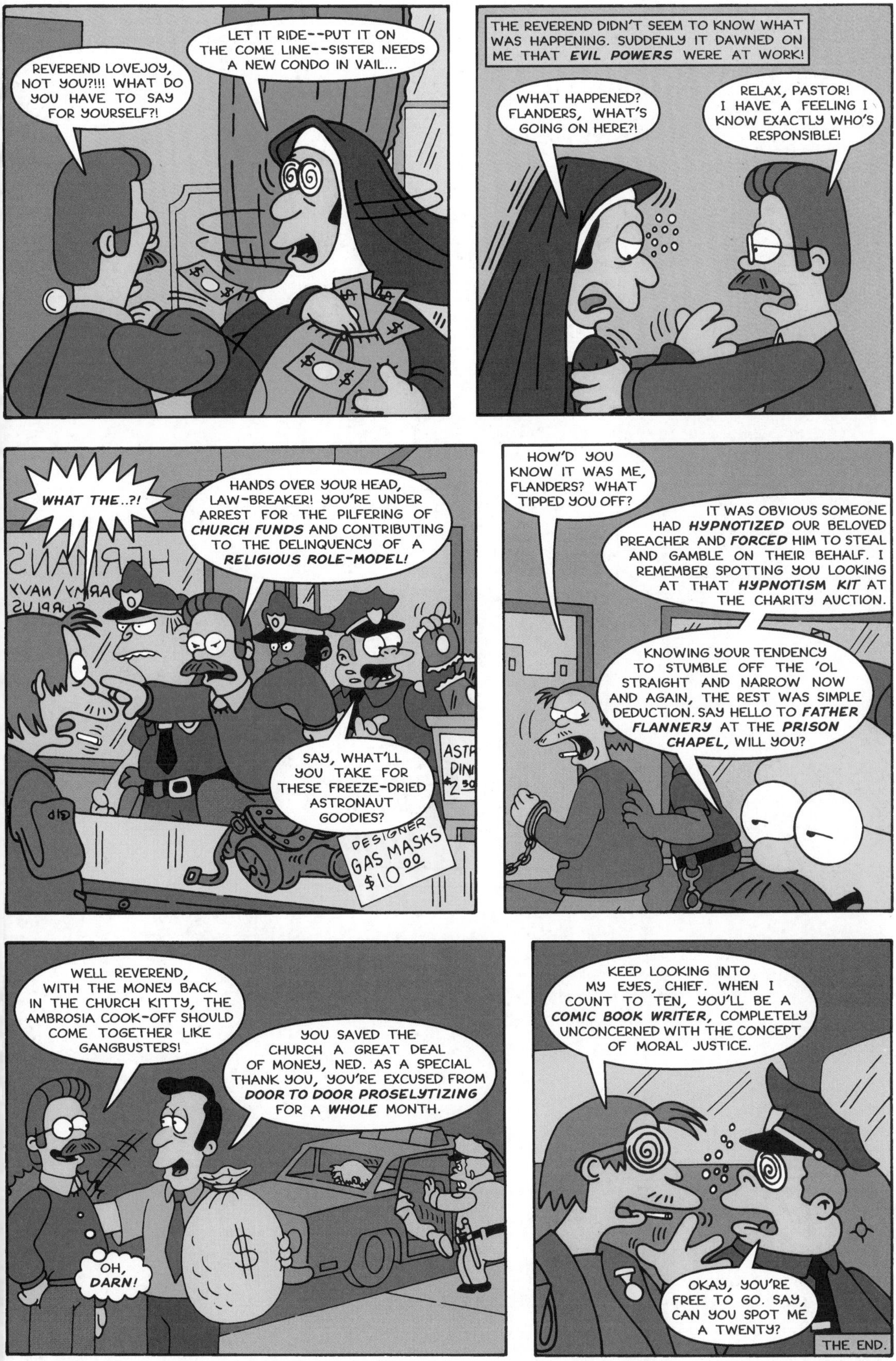
REVEREND LOVEJOY, NOT YOU?!!! WHAT DO YOU HAVE TO SAY FOR YOURSELF?!
LET IT RIDE--PUT IT ON THE COME LINE--SISTER NEEDS A NEW CONDO IN VAIL...
THE REVEREND DIDN'T SEEM TO KNOW WHAT WAS HAPPENING. SUDDENLY IT DAWNED ON ME THAT EVIL POWERS WERE AT WORK!
WHAT HAPPENED? FLANDERS, WHAT'S GOING ON HERE?!
RELAX, PASTOR! I HAVE A FEELING I KNOW EXACTLY WHO'S RESPONSIBLE!
WHAT THE..?!
HANDS OVER YOUR HEAD, LAW-BREAKER! YOU'RE UNDER ARREST FOR THE PILFERING OF CHURCH FUNDS AND CONTRIBUTING TO THE DELINQUENCY OF A RELIGIOUS ROLE-MODEL!
HERMAN'S ARMY/NAVY SURPLUS
SAY, WHAT'LL YOU TAKE FOR THESE FREEZE-DRIED ASTRONAUT GOODIES?
DESIGNER GAS MASKS $10.00
HOW'D YOU KNOW IT WAS ME, FLANDERS? WHAT TIPPED YOU OFF?
IT WAS OBVIOUS SOMEONE HAD HYPNOTIZED OUR BELOVED PREACHER AND FORCED HIM TO STEAL AND GAMBLE ON THEIR BEHALF. I REMEMBER SPOTTING YOU LOOKING AT THAT HYPNOTISM KIT AT THE CHARITY AUCTION.
KNOWING YOUR TENDENCY TO STUMBLE OFF THE 'OL STRAIGHT AND NARROW NOW AND AGAIN, THE REST WAS SIMPLE DEDUCTION. SAY HELLO TO FATHER FLANNERY AT THE PRISON CHAPEL, WILL YOU?
WELL REVEREND, WITH THE MONEY BACK IN THE CHURCH KITTY, THE AMBROSIA COOK-OFF SHOULD COME TOGETHER LIKE GANGBUSTERS!
YOU SAVED THE CHURCH A GREAT DEAL OF MONEY, NED. AS A SPECIAL THANK YOU, YOU'RE EXCUSED FROM DOOR TO DOOR PROSELYTIZING FOR A WHOLE MONTH.
OH, DARN!
KEEP LOOKING INTO MY EYES, CHIEF. WHEN I COUNT TO TEN, YOU'LL BE A COMIC BOOK WRITER, COMPLETELY UNCONCERNED WITH THE CONCEPT OF MORAL JUSTICE.
OKAY, YOU'RE FREE TO GO. SAY, CAN YOU SPOT ME A TWENTY?
THE END.

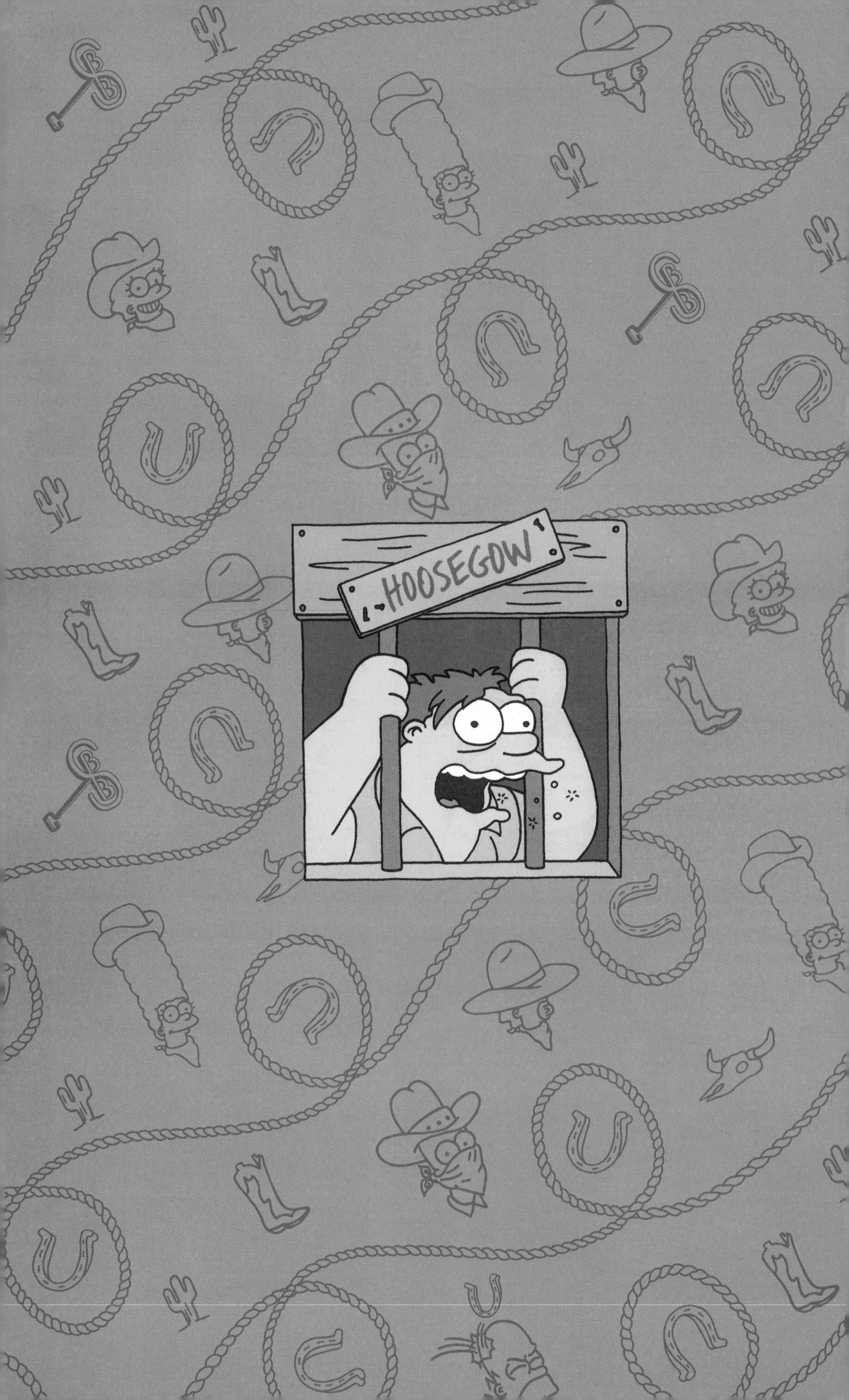
HOOSEGOW

BONGO COMICS GROUP
#29
APPROVED BY THE COMICS CODE AUTHORITY
SIMPSONS COMICS
S
GROENING

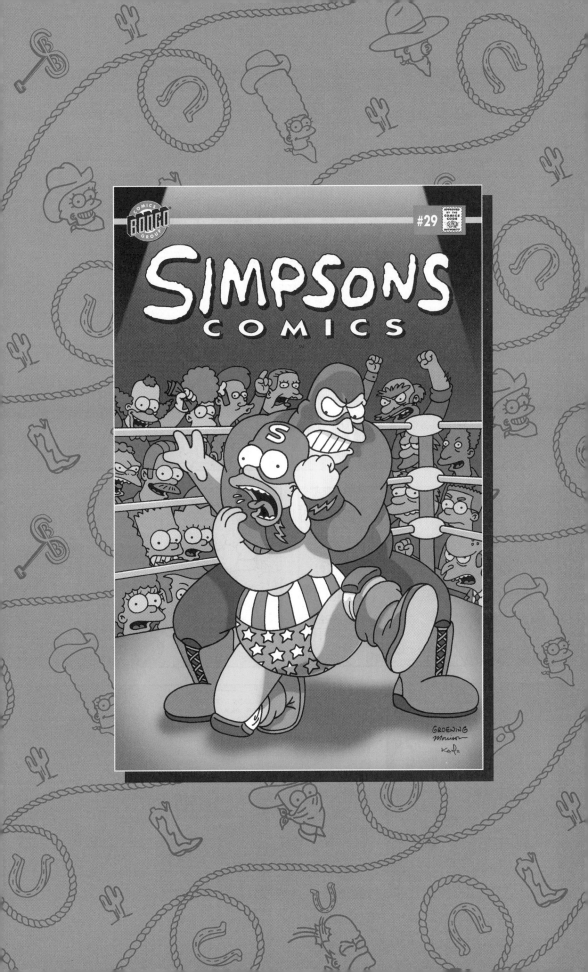

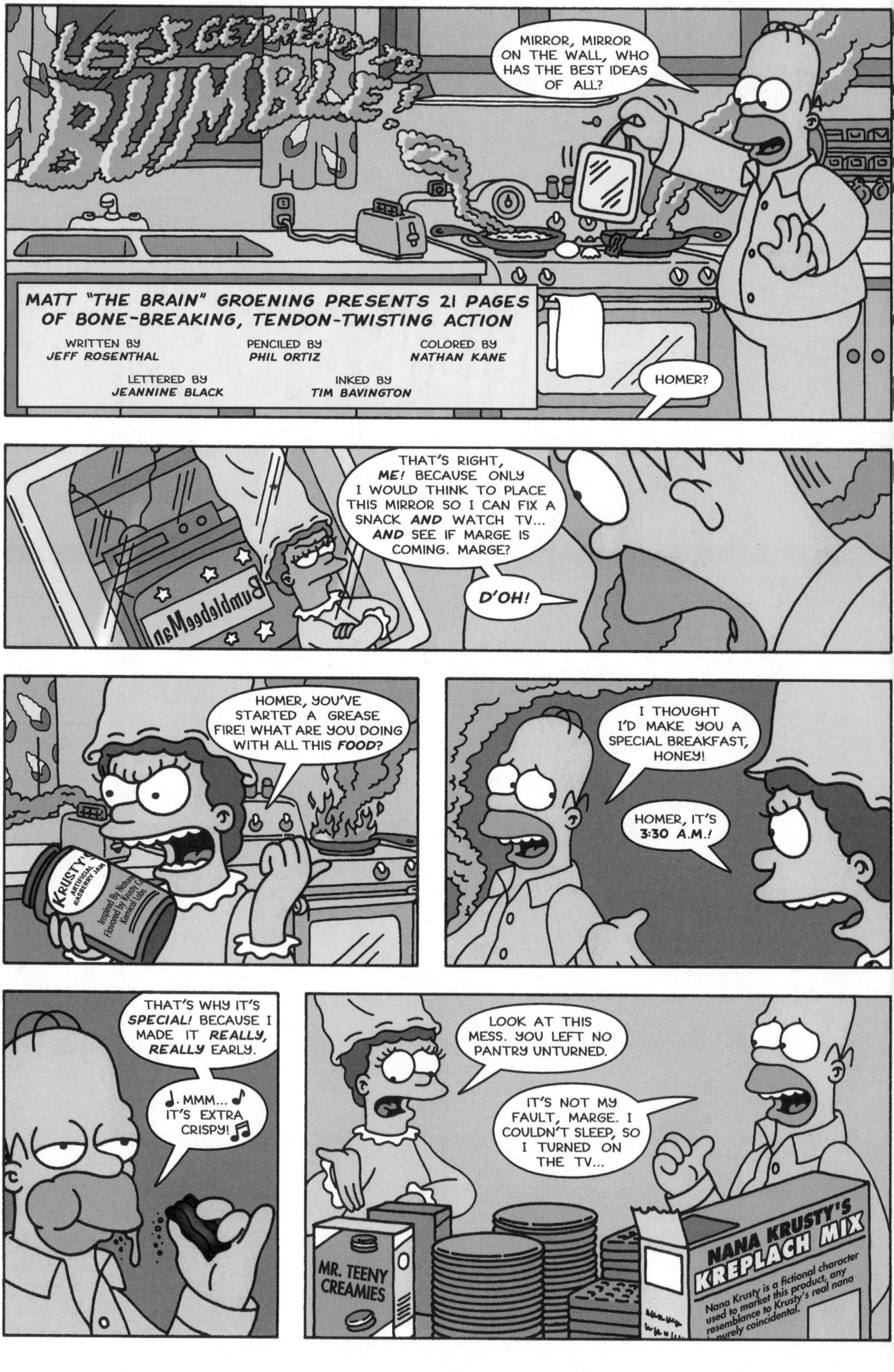
LET'S GET READY TO BUMBLE!
MIRROR, MIRROR ON THE WALL, WHO HAS THE BEST IDEAS OF ALL?
MATT "THE BRAIN" GROENING PRESENTS 21 PAGES OF BONE-BREAKING, TENDON-TWISTING ACTION
WRITTEN BY JEFF ROSENTHAL
PENCILED BY PHIL ORTIZ
COLORED BY NATHAN KANE
LETTERED BY JEANNINE BLACK
INKED BY TIM BAVINGTON
HOMER?
THAT'S RIGHT, *ME!* BECAUSE ONLY I WOULD THINK TO PLACE THIS MIRROR SO I CAN FIX A SNACK *AND* WATCH TV... *AND* SEE IF MARGE IS COMING. MARGE?
D'OH!
HOMER, YOU'VE STARTED A GREASE FIRE! WHAT ARE YOU DOING WITH ALL THIS *FOOD*?
KRUSTY'S ARTIFICIAL RASBERRY JAM
I THOUGHT I'D MAKE YOU A SPECIAL BREAKFAST, HONEY!
HOMER, IT'S **3:30 A.M.!**
THAT'S WHY IT'S *SPECIAL!* BECAUSE I MADE IT *REALLY, REALLY* EARLY.
♩. MMM... ♪ IT'S EXTRA CRISPY! ♫
LOOK AT THIS MESS. YOU LEFT NO PANTRY UNTURNED.
IT'S NOT MY FAULT, MARGE. I COULDN'T SLEEP, SO I TURNED ON THE TV...
MR. TEENY CREAMIES
NANA KRUSTY'S KREPLACH MIX
Nana Krusty is a fictional character used to market this product, any resemblance to Krusty's real nana is purely coincidental.

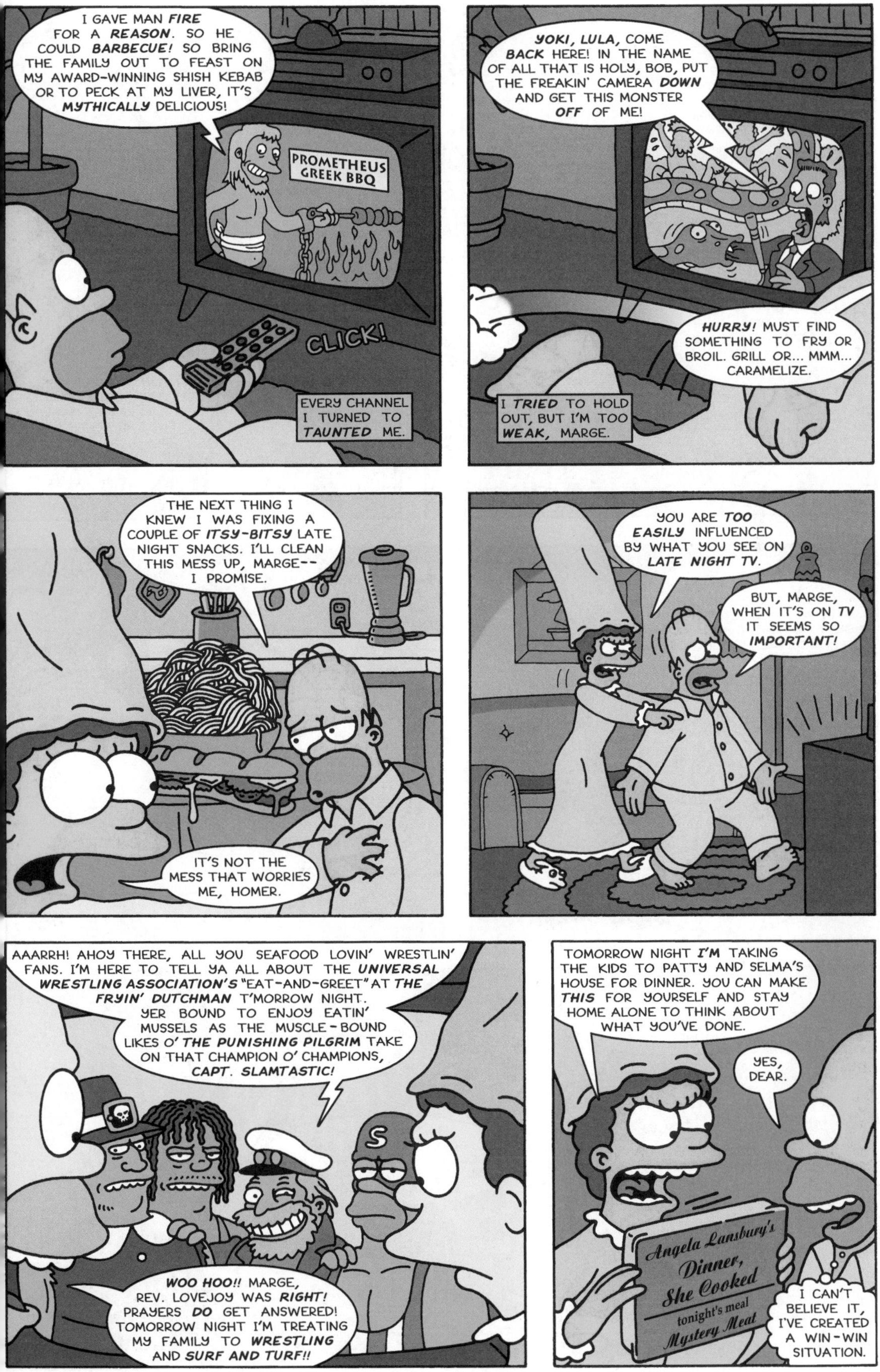
I GAVE MAN FIRE FOR A REASON. SO HE COULD BARBECUE! SO BRING THE FAMILY OUT TO FEAST ON MY AWARD-WINNING SHISH KEBAB OR TO PECK AT MY LIVER, IT'S MYTHICALLY DELICIOUS!
PROMETHEUS GREEK BBQ
CLICK!
EVERY CHANNEL I TURNED TO TAUNTED ME.
YOKI, LULA, COME BACK HERE! IN THE NAME OF ALL THAT IS HOLY, BOB, PUT THE FREAKIN' CAMERA DOWN AND GET THIS MONSTER OFF OF ME!
HURRY! MUST FIND SOMETHING TO FRY OR BROIL. GRILL OR... MMM... CARAMELIZE.
I TRIED TO HOLD OUT, BUT I'M TOO WEAK, MARGE.
THE NEXT THING I KNEW I WAS FIXING A COUPLE OF ITSY-BITSY LATE NIGHT SNACKS. I'LL CLEAN THIS MESS UP, MARGE-- I PROMISE.
IT'S NOT THE MESS THAT WORRIES ME, HOMER.
YOU ARE TOO EASILY INFLUENCED BY WHAT YOU SEE ON LATE NIGHT TV.
BUT, MARGE, WHEN IT'S ON TV IT SEEMS SO IMPORTANT!
AAARRH! AHOY THERE, ALL YOU SEAFOOD LOVIN' WRESTLIN' FANS. I'M HERE TO TELL YA ALL ABOUT THE UNIVERSAL WRESTLING ASSOCIATION'S "EAT-AND-GREET" AT THE FRYIN' DUTCHMAN T'MORROW NIGHT. YER BOUND TO ENJOY EATIN' MUSSELS AS THE MUSCLE-BOUND LIKES O' THE PUNISHING PILGRIM TAKE ON THAT CHAMPION O' CHAMPIONS, CAPT. SLAMTASTIC!
S
WOO HOO!! MARGE, REV. LOVEJOY WAS RIGHT! PRAYERS DO GET ANSWERED! TOMORROW NIGHT I'M TREATING MY FAMILY TO WRESTLING AND SURF AND TURF!!
TOMORROW NIGHT I'M TAKING THE KIDS TO PATTY AND SELMA'S HOUSE FOR DINNER. YOU CAN MAKE THIS FOR YOURSELF AND STAY HOME ALONE TO THINK ABOUT WHAT YOU'VE DONE.
YES, DEAR.
Angela Lansbury's Dinner, She Cooked
tonight's meal Mystery Meat
I CAN'T BELIEVE IT, I'VE CREATED A WIN-WIN SITUATION.

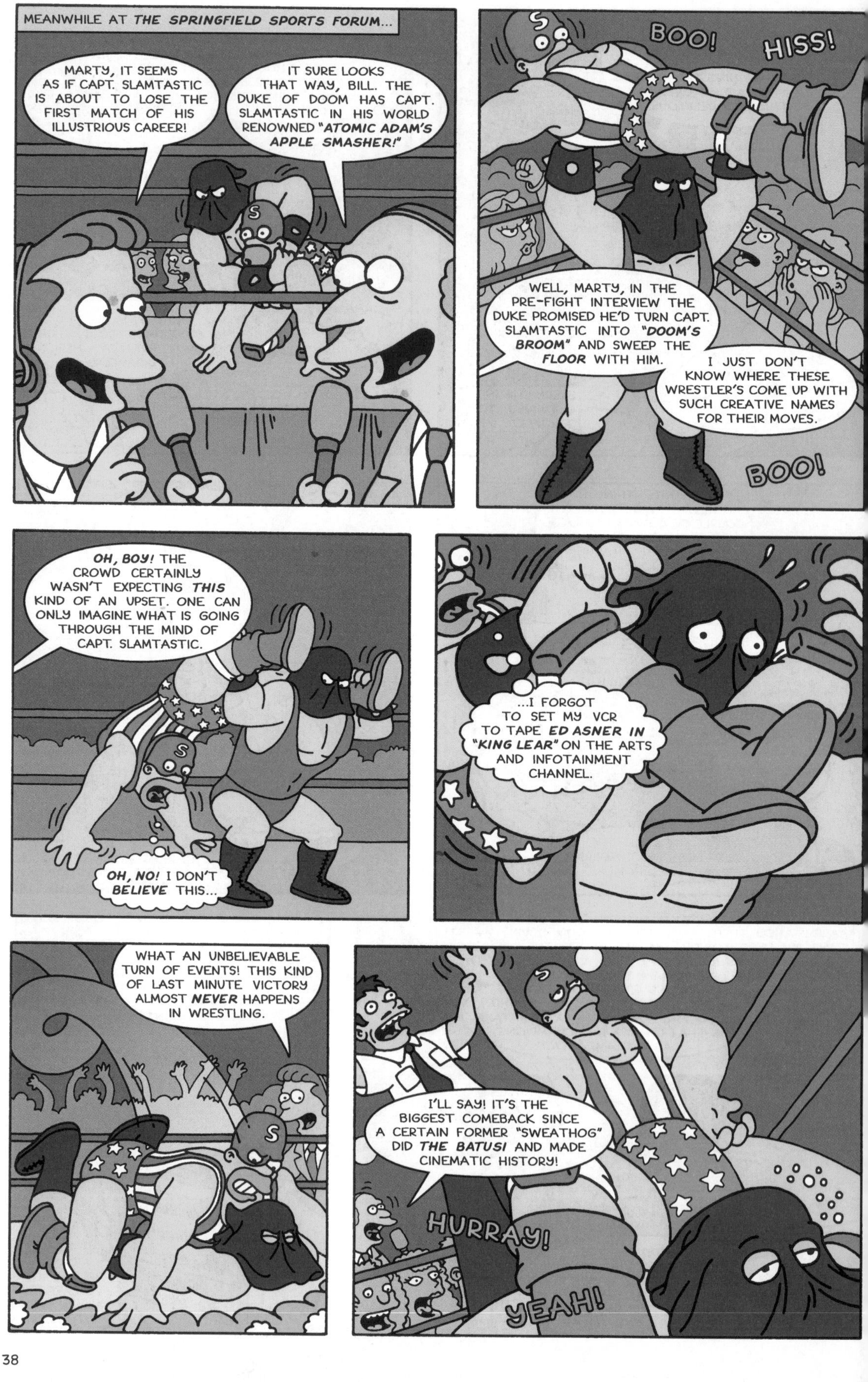
MEANWHILE AT THE SPRINGFIELD SPORTS FORUM...
MARTY, IT SEEMS AS IF CAPT. SLAMTASTIC IS ABOUT TO LOSE THE FIRST MATCH OF HIS ILLUSTRIOUS CAREER!
IT SURE LOOKS THAT WAY, BILL. THE DUKE OF DOOM HAS CAPT. SLAMTASTIC IN HIS WORLD RENOWNED "ATOMIC ADAM'S APPLE SMASHER!"
BOO!
HISS!
WELL, MARTY, IN THE PRE-FIGHT INTERVIEW THE DUKE PROMISED HE'D TURN CAPT. SLAMTASTIC INTO "DOOM'S BROOM" AND SWEEP THE FLOOR WITH HIM.
I JUST DON'T KNOW WHERE THESE WRESTLER'S COME UP WITH SUCH CREATIVE NAMES FOR THEIR MOVES.
BOO!
OH, BOY! THE CROWD CERTAINLY WASN'T EXPECTING THIS KIND OF AN UPSET. ONE CAN ONLY IMAGINE WHAT IS GOING THROUGH THE MIND OF CAPT. SLAMTASTIC.
OH, NO! I DON'T BELIEVE THIS...
...I FORGOT TO SET MY VCR TO TAPE ED ASNER IN "KING LEAR" ON THE ARTS AND INFOTAINMENT CHANNEL.
WHAT AN UNBELIEVABLE TURN OF EVENTS! THIS KIND OF LAST MINUTE VICTORY ALMOST NEVER HAPPENS IN WRESTLING.
I'LL SAY! IT'S THE BIGGEST COMEBACK SINCE A CERTAIN FORMER "SWEATHOG" DID THE BATUSI AND MADE CINEMATIC HISTORY!
HURRAY!
YEAH!

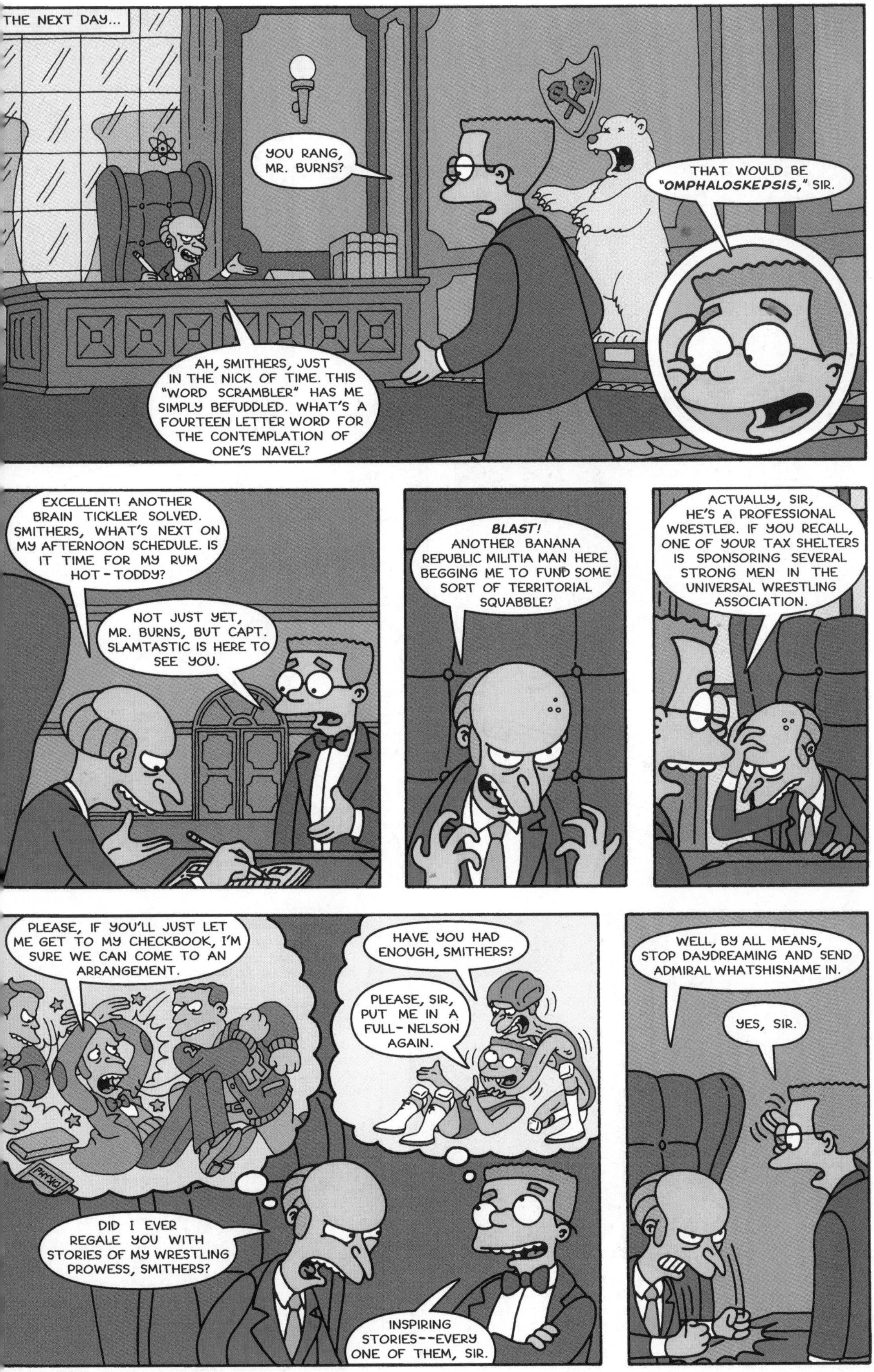

THE NEXT DAY...
YOU RANG, MR. BURNS?
AH, SMITHERS, JUST IN THE NICK OF TIME. THIS "WORD SCRAMBLER" HAS ME SIMPLY BEFUDDLED. WHAT'S A FOURTEEN LETTER WORD FOR THE CONTEMPLATION OF ONE'S NAVEL?
THAT WOULD BE "OMPHALOSKEPSIS," SIR.
EXCELLENT! ANOTHER BRAIN TICKLER SOLVED. SMITHERS, WHAT'S NEXT ON MY AFTERNOON SCHEDULE. IS IT TIME FOR MY RUM HOT-TODDY?
NOT JUST YET, MR. BURNS, BUT CAPT. SLAMTASTIC IS HERE TO SEE YOU.
BLAST! ANOTHER BANANA REPUBLIC MILITIA MAN HERE BEGGING ME TO FUND SOME SORT OF TERRITORIAL SQUABBLE?
ACTUALLY, SIR, HE'S A PROFESSIONAL WRESTLER. IF YOU RECALL, ONE OF YOUR TAX SHELTERS IS SPONSORING SEVERAL STRONG MEN IN THE UNIVERSAL WRESTLING ASSOCIATION.
PLEASE, IF YOU'LL JUST LET ME GET TO MY CHECKBOOK, I'M SURE WE CAN COME TO AN ARRANGEMENT.
PHYSICS
DID I EVER REGALE YOU WITH STORIES OF MY WRESTLING PROWESS, SMITHERS?
HAVE YOU HAD ENOUGH, SMITHERS?
PLEASE, SIR, PUT ME IN A FULL-NELSON AGAIN.
INSPIRING STORIES--EVERY ONE OF THEM, SIR.
WELL, BY ALL MEANS, STOP DAYDREAMING AND SEND ADMIRAL WHATSHISNAME IN.
YES, SIR.

YOU'VE HAD QUITE A CAREER, CAPTAIN **SPAM**TASTIC. TO WHAT DO YOU ATTRIBUTE YOUR UNFLAGGING SUCCESS?

YOU KNOW, MR. BURNS... THE FACT THAT ALL THE FIGHTS ARE *FIXED*.

THEY'RE *WHAT!?!* THIS IS AN *OUTRAGE!* WHO IS THE TWO-BIT SHILL WHO WOULD *PERPETRATE* THIS KIND OF SHAM?

I'M AFRAID *YOU ARE*, SIR.

THE MAULER OF MALTA -$500.

THE ZIMBARBNIAN ZEPHYR -$1,000.

THE ALASKAN TASKMASTER -$450.

THE DUKE OF DOOM -$500.

YOU SEE, BY INSURING CAPTAIN SLAMTASTIC'S SUCCESS IN THE RING, WE INCREASE THE POPULARITY OF HIS MERCHANDISE. THIS BRINGS IN APPROXIMATELY 3.2 MILLION A YEAR AND CHANGE *AND* IS OWNED BY *BURNS, INC.*

CAPT. SLAMTASTIC VS. Pharmacist Phil IN "SAY NO TO DRUGS."

EXCELLENT, SMITHERS, *EXCELLENT!* BUT WHY DIDN'T I *KNOW* ABOUT THIS?

AS I SAID, SIR, IT *ONLY* BRINGS IN 3.2 MILLION A YEAR AND CHANGE. I DIDN'T WANT TO BOTHER YOU WITH AN INVESTMENT THAT SMALL.

SO, MY GOOD CAPTAIN, WHAT BRINGS *YOU* HERE? HAVE YOU COME TO IMPART GRATIS TO THE HAND THAT FEEDS OR BEG FOR A LARGER PERCENTAGE OF THE PALTRY SUM I MAKE FROM YOUR LIKENESS?

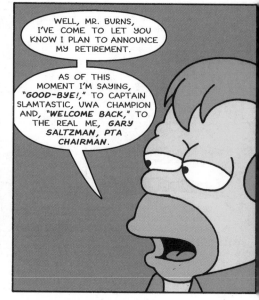

WELL, MR. BURNS, I'VE COME TO LET YOU KNOW I PLAN TO ANNOUNCE MY RETIREMENT.

AS OF THIS MOMENT I'M SAYING, *"GOOD-BYE!,"* TO CAPTAIN SLAMTASTIC, UWA CHAMPION AND, *"WELCOME BACK,"* TO THE REAL ME, *GARY SALTZMAN*, PTA CHAIRMAN.

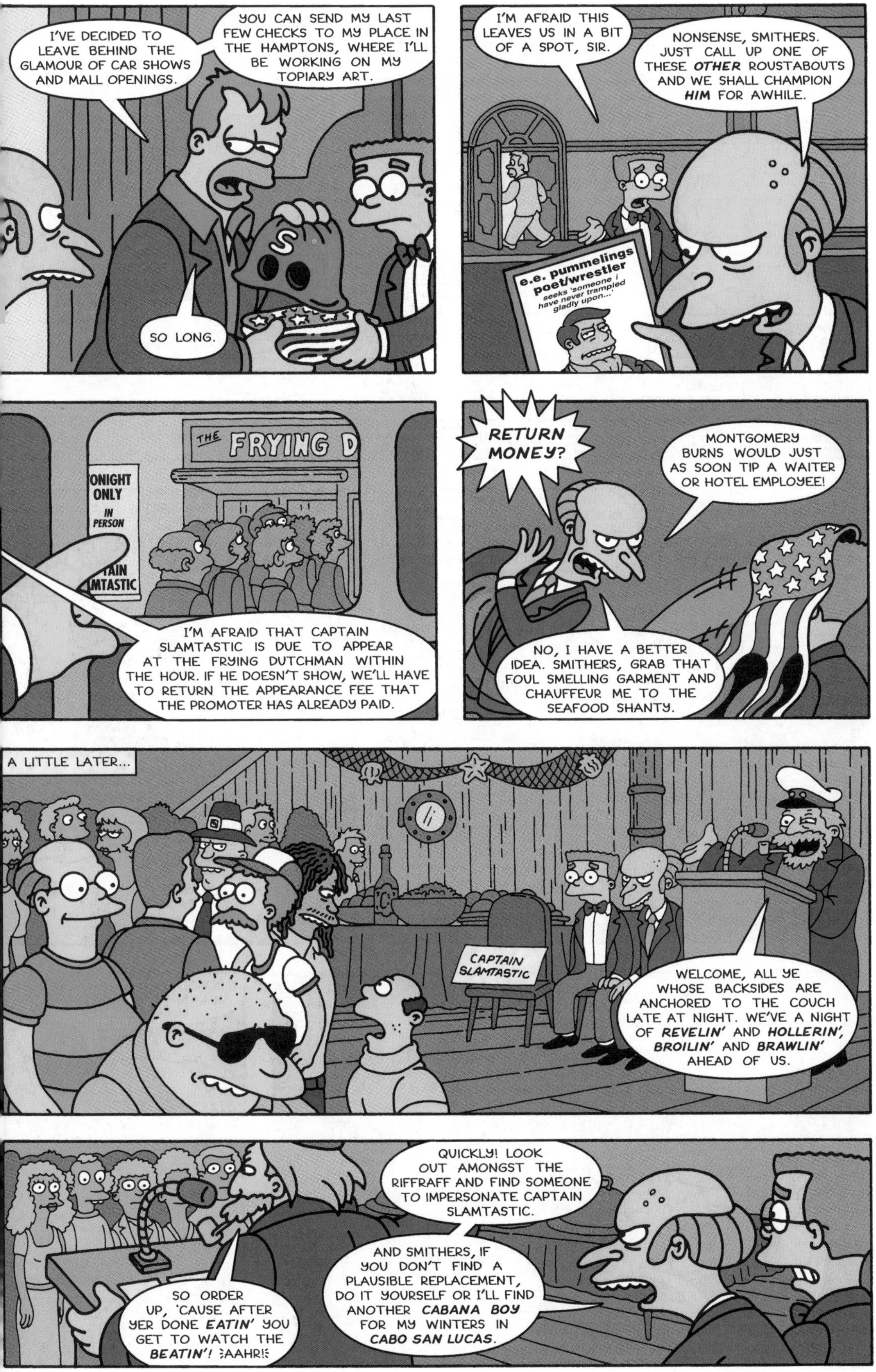

I'VE DECIDED TO LEAVE BEHIND THE GLAMOUR OF CAR SHOWS AND MALL OPENINGS.
YOU CAN SEND MY LAST FEW CHECKS TO MY PLACE IN THE HAMPTONS, WHERE I'LL BE WORKING ON MY TOPIARY ART.
SO LONG.
I'M AFRAID THIS LEAVES US IN A BIT OF A SPOT, SIR.
NONSENSE, SMITHERS. JUST CALL UP ONE OF THESE *OTHER* ROUSTABOUTS AND WE SHALL CHAMPION *HIM* FOR AWHILE.
e.e. pummelings
poet/wrestler
seeks 'someone i have never trampled gladly upon...'
THE FRYING D
ONLY
IN PERSON
I'M AFRAID THAT CAPTAIN SLAMTASTIC IS DUE TO APPEAR AT THE FRYING DUTCHMAN WITHIN THE HOUR. IF HE DOESN'T SHOW, WE'LL HAVE TO RETURN THE APPEARANCE FEE THAT THE PROMOTER HAS ALREADY PAID.
RETURN MONEY?
MONTGOMERY BURNS WOULD JUST AS SOON TIP A WAITER OR HOTEL EMPLOYEE!
NO, I HAVE A BETTER IDEA. SMITHERS, GRAB THAT FOUL SMELLING GARMENT AND CHAUFFEUR ME TO THE SEAFOOD SHANTY.
A LITTLE LATER...
CAPTAIN SLAMTASTIC
WELCOME, ALL YE WHOSE BACKSIDES ARE ANCHORED TO THE COUCH LATE AT NIGHT. WE'VE A NIGHT OF *REVELIN'* AND *HOLLERIN'*, *BROILIN'* AND *BRAWLIN'* AHEAD OF US.
SO ORDER UP, 'CAUSE AFTER YER DONE *EATIN'* YOU GET TO WATCH THE *BEATIN'*! AAHR!!
QUICKLY! LOOK OUT AMONGST THE RIFFRAFF AND FIND SOMEONE TO IMPERSONATE CAPTAIN SLAMTASTIC.
AND SMITHERS, IF YOU DON'T FIND A PLAUSIBLE REPLACEMENT, DO IT YOURSELF OR I'LL FIND ANOTHER *CABANA BOY* FOR MY WINTERS IN *CABO SAN LUCAS*.

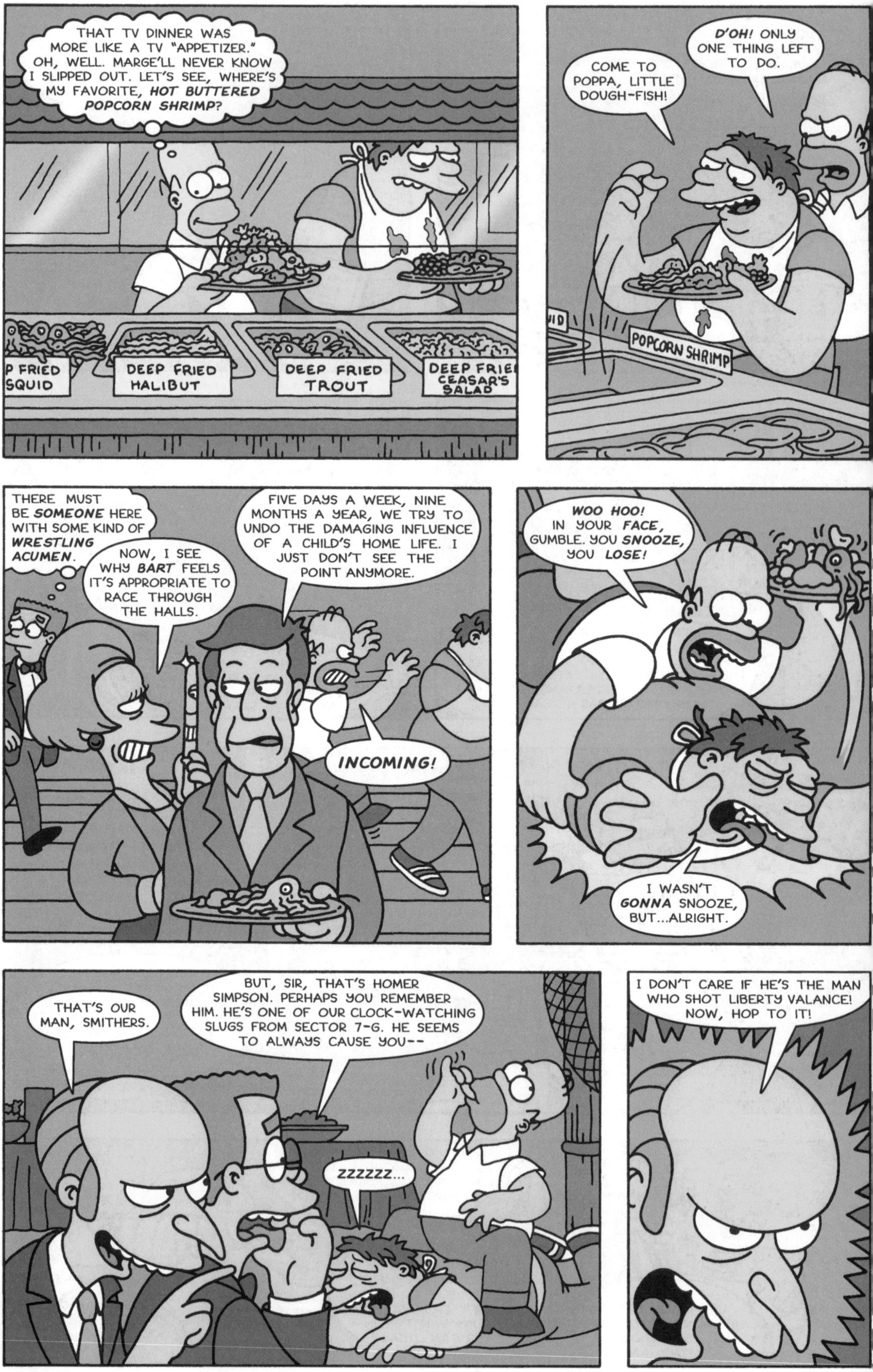

THAT TV DINNER WAS MORE LIKE A TV "APPETIZER." OH, WELL. MARGE'LL NEVER KNOW I SLIPPED OUT. LET'S SEE, WHERE'S MY FAVORITE, *HOT BUTTERED POPCORN SHRIMP*?
P FRIED SQUID
DEEP FRIED HALIBUT
DEEP FRIED TROUT
DEEP FRIE CEASAR'S SALAD
COME TO POPPA, LITTLE DOUGH-FISH!
D'OH! ONLY ONE THING LEFT TO DO.
ID
POPCORN SHRIMP
THERE MUST BE *SOMEONE* HERE WITH SOME KIND OF *WRESTLING ACUMEN*.
NOW, I SEE WHY *BART* FEELS IT'S APPROPRIATE TO RACE THROUGH THE HALLS.
FIVE DAYS A WEEK, NINE MONTHS A YEAR, WE TRY TO UNDO THE DAMAGING INFLUENCE OF A CHILD'S HOME LIFE. I JUST DON'T SEE THE POINT ANYMORE.
INCOMING!
WOO HOO! IN YOUR *FACE*, GUMBLE. YOU *SNOOZE*, YOU *LOSE*!
I WASN'T *GONNA* SNOOZE, BUT...ALRIGHT.
THAT'S OUR MAN, SMITHERS.
BUT, SIR, THAT'S HOMER SIMPSON. PERHAPS YOU REMEMBER HIM. HE'S ONE OF OUR CLOCK-WATCHING SLUGS FROM SECTOR 7-G. HE SEEMS TO ALWAYS CAUSE YOU--
ZZZZZZ...
I DON'T CARE IF HE'S THE MAN WHO SHOT LIBERTY VALANCE! NOW, HOP TO IT!

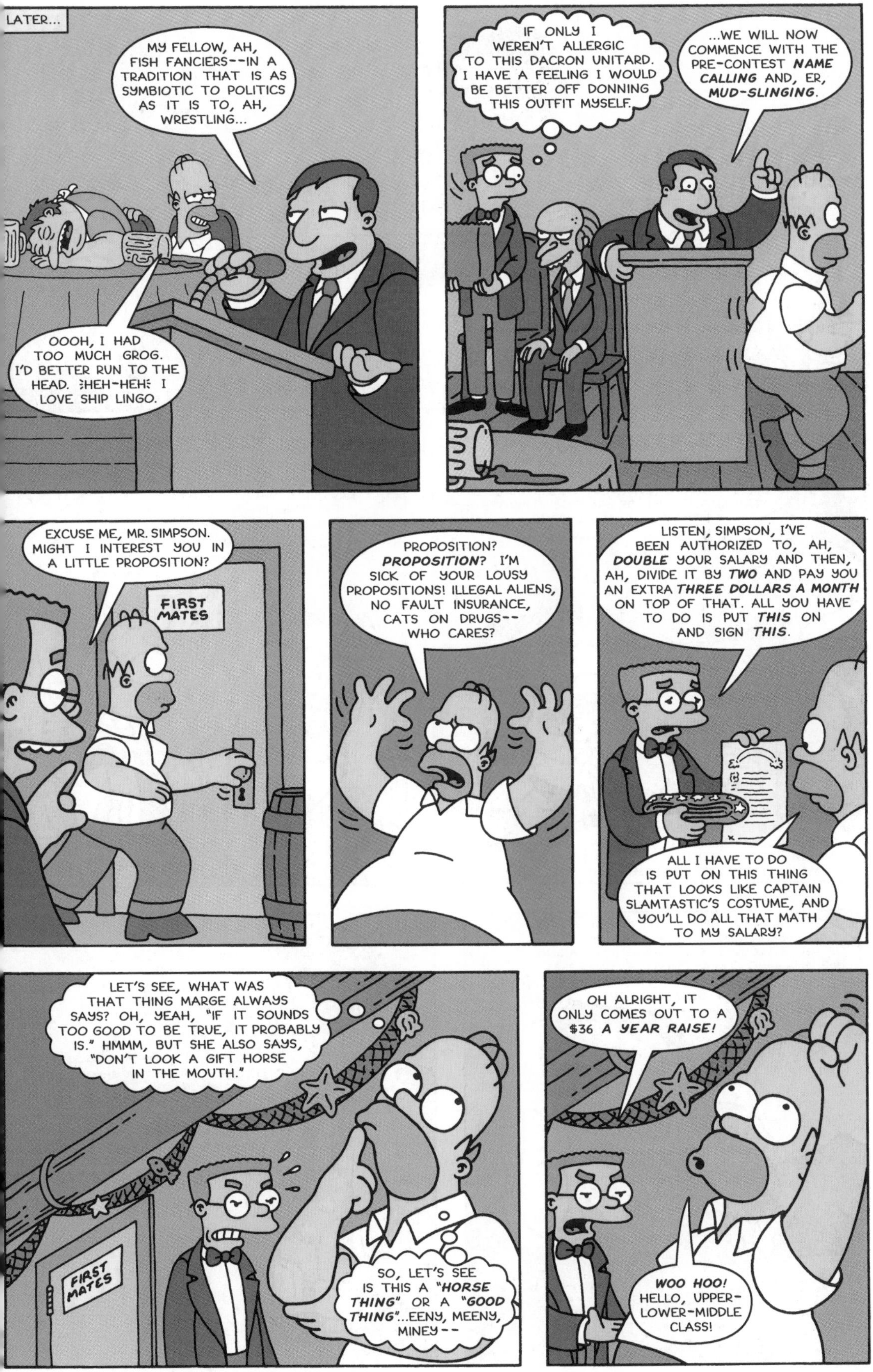
LATER...
MY FELLOW, AH, FISH FANCIERS--IN A TRADITION THAT IS AS SYMBIOTIC TO POLITICS AS IT IS TO, AH, WRESTLING...
OOOH, I HAD TOO MUCH GROG. I'D BETTER RUN TO THE HEAD. HEH-HEH I LOVE SHIP LINGO.
IF ONLY I WEREN'T ALLERGIC TO THIS DACRON UNITARD. I HAVE A FEELING I WOULD BE BETTER OFF DONNING THIS OUTFIT MYSELF.
...WE WILL NOW COMMENCE WITH THE PRE-CONTEST NAME CALLING AND, ER, MUD-SLINGING.
EXCUSE ME, MR. SIMPSON. MIGHT I INTEREST YOU IN A LITTLE PROPOSITION?
FIRST MATES
PROPOSITION? PROPOSITION? I'M SICK OF YOUR LOUSY PROPOSITIONS! ILLEGAL ALIENS, NO FAULT INSURANCE, CATS ON DRUGS-- WHO CARES?
LISTEN, SIMPSON, I'VE BEEN AUTHORIZED TO, AH, DOUBLE YOUR SALARY AND THEN, AH, DIVIDE IT BY TWO AND PAY YOU AN EXTRA THREE DOLLARS A MONTH ON TOP OF THAT. ALL YOU HAVE TO DO IS PUT THIS ON AND SIGN THIS.
ALL I HAVE TO DO IS PUT ON THIS THING THAT LOOKS LIKE CAPTAIN SLAMTASTIC'S COSTUME, AND YOU'LL DO ALL THAT MATH TO MY SALARY?
LET'S SEE, WHAT WAS THAT THING MARGE ALWAYS SAYS? OH, YEAH, "IF IT SOUNDS TOO GOOD TO BE TRUE, IT PROBABLY IS." HMMM, BUT SHE ALSO SAYS, "DON'T LOOK A GIFT HORSE IN THE MOUTH."
FIRST MATES
SO, LET'S SEE IS THIS A "HORSE THING" OR A "GOOD THING"...EENY, MEENY, MINEY--
OH ALRIGHT, IT ONLY COMES OUT TO A $36 A YEAR RAISE!
WOO HOO! HELLO, UPPER-LOWER-MIDDLE CLASS!

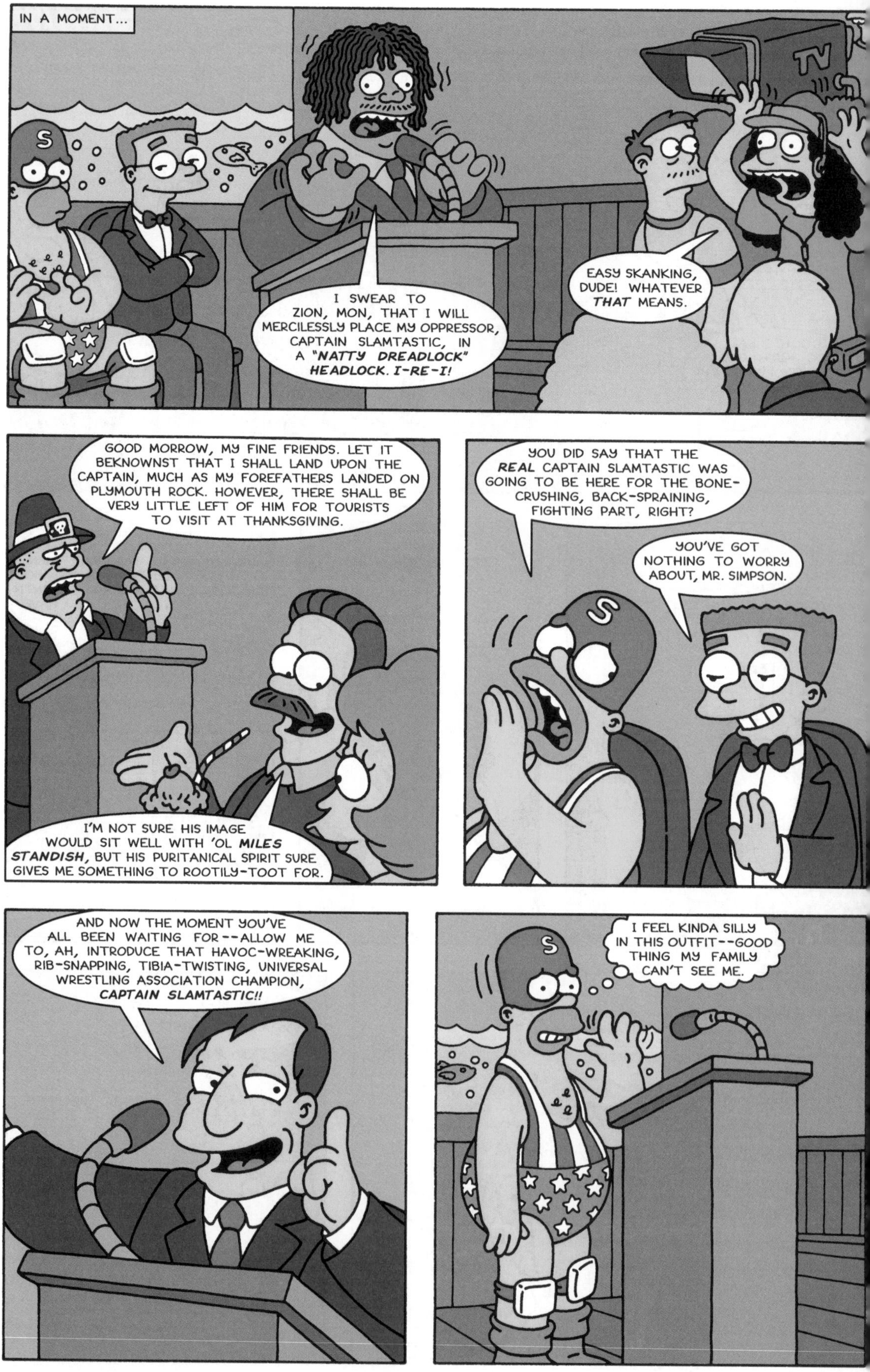
IN A MOMENT...
I SWEAR TO ZION, MON, THAT I WILL MERCILESSLY PLACE MY OPPRESSOR, CAPTAIN SLAMTASTIC, IN A "NATTY DREADLOCK" HEADLOCK. I-RE-I!
EASY SKANKING, DUDE! WHATEVER THAT MEANS.
TV
GOOD MORROW, MY FINE FRIENDS. LET IT BEKNOWNST THAT I SHALL LAND UPON THE CAPTAIN, MUCH AS MY FOREFATHERS LANDED ON PLYMOUTH ROCK. HOWEVER, THERE SHALL BE VERY LITTLE LEFT OF HIM FOR TOURISTS TO VISIT AT THANKSGIVING.
I'M NOT SURE HIS IMAGE WOULD SIT WELL WITH 'OL MILES STANDISH, BUT HIS PURITANICAL SPIRIT SURE GIVES ME SOMETHING TO ROOTILY-TOOT FOR.
YOU DID SAY THAT THE REAL CAPTAIN SLAMTASTIC WAS GOING TO BE HERE FOR THE BONE-CRUSHING, BACK-SPRAINING, FIGHTING PART, RIGHT?
YOU'VE GOT NOTHING TO WORRY ABOUT, MR. SIMPSON.
AND NOW THE MOMENT YOU'VE ALL BEEN WAITING FOR--ALLOW ME TO, AH, INTRODUCE THAT HAVOC-WREAKING, RIB-SNAPPING, TIBIA-TWISTING, UNIVERSAL WRESTLING ASSOCIATION CHAMPION, CAPTAIN SLAMTASTIC!!
I FEEL KINDA SILLY IN THIS OUTFIT--GOOD THING MY FAMILY CAN'T SEE ME.

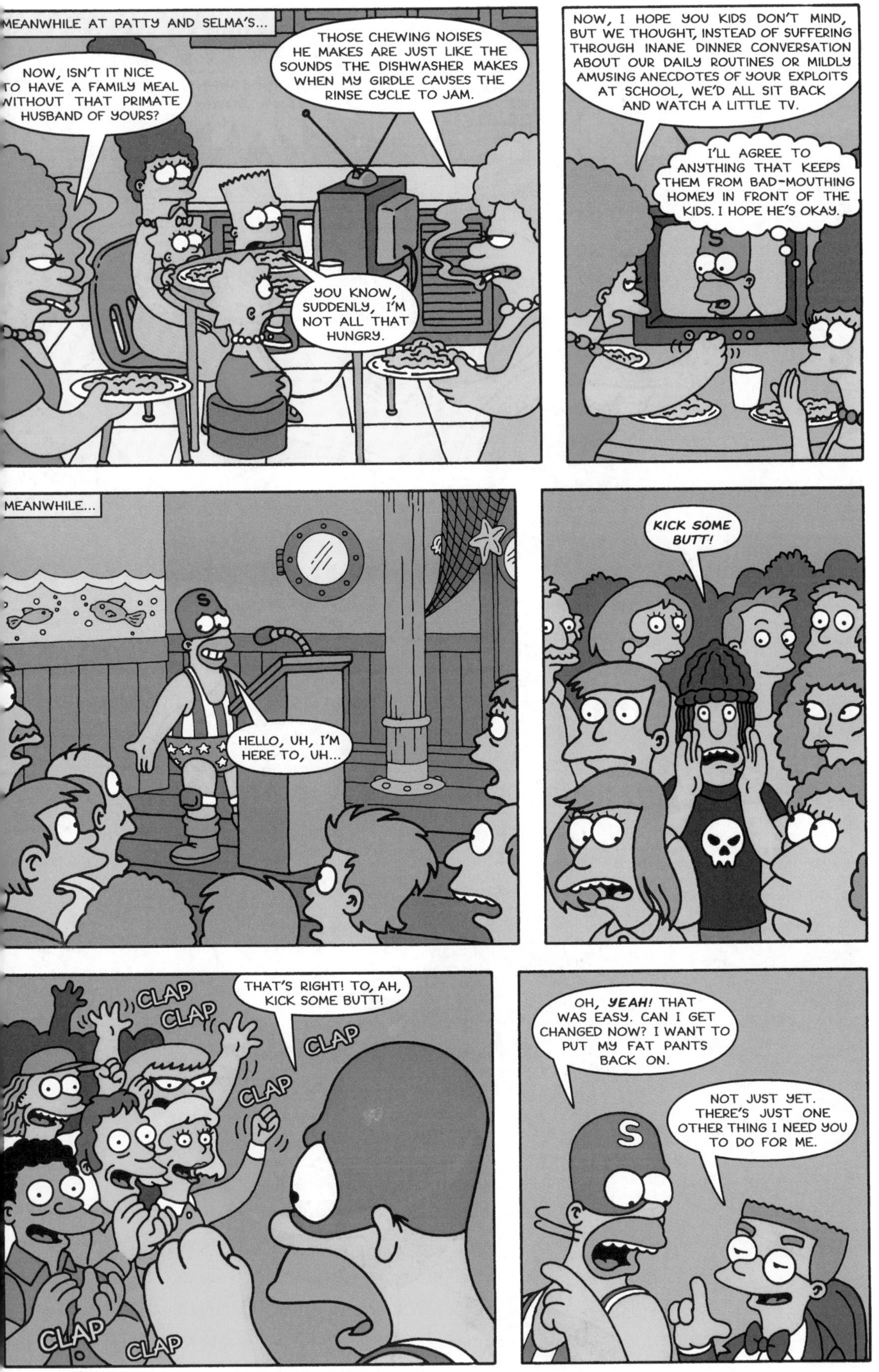
MEANWHILE AT PATTY AND SELMA'S...
NOW, ISN'T IT NICE TO HAVE A FAMILY MEAL WITHOUT THAT PRIMATE HUSBAND OF YOURS?
THOSE CHEWING NOISES HE MAKES ARE JUST LIKE THE SOUNDS THE DISHWASHER MAKES WHEN MY GIRDLE CAUSES THE RINSE CYCLE TO JAM.
YOU KNOW, SUDDENLY, I'M NOT ALL THAT HUNGRY.
NOW, I HOPE YOU KIDS DON'T MIND, BUT WE THOUGHT, INSTEAD OF SUFFERING THROUGH INANE DINNER CONVERSATION ABOUT OUR DAILY ROUTINES OR MILDLY AMUSING ANECDOTES OF YOUR EXPLOITS AT SCHOOL, WE'D ALL SIT BACK AND WATCH A LITTLE TV.
I'LL AGREE TO ANYTHING THAT KEEPS THEM FROM BAD-MOUTHING HOMEY IN FRONT OF THE KIDS. I HOPE HE'S OKAY.
MEANWHILE...
HELLO, UH, I'M HERE TO, UH...
KICK SOME BUTT!
THAT'S RIGHT! TO, AH, KICK SOME BUTT!
CLAP CLAP CLAP CLAP CLAP CLAP
OH, YEAH! THAT WAS EASY. CAN I GET CHANGED NOW? I WANT TO PUT MY FAT PANTS BACK ON.
NOT JUST YET. THERE'S JUST ONE OTHER THING I NEED YOU TO DO FOR ME.

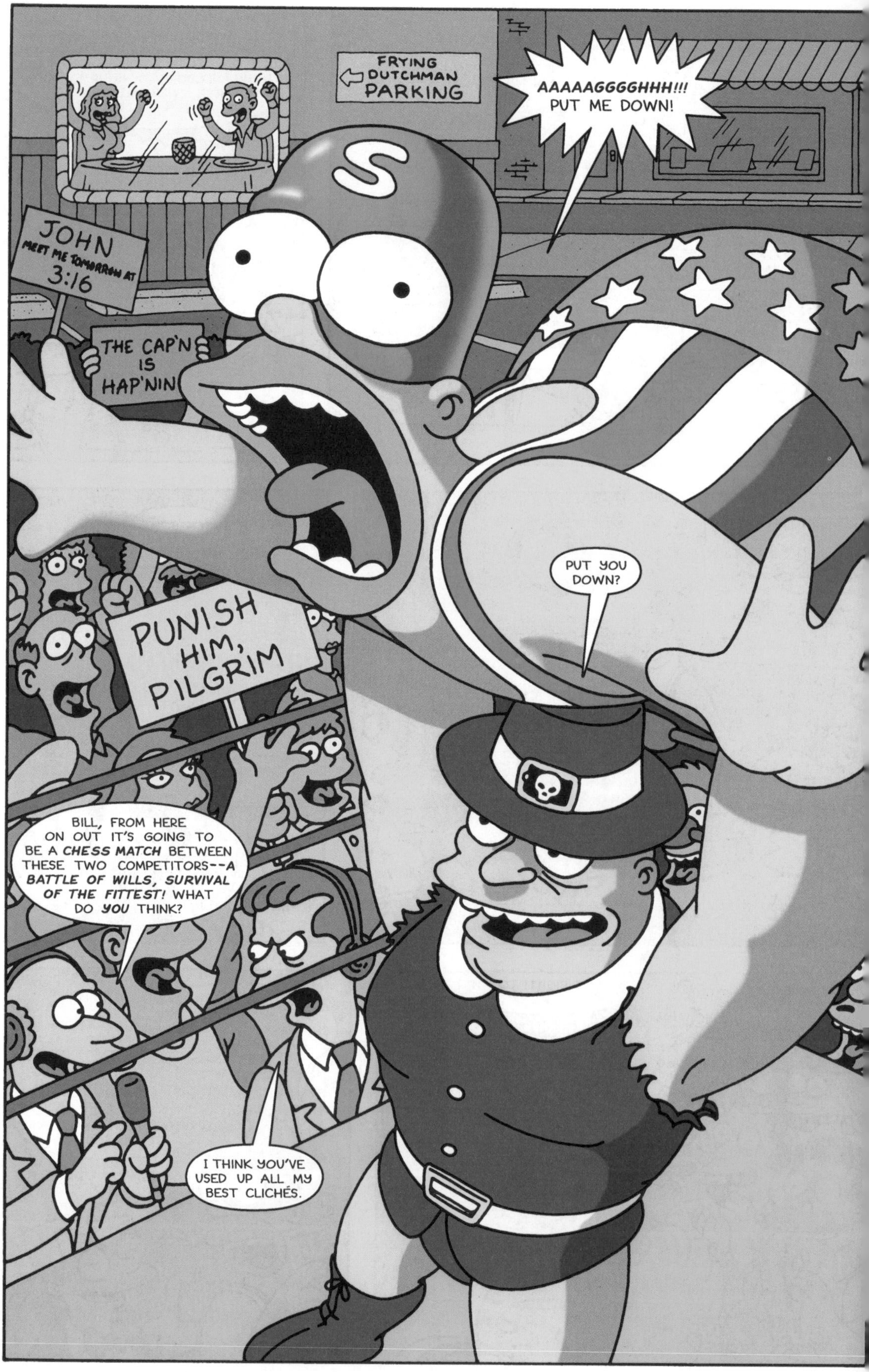
FRYING DUTCHMAN PARKING
AAAAAGGGGHHH!!! PUT ME DOWN!
JOHN MEET ME TOMORROW AT 3:16
THE CAP'N IS HAP'NIN
PUNISH HIM, PILGRIM
PUT YOU DOWN?
BILL, FROM HERE ON OUT IT'S GOING TO BE A CHESS MATCH BETWEEN THESE TWO COMPETITORS--A BATTLE OF WILLS, SURVIVAL OF THE FITTEST! WHAT DO YOU THINK?
I THINK YOU'VE USED UP ALL MY BEST CLICHÉS.

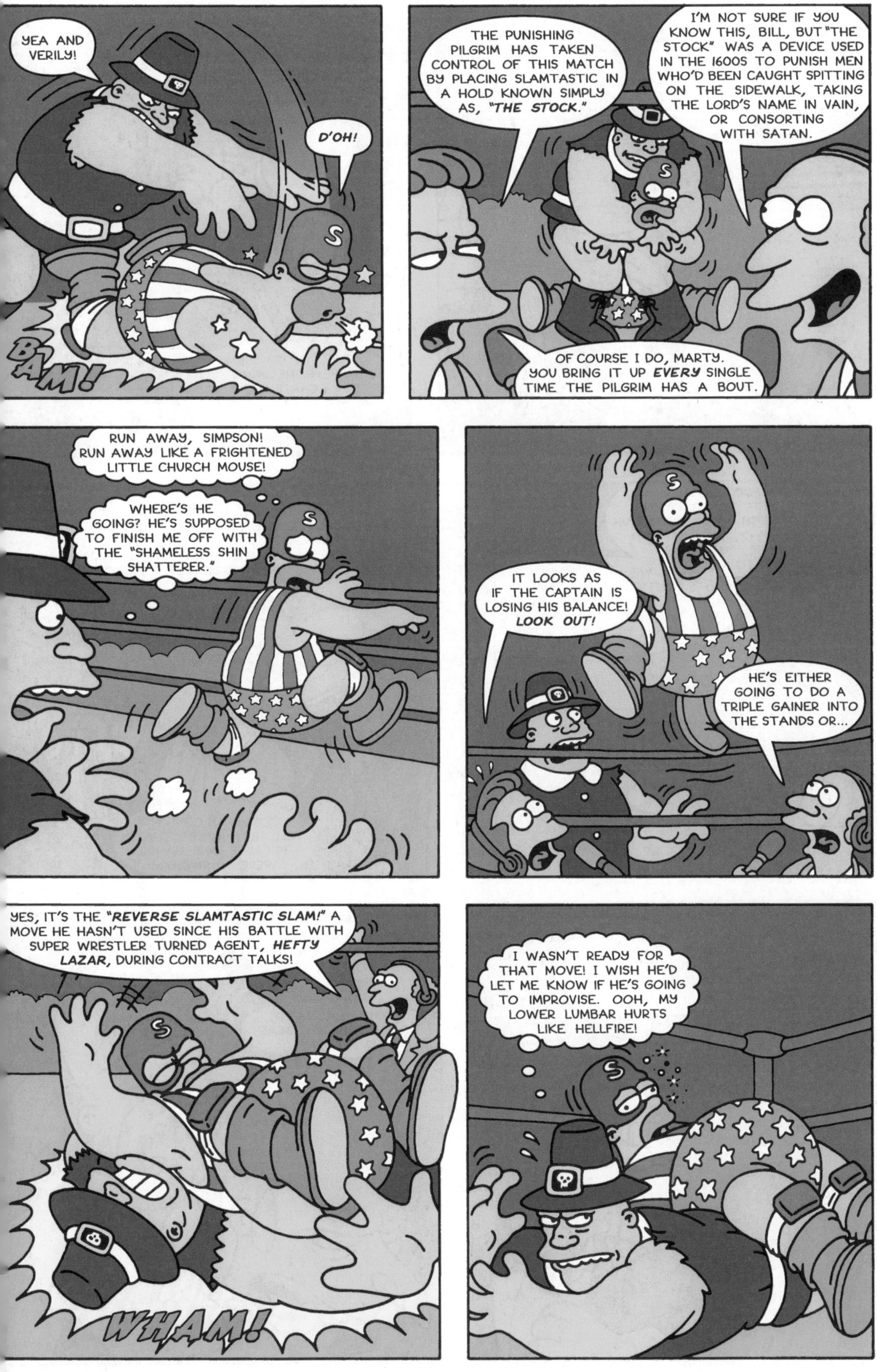

YEA AND VERILY!
D'OH!
BAM!
THE PUNISHING PILGRIM HAS TAKEN CONTROL OF THIS MATCH BY PLACING SLAMTASTIC IN A HOLD KNOWN SIMPLY AS, "THE STOCK."
I'M NOT SURE IF YOU KNOW THIS, BILL, BUT "THE STOCK" WAS A DEVICE USED IN THE 1600S TO PUNISH MEN WHO'D BEEN CAUGHT SPITTING ON THE SIDEWALK, TAKING THE LORD'S NAME IN VAIN, OR CONSORTING WITH SATAN.
OF COURSE I DO, MARTY. YOU BRING IT UP EVERY SINGLE TIME THE PILGRIM HAS A BOUT.
RUN AWAY, SIMPSON! RUN AWAY LIKE A FRIGHTENED LITTLE CHURCH MOUSE!
WHERE'S HE GOING? HE'S SUPPOSED TO FINISH ME OFF WITH THE "SHAMELESS SHIN SHATTERER."
IT LOOKS AS IF THE CAPTAIN IS LOSING HIS BALANCE! LOOK OUT!
HE'S EITHER GOING TO DO A TRIPLE GAINER INTO THE STANDS OR...
YES, IT'S THE "REVERSE SLAMTASTIC SLAM!" A MOVE HE HASN'T USED SINCE HIS BATTLE WITH SUPER WRESTLER TURNED AGENT, HEFTY LAZAR, DURING CONTRACT TALKS!
WHAM!
I WASN'T READY FOR THAT MOVE! I WISH HE'D LET ME KNOW IF HE'S GOING TO IMPROVISE. OOH, MY LOWER LUMBAR HURTS LIKE HELLFIRE!

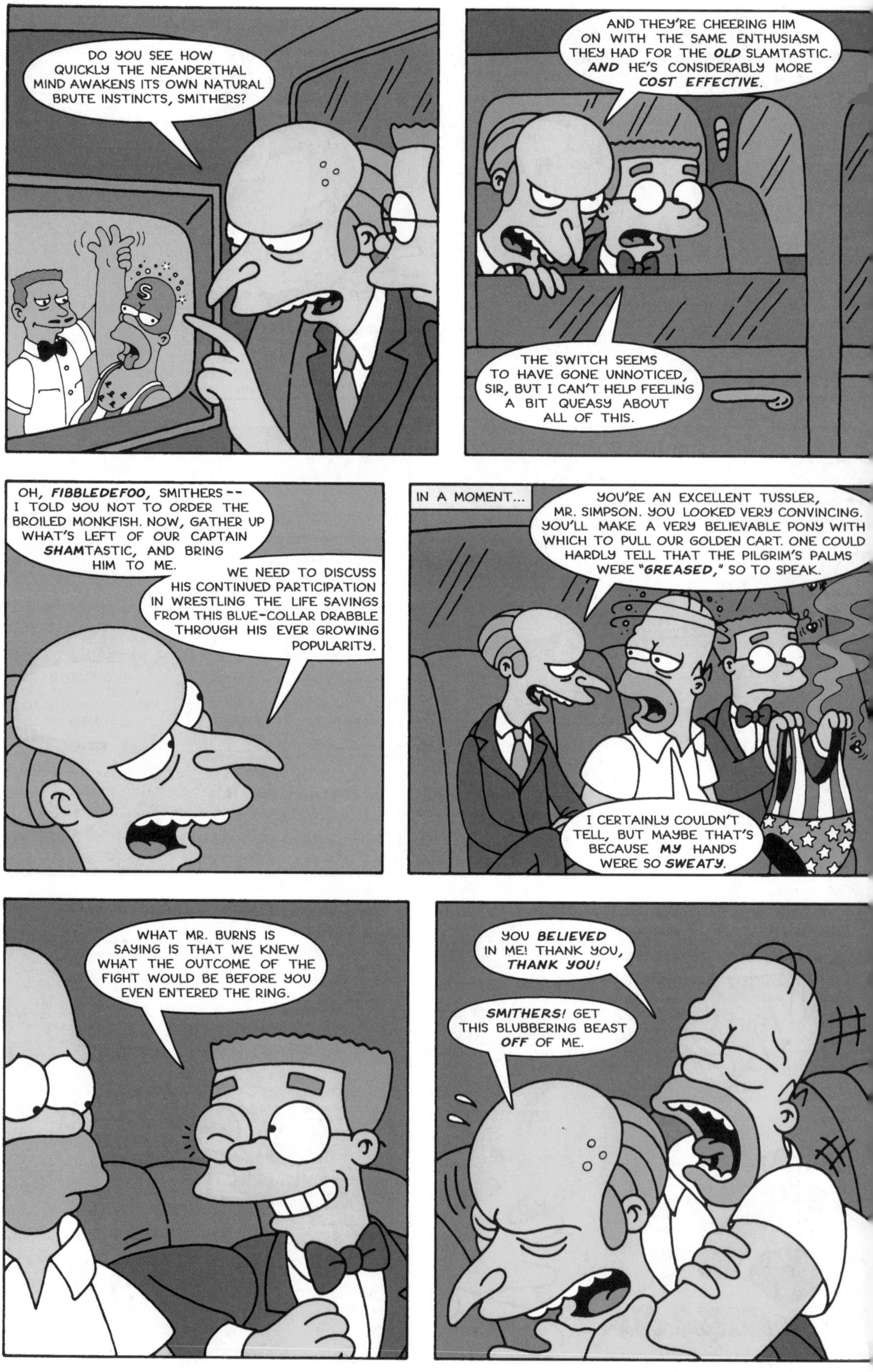
DO YOU SEE HOW QUICKLY THE NEANDERTHAL MIND AWAKENS ITS OWN NATURAL BRUTE INSTINCTS, SMITHERS?
AND THEY'RE CHEERING HIM ON WITH THE SAME ENTHUSIASM THEY HAD FOR THE OLD SLAMTASTIC. AND HE'S CONSIDERABLY MORE COST EFFECTIVE.
THE SWITCH SEEMS TO HAVE GONE UNNOTICED, SIR, BUT I CAN'T HELP FEELING A BIT QUEASY ABOUT ALL OF THIS.
OH, FIBBLEDEFOO, SMITHERS-- I TOLD YOU NOT TO ORDER THE BROILED MONKFISH. NOW, GATHER UP WHAT'S LEFT OF OUR CAPTAIN SHAMTASTIC, AND BRING HIM TO ME.
WE NEED TO DISCUSS HIS CONTINUED PARTICIPATION IN WRESTLING THE LIFE SAVINGS FROM THIS BLUE-COLLAR DRABBLE THROUGH HIS EVER GROWING POPULARITY.
IN A MOMENT...
YOU'RE AN EXCELLENT TUSSLER, MR. SIMPSON. YOU LOOKED VERY CONVINCING. YOU'LL MAKE A VERY BELIEVABLE PONY WITH WHICH TO PULL OUR GOLDEN CART. ONE COULD HARDLY TELL THAT THE PILGRIM'S PALMS WERE "GREASED," SO TO SPEAK.
I CERTAINLY COULDN'T TELL, BUT MAYBE THAT'S BECAUSE MY HANDS WERE SO SWEATY.
WHAT MR. BURNS IS SAYING IS THAT WE KNEW WHAT THE OUTCOME OF THE FIGHT WOULD BE BEFORE YOU EVEN ENTERED THE RING.
YOU BELIEVED IN ME! THANK YOU, THANK YOU!
SMITHERS! GET THIS BLUBBERING BEAST OFF OF ME.

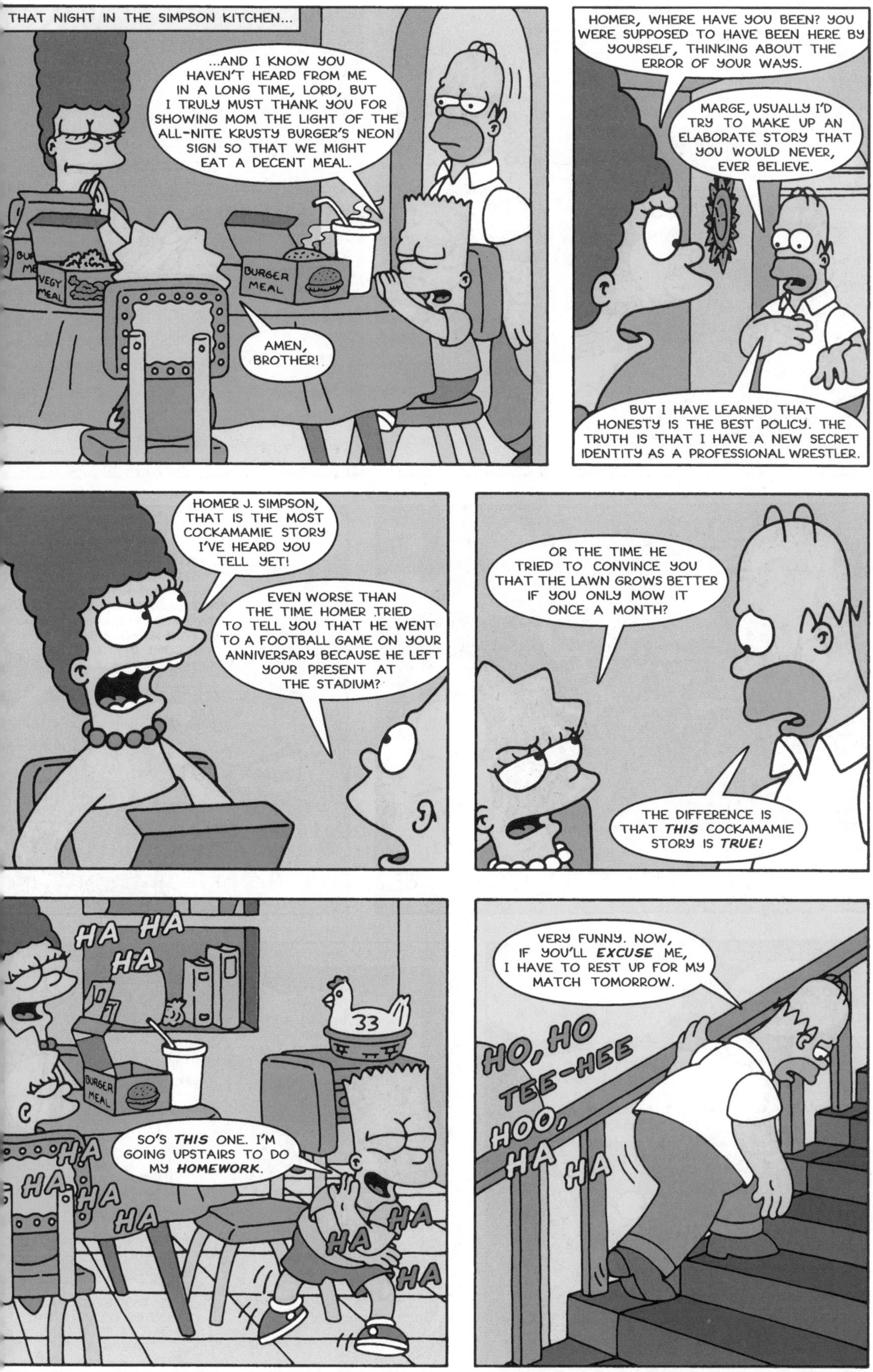
THAT NIGHT IN THE SIMPSON KITCHEN...
...AND I KNOW YOU HAVEN'T HEARD FROM ME IN A LONG TIME, LORD, BUT I TRULY MUST THANK YOU FOR SHOWING MOM THE LIGHT OF THE ALL-NITE KRUSTY BURGER'S NEON SIGN SO THAT WE MIGHT EAT A DECENT MEAL.
VEGY MEAL
BURGER MEAL
AMEN, BROTHER!
HOMER, WHERE HAVE YOU BEEN? YOU WERE SUPPOSED TO HAVE BEEN HERE BY YOURSELF, THINKING ABOUT THE ERROR OF YOUR WAYS.
MARGE, USUALLY I'D TRY TO MAKE UP AN ELABORATE STORY THAT YOU WOULD NEVER, EVER BELIEVE.
BUT I HAVE LEARNED THAT HONESTY IS THE BEST POLICY. THE TRUTH IS THAT I HAVE A NEW SECRET IDENTITY AS A PROFESSIONAL WRESTLER.
HOMER J. SIMPSON, THAT IS THE MOST COCKAMAMIE STORY I'VE HEARD YOU TELL YET!
EVEN WORSE THAN THE TIME HOMER TRIED TO TELL YOU THAT HE WENT TO A FOOTBALL GAME ON YOUR ANNIVERSARY BECAUSE HE LEFT YOUR PRESENT AT THE STADIUM?
OR THE TIME HE TRIED TO CONVINCE YOU THAT THE LAWN GROWS BETTER IF YOU ONLY MOW IT ONCE A MONTH?
THE DIFFERENCE IS THAT *THIS* COCKAMAMIE STORY IS *TRUE!*
HA HA HA
33
BURGER MEAL
SO'S *THIS* ONE. I'M GOING UPSTAIRS TO DO MY *HOMEWORK*.
HA HA HA HA HA HA HA
VERY FUNNY. NOW, IF YOU'LL *EXCUSE* ME, I HAVE TO REST UP FOR MY MATCH TOMORROW.
HO, HO TEE-HEE HOO, HA HA

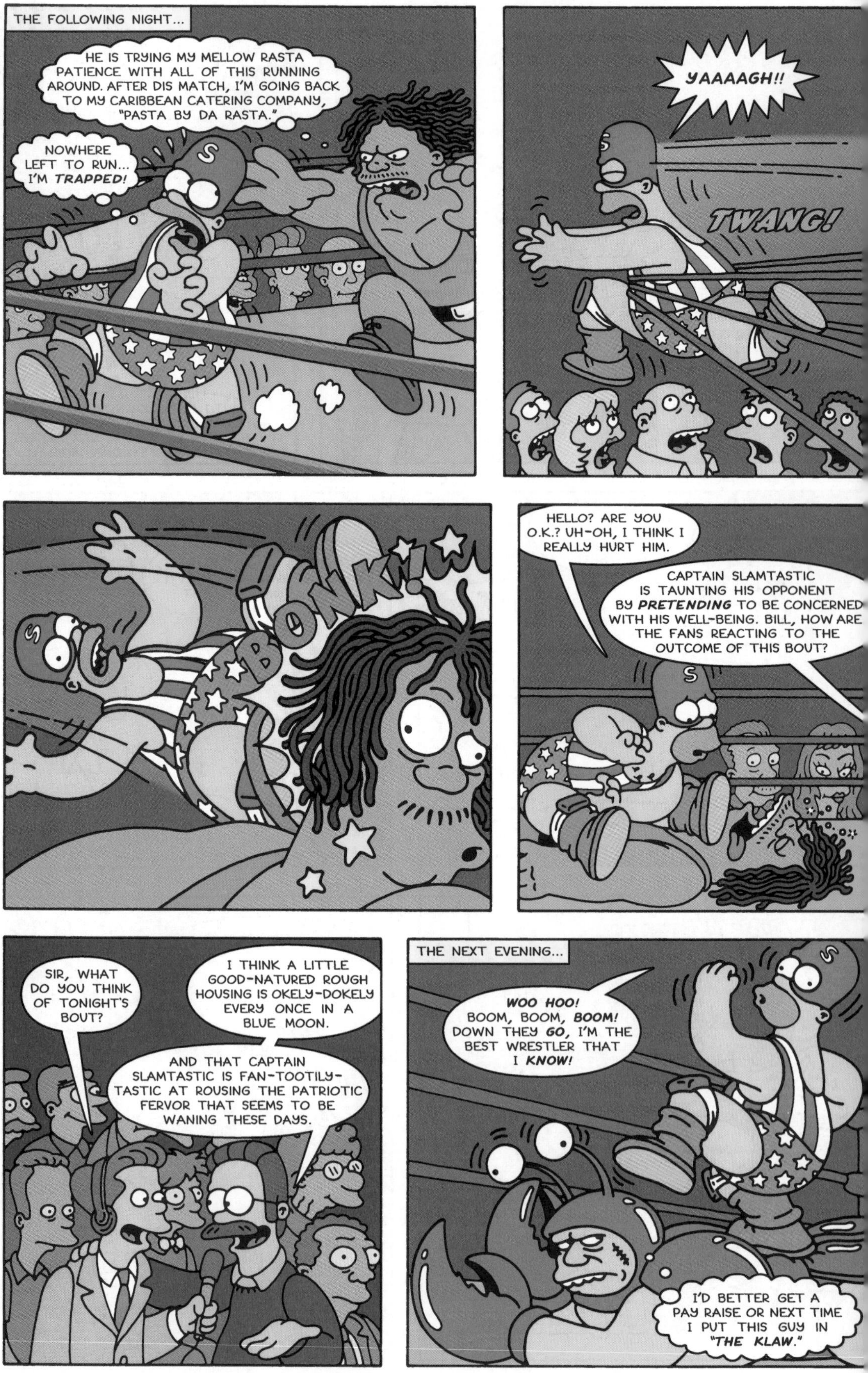
THE FOLLOWING NIGHT...
HE IS TRYING MY MELLOW RASTA PATIENCE WITH ALL OF THIS RUNNING AROUND. AFTER DIS MATCH, I'M GOING BACK TO MY CARIBBEAN CATERING COMPANY, "PASTA BY DA RASTA."
NOWHERE LEFT TO RUN... I'M ***TRAPPED!***
YAAAAGH!!
TWANG!
BONK!
HELLO? ARE YOU O.K.? UH-OH, I THINK I REALLY HURT HIM.
CAPTAIN SLAMTASTIC IS TAUNTING HIS OPPONENT BY ***PRETENDING*** TO BE CONCERNED WITH HIS WELL-BEING. BILL, HOW ARE THE FANS REACTING TO THE OUTCOME OF THIS BOUT?
SIR, WHAT DO YOU THINK OF TONIGHT'S BOUT?
I THINK A LITTLE GOOD-NATURED ROUGH HOUSING IS OKELY-DOKELY EVERY ONCE IN A BLUE MOON.
AND THAT CAPTAIN SLAMTASTIC IS FAN-TOOTILY-TASTIC AT ROUSING THE PATRIOTIC FERVOR THAT SEEMS TO BE WANING THESE DAYS.
THE NEXT EVENING...
WOO HOO! BOOM, BOOM, ***BOOM!*** DOWN THEY ***GO***, I'M THE BEST WRESTLER THAT I ***KNOW!***
I'D BETTER GET A PAY RAISE OR NEXT TIME I PUT THIS GUY IN ***"THE KLAW."***

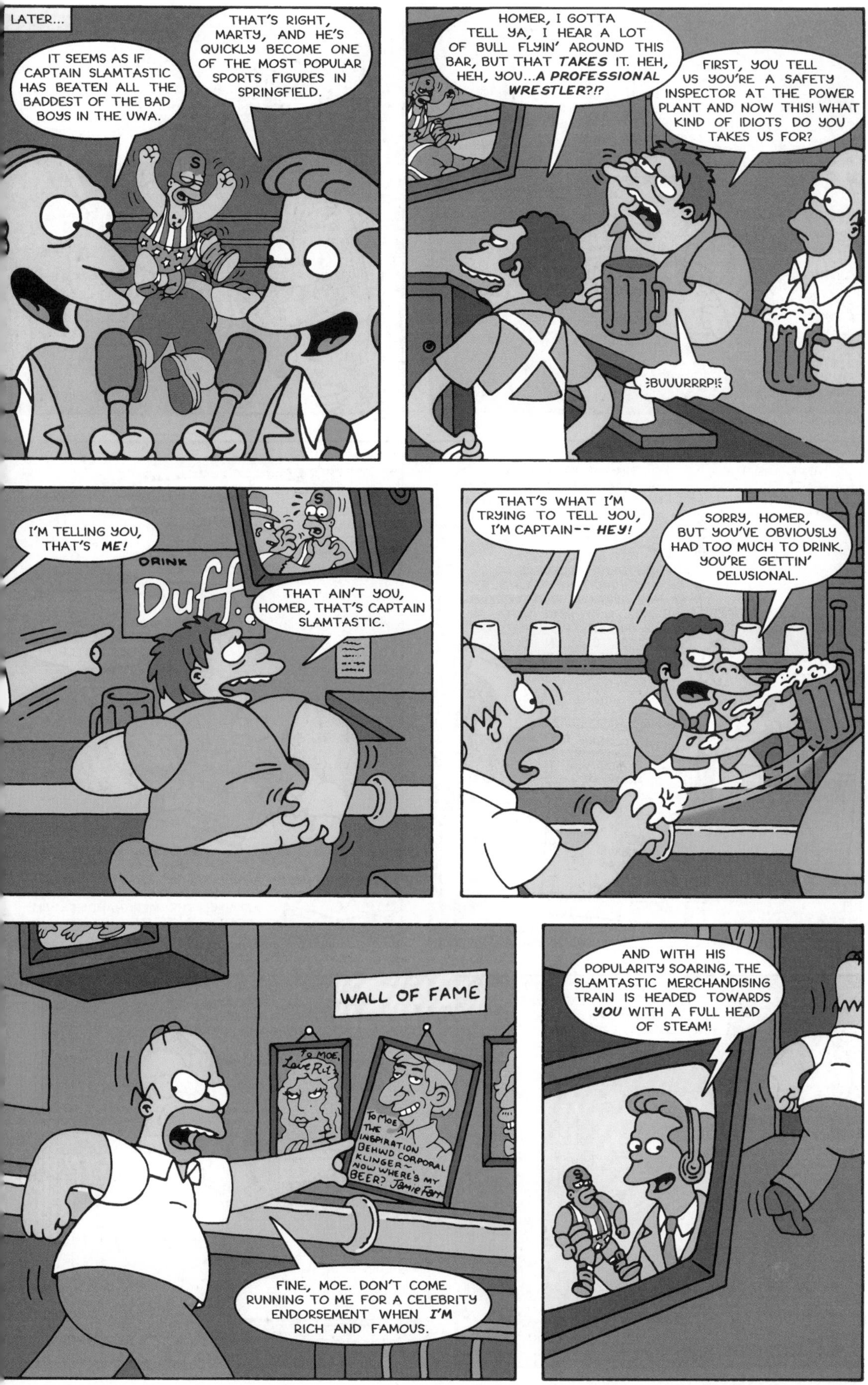

LATER...
IT SEEMS AS IF CAPTAIN SLAMTASTIC HAS BEATEN ALL THE BADDEST OF THE BAD BOYS IN THE UWA.
THAT'S RIGHT, MARTY, AND HE'S QUICKLY BECOME ONE OF THE MOST POPULAR SPORTS FIGURES IN SPRINGFIELD.
HOMER, I GOTTA TELL YA, I HEAR A LOT OF BULL FLYIN' AROUND THIS BAR, BUT THAT *TAKES* IT. HEH, HEH, YOU...*A PROFESSIONAL WRESTLER*?!?
FIRST, YOU TELL US YOU'RE A SAFETY INSPECTOR AT THE POWER PLANT AND NOW THIS! WHAT KIND OF IDIOTS DO YOU TAKES US FOR?
BUUURRRP!
I'M TELLING YOU, THAT'S *ME!*
DRINK
Duff
THAT AIN'T YOU, HOMER, THAT'S CAPTAIN SLAMTASTIC.
THAT'S WHAT I'M TRYING TO TELL YOU, I'M CAPTAIN-- *HEY!*
SORRY, HOMER, BUT YOU'VE OBVIOUSLY HAD TOO MUCH TO DRINK. YOU'RE GETTIN' DELUSIONAL.
WALL OF FAME
TO MOE THE INSPIRATION BEHIND CORPORAL KLINGER~ NOW WHERE'S MY BEER?
FINE, MOE. DON'T COME RUNNING TO ME FOR A CELEBRITY ENDORSEMENT WHEN *I'M* RICH AND FAMOUS.
AND WITH HIS POPULARITY SOARING, THE SLAMTASTIC MERCHANDISING TRAIN IS HEADED TOWARDS *YOU* WITH A FULL HEAD OF STEAM!

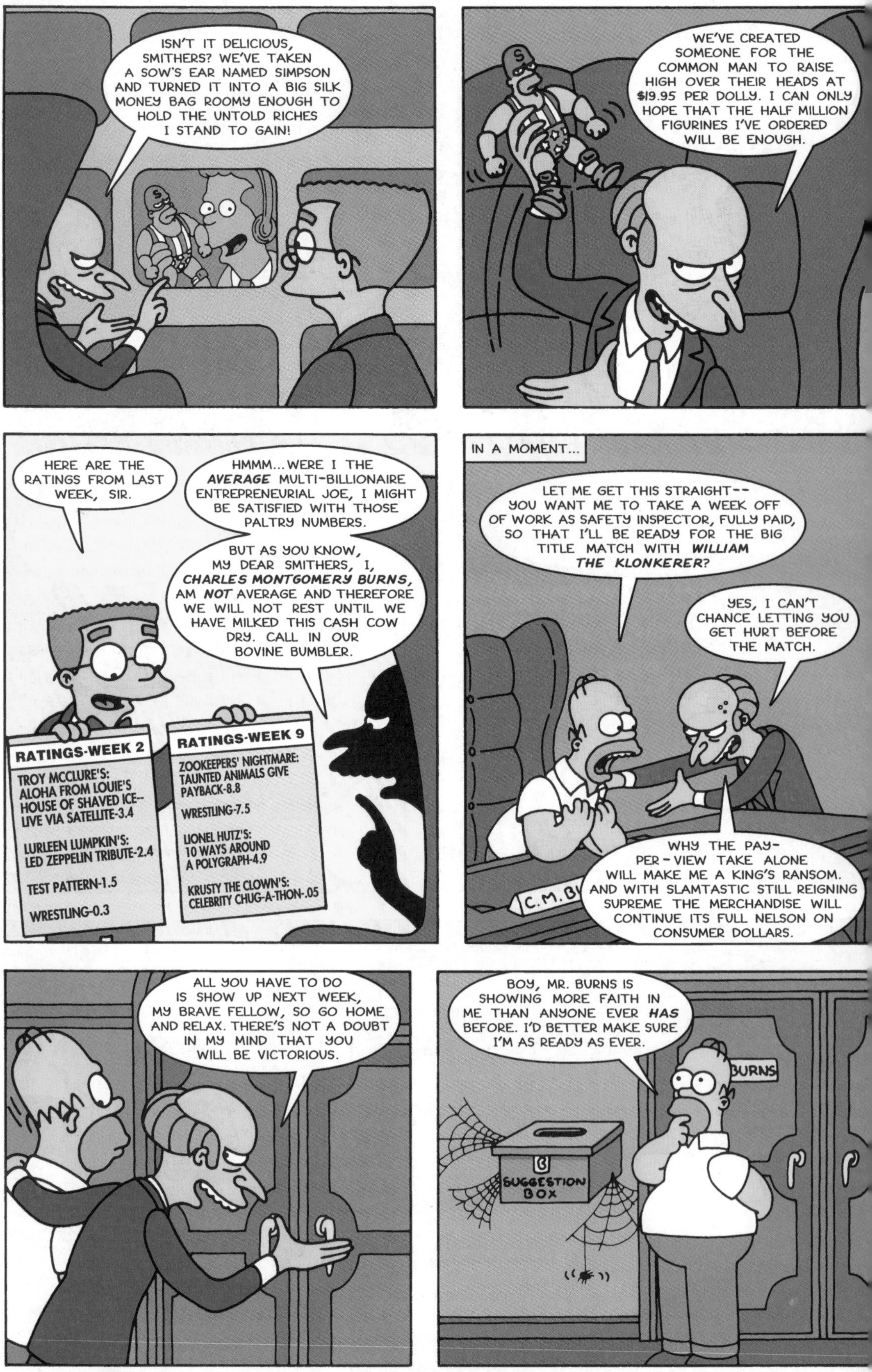
ISN'T IT DELICIOUS, SMITHERS? WE'VE TAKEN A SOW'S EAR NAMED SIMPSON AND TURNED IT INTO A BIG SILK MONEY BAG ROOMY ENOUGH TO HOLD THE UNTOLD RICHES I STAND TO GAIN!
WE'VE CREATED SOMEONE FOR THE COMMON MAN TO RAISE HIGH OVER THEIR HEADS AT $19.95 PER DOLLY. I CAN ONLY HOPE THAT THE HALF MILLION FIGURINES I'VE ORDERED WILL BE ENOUGH.
HERE ARE THE RATINGS FROM LAST WEEK, SIR.
HMMM... WERE I THE *AVERAGE* MULTI-BILLIONAIRE ENTREPRENEURIAL JOE, I MIGHT BE SATISFIED WITH THOSE PALTRY NUMBERS.
BUT AS YOU KNOW, MY DEAR SMITHERS, I, ***CHARLES MONTGOMERY BURNS,*** AM ***NOT*** AVERAGE AND THEREFORE WE WILL NOT REST UNTIL WE HAVE MILKED THIS CASH COW DRY. CALL IN OUR BOVINE BUMBLER.
RATINGS-WEEK 2
TROY MCCLURE'S: ALOHA FROM LOUIE'S HOUSE OF SHAVED ICE--LIVE VIA SATELLITE-3.4
LURLEEN LUMPKIN'S: LED ZEPPELIN TRIBUTE-2.4
TEST PATTERN-1.5
WRESTLING-0.3
RATINGS-WEEK 9
ZOOKEEPERS' NIGHTMARE: TAUNTED ANIMALS GIVE PAYBACK-8.8
WRESTLING-7.5
LIONEL HUTZ'S: 10 WAYS AROUND A POLYGRAPH-4.9
KRUSTY THE CLOWN'S: CELEBRITY CHUG-A-THON-.05
IN A MOMENT...
LET ME GET THIS STRAIGHT-- YOU WANT ME TO TAKE A WEEK OFF OF WORK AS SAFETY INSPECTOR, FULLY PAID, SO THAT I'LL BE READY FOR THE BIG TITLE MATCH WITH ***WILLIAM THE KLONKERER***?
YES, I CAN'T CHANCE LETTING YOU GET HURT BEFORE THE MATCH.
WHY THE PAY-PER-VIEW TAKE ALONE WILL MAKE ME A KING'S RANSOM. AND WITH SLAMTASTIC STILL REIGNING SUPREME THE MERCHANDISE WILL CONTINUE ITS FULL NELSON ON CONSUMER DOLLARS.
ALL YOU HAVE TO DO IS SHOW UP NEXT WEEK, MY BRAVE FELLOW, SO GO HOME AND RELAX. THERE'S NOT A DOUBT IN MY MIND THAT YOU WILL BE VICTORIOUS.
BOY, MR. BURNS IS SHOWING MORE FAITH IN ME THAN ANYONE EVER ***HAS*** BEFORE. I'D BETTER MAKE SURE I'M AS READY AS EVER.
BURNS
SUGGESTION BOX

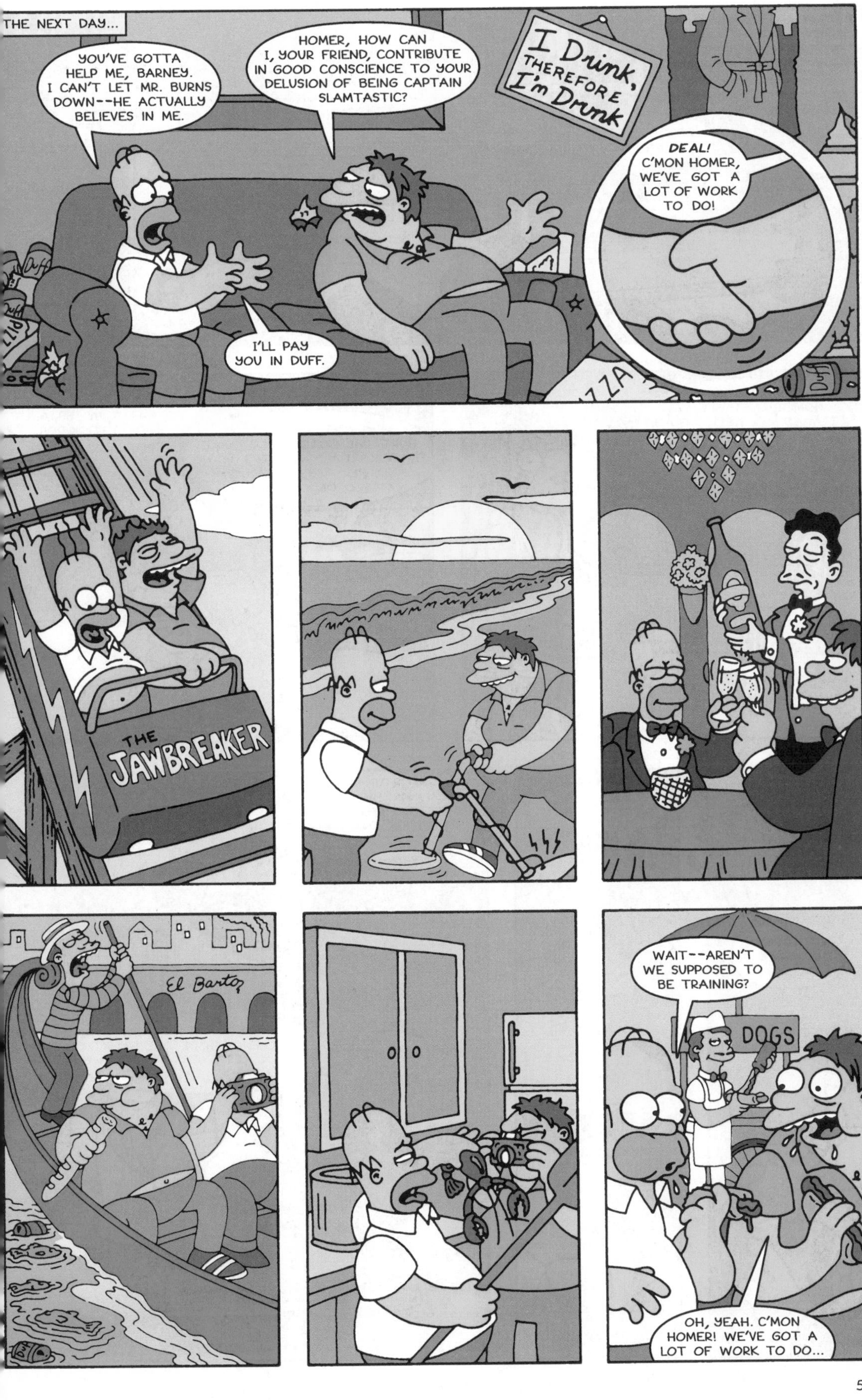
THE NEXT DAY...
YOU'VE GOTTA HELP ME, BARNEY. I CAN'T LET MR. BURNS DOWN--HE ACTUALLY BELIEVES IN ME.
HOMER, HOW CAN I, YOUR FRIEND, CONTRIBUTE IN GOOD CONSCIENCE TO YOUR DELUSION OF BEING CAPTAIN SLAMTASTIC?
I Drink, THEREFORE I'm Drunk
I'LL PAY YOU IN DUFF.
DEAL! C'MON HOMER, WE'VE GOT A LOT OF WORK TO DO!
THE JAWBREAKER
El Barto
WAIT--AREN'T WE SUPPOSED TO BE TRAINING?
DOGS
OH, YEAH. C'MON HOMER! WE'VE GOT A LOT OF WORK TO DO...

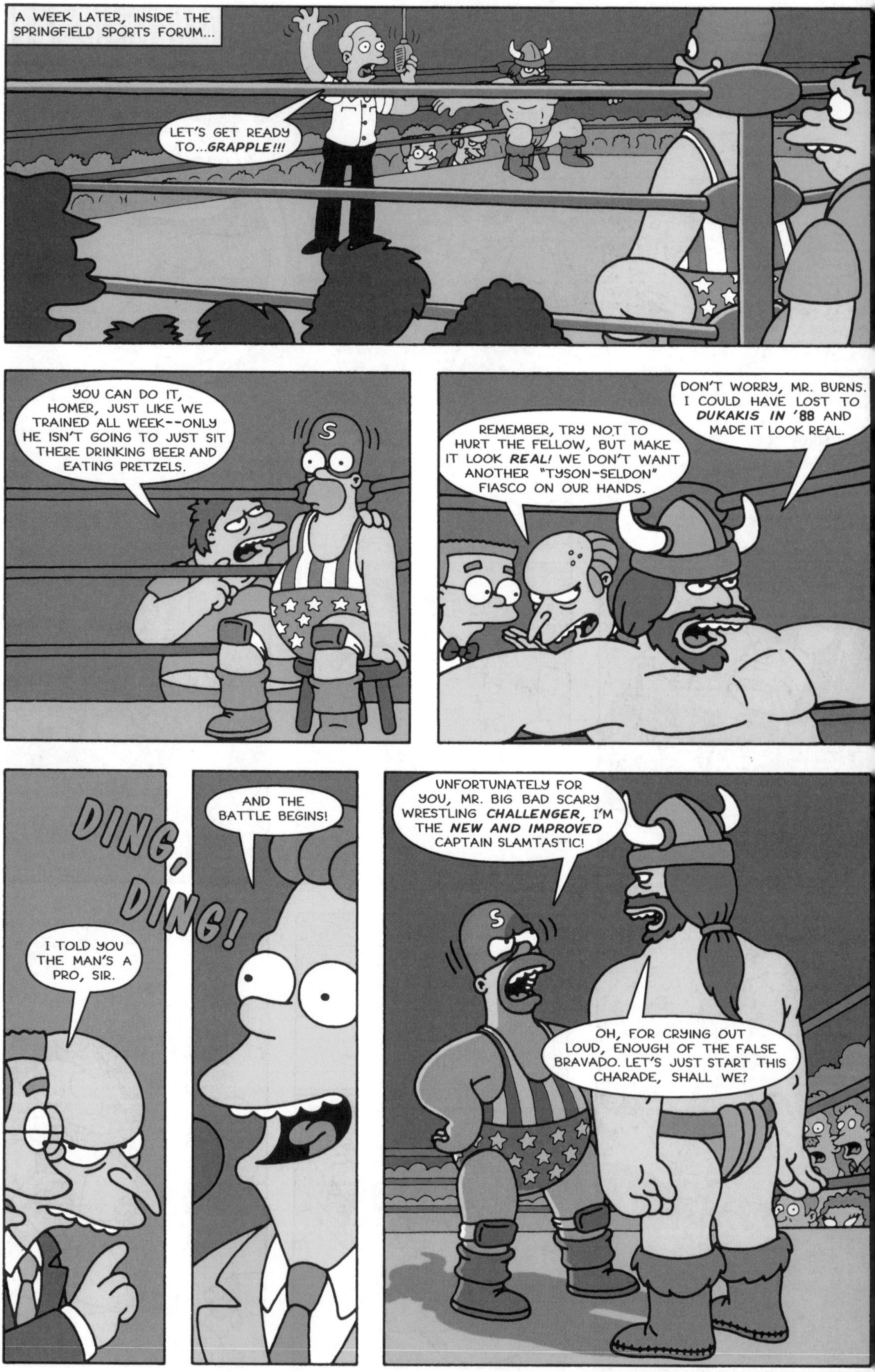
A WEEK LATER, INSIDE THE SPRINGFIELD SPORTS FORUM...
LET'S GET READY TO...GRAPPLE!!!
YOU CAN DO IT, HOMER, JUST LIKE WE TRAINED ALL WEEK--ONLY HE ISN'T GOING TO JUST SIT THERE DRINKING BEER AND EATING PRETZELS.
REMEMBER, TRY NOT TO HURT THE FELLOW, BUT MAKE IT LOOK REAL! WE DON'T WANT ANOTHER "TYSON-SELDON" FIASCO ON OUR HANDS.
DON'T WORRY, MR. BURNS. I COULD HAVE LOST TO DUKAKIS IN '88 AND MADE IT LOOK REAL.
DING, DING!
I TOLD YOU THE MAN'S A PRO, SIR.
AND THE BATTLE BEGINS!
UNFORTUNATELY FOR YOU, MR. BIG BAD SCARY WRESTLING CHALLENGER, I'M THE NEW AND IMPROVED CAPTAIN SLAMTASTIC!
OH, FOR CRYING OUT LOUD, ENOUGH OF THE FALSE BRAVADO. LET'S JUST START THIS CHARADE, SHALL WE?

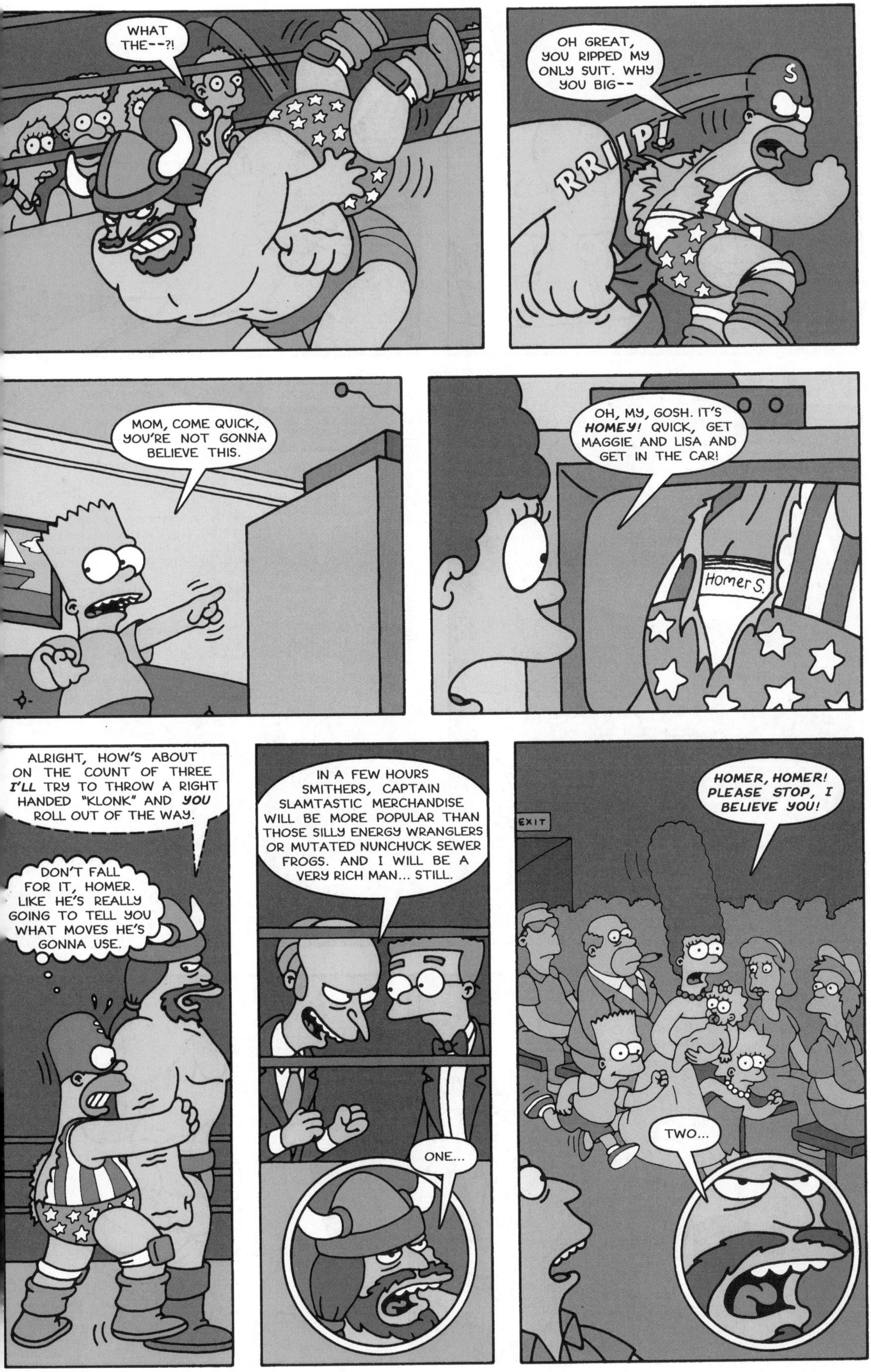

WHAT THE--?!
OH GREAT, YOU RIPPED MY ONLY SUIT. WHY YOU BIG--
RRIIP!
MOM, COME QUICK, YOU'RE NOT GONNA BELIEVE THIS.
OH, MY, GOSH. IT'S HOMEY! QUICK, GET MAGGIE AND LISA AND GET IN THE CAR!
Homer S.
ALRIGHT, HOW'S ABOUT ON THE COUNT OF THREE I'LL TRY TO THROW A RIGHT HANDED "KLONK" AND YOU ROLL OUT OF THE WAY.
DON'T FALL FOR IT, HOMER. LIKE HE'S REALLY GOING TO TELL YOU WHAT MOVES HE'S GONNA USE.
IN A FEW HOURS SMITHERS, CAPTAIN SLAMTASTIC MERCHANDISE WILL BE MORE POPULAR THAN THOSE SILLY ENERGY WRANGLERS OR MUTATED NUNCHUCK SEWER FROGS. AND I WILL BE A VERY RICH MAN... STILL.
ONE...
EXIT
HOMER, HOMER! PLEASE STOP, I BELIEVE YOU!
TWO...

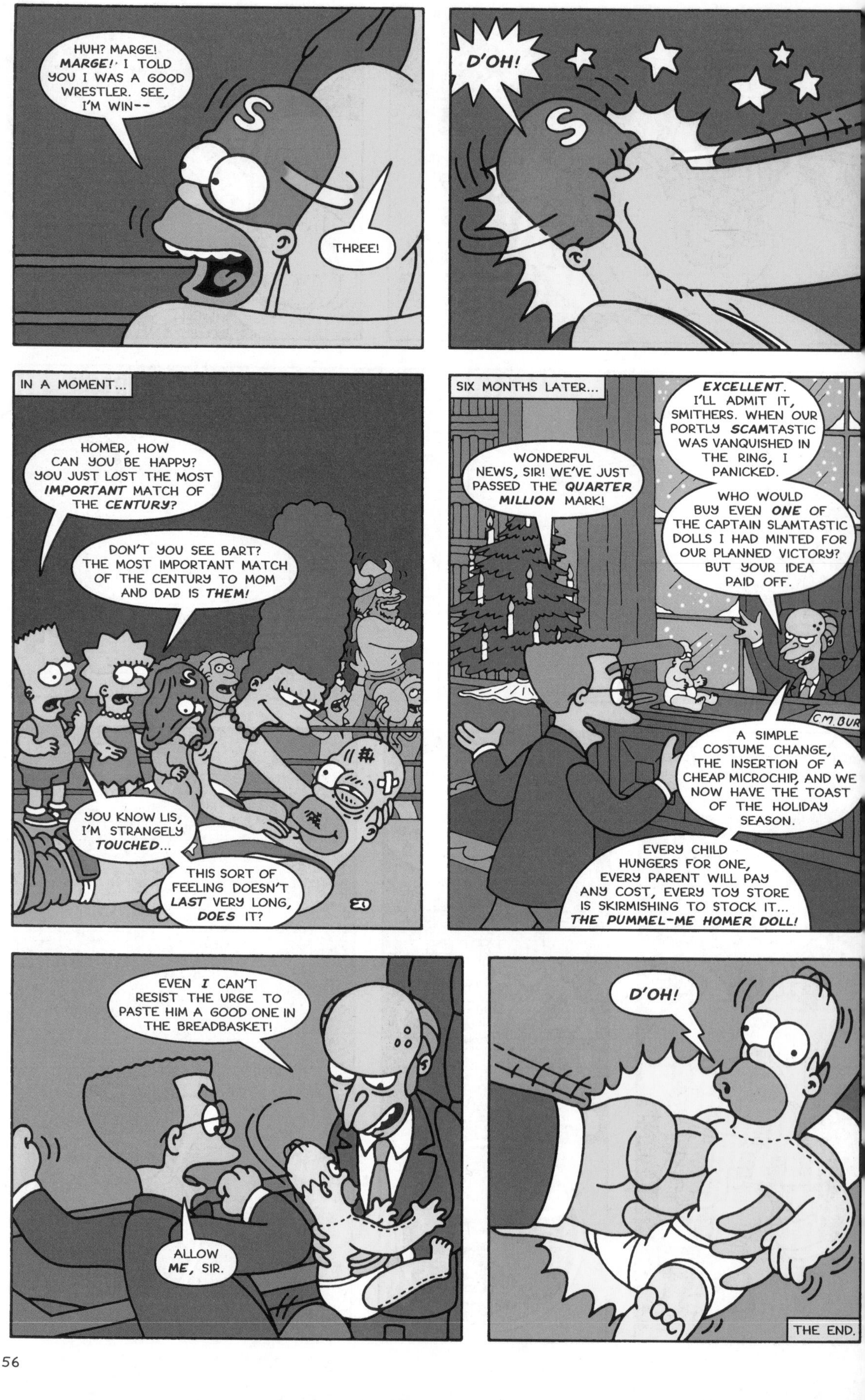
HUH? MARGE! MARGE! I TOLD YOU I WAS A GOOD WRESTLER. SEE, I'M WIN--
THREE!
D'OH!
IN A MOMENT...
HOMER, HOW CAN YOU BE HAPPY? YOU JUST LOST THE MOST IMPORTANT MATCH OF THE CENTURY?
DON'T YOU SEE BART? THE MOST IMPORTANT MATCH OF THE CENTURY TO MOM AND DAD IS THEM!
YOU KNOW LIS, I'M STRANGELY TOUCHED...
THIS SORT OF FEELING DOESN'T LAST VERY LONG, DOES IT?
SIX MONTHS LATER...
WONDERFUL NEWS, SIR! WE'VE JUST PASSED THE QUARTER MILLION MARK!
EXCELLENT. I'LL ADMIT IT, SMITHERS. WHEN OUR PORTLY SCAMTASTIC WAS VANQUISHED IN THE RING, I PANICKED.
WHO WOULD BUY EVEN ONE OF THE CAPTAIN SLAMTASTIC DOLLS I HAD MINTED FOR OUR PLANNED VICTORY? BUT YOUR IDEA PAID OFF.
A SIMPLE COSTUME CHANGE, THE INSERTION OF A CHEAP MICROCHIP, AND WE NOW HAVE THE TOAST OF THE HOLIDAY SEASON.
EVERY CHILD HUNGERS FOR ONE, EVERY PARENT WILL PAY ANY COST, EVERY TOY STORE IS SKIRMISHING TO STOCK IT... THE PUMMEL-ME HOMER DOLL!
EVEN I CAN'T RESIST THE URGE TO PASTE HIM A GOOD ONE IN THE BREADBASKET!
ALLOW ME, SIR.
D'OH!
THE END.

MAGGIE SIMPSON *IN* "BRINGING DOWN BABY"

SPRINGFIELD "DAZE" ANNUAL PICNIC

WHAT A LOVELY DAY FOR A PICNIC!

STORY & ART	LETTERS	COLORS	BARRED FROM PICNIC AFTER LAST YEAR'S "INCIDENT"
BILL MORRISON	JEANNINE BLACK	NATHAN KANE	MATT GROENING

THIS LOOKS LIKE A GOOD SPOT.

HERE, MAGGIE, YOU PLAY WITH YOUR RATTLE WHILE I FIX YOU A JAR OF "BABY'S FIRST PICNIC FOOD."

PFFFT!

I THINK WE'LL TRY THE *PURÉED CHILI DOG.*

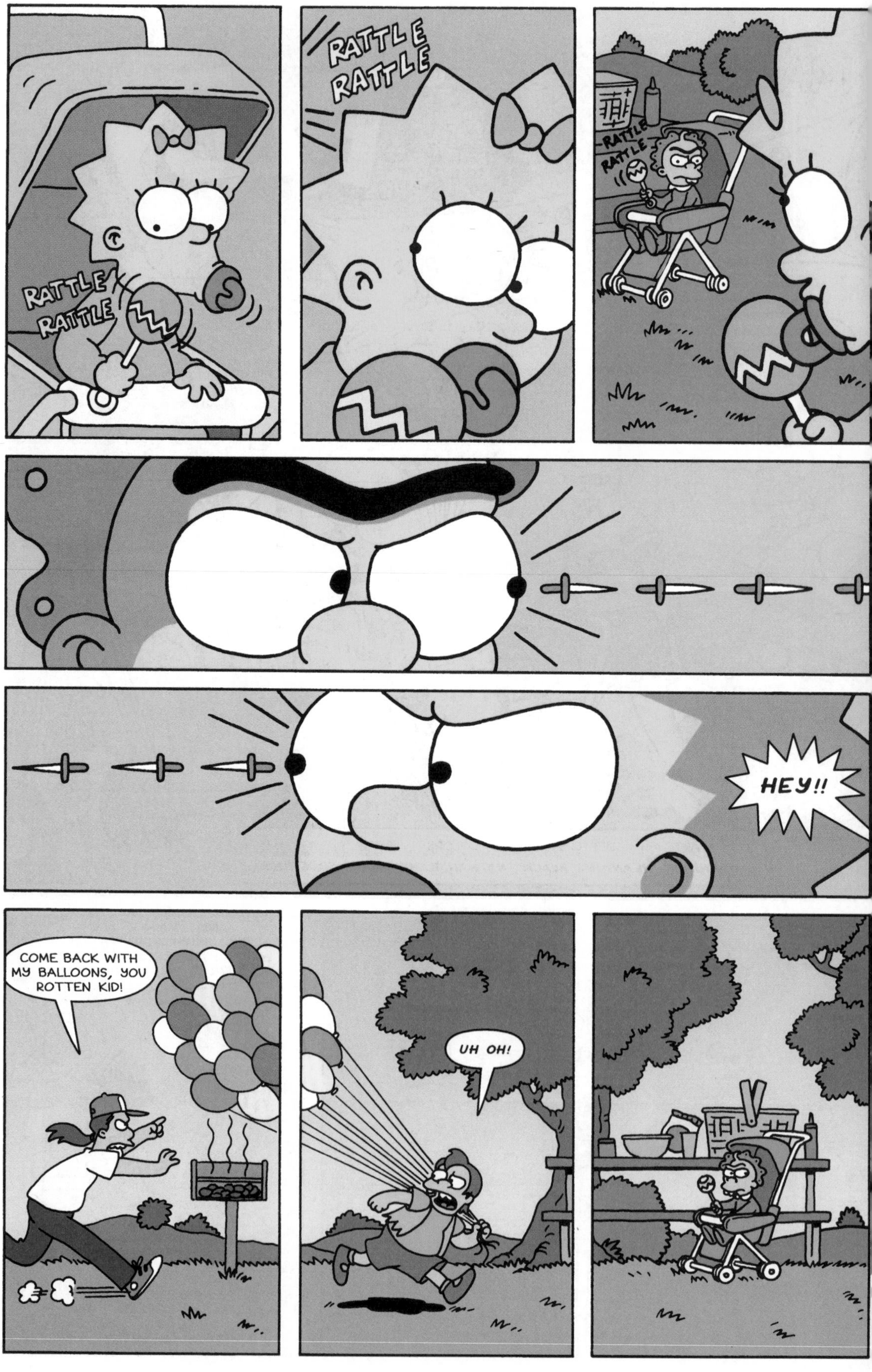
RATTLE RATTLE
RATTLE RATTLE
RATTLE RATTLE
HEY!!
COME BACK WITH MY BALLOONS, YOU ROTTEN KID!
UH OH!

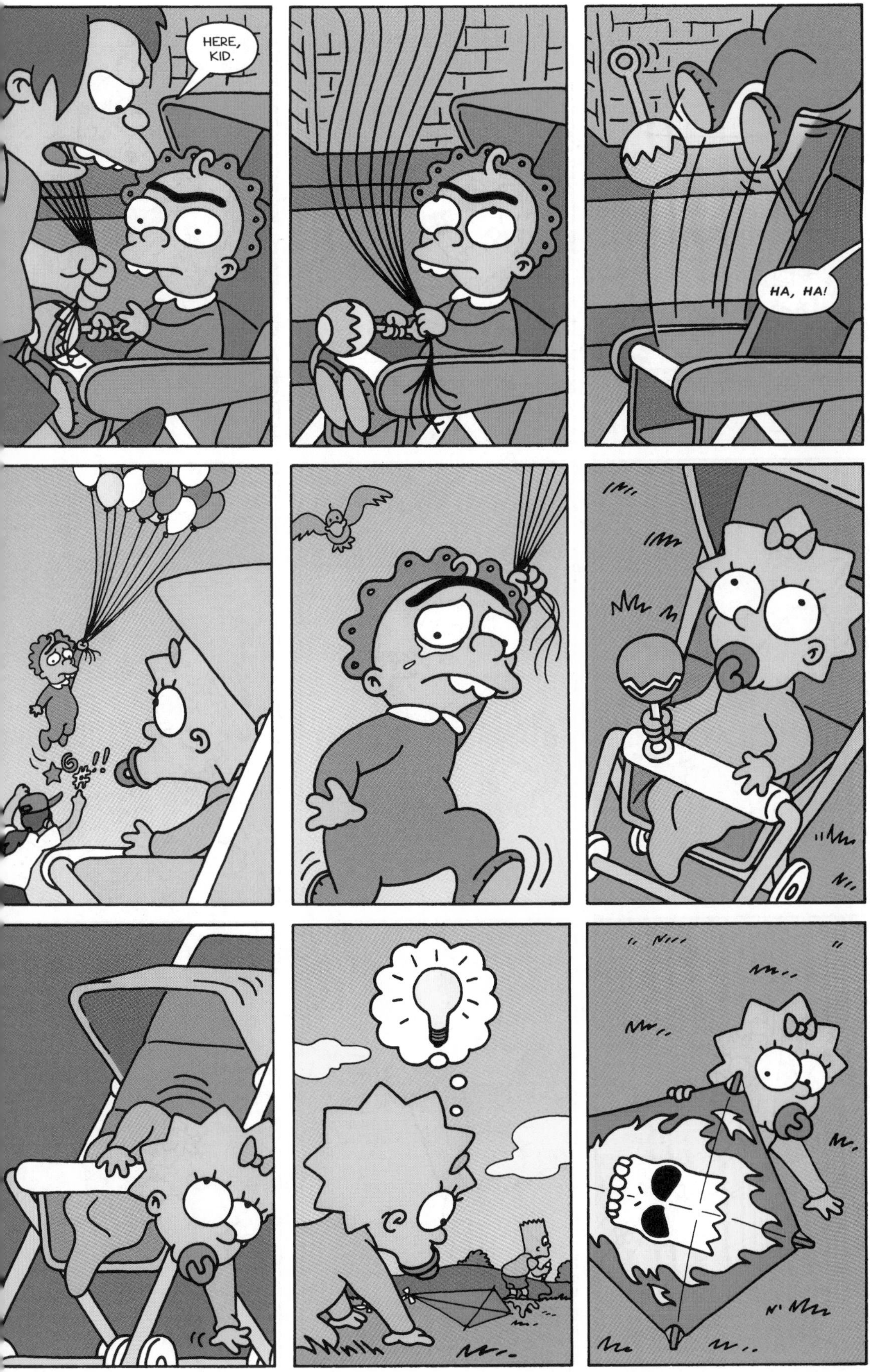
HERE, KID.
HA, HA!

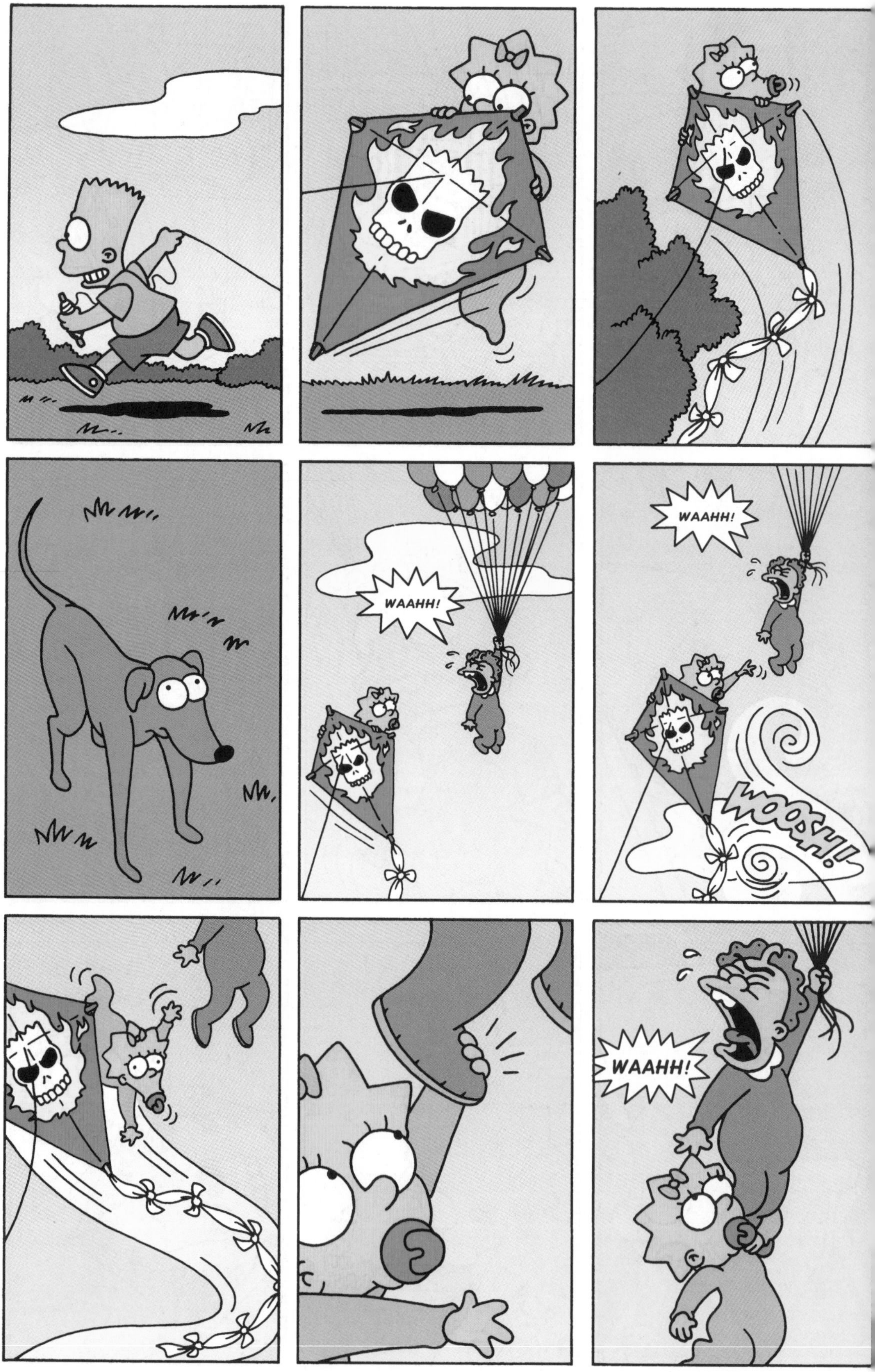
WAAHH!
WAAHH!
WOOSH!!
WAAHH!

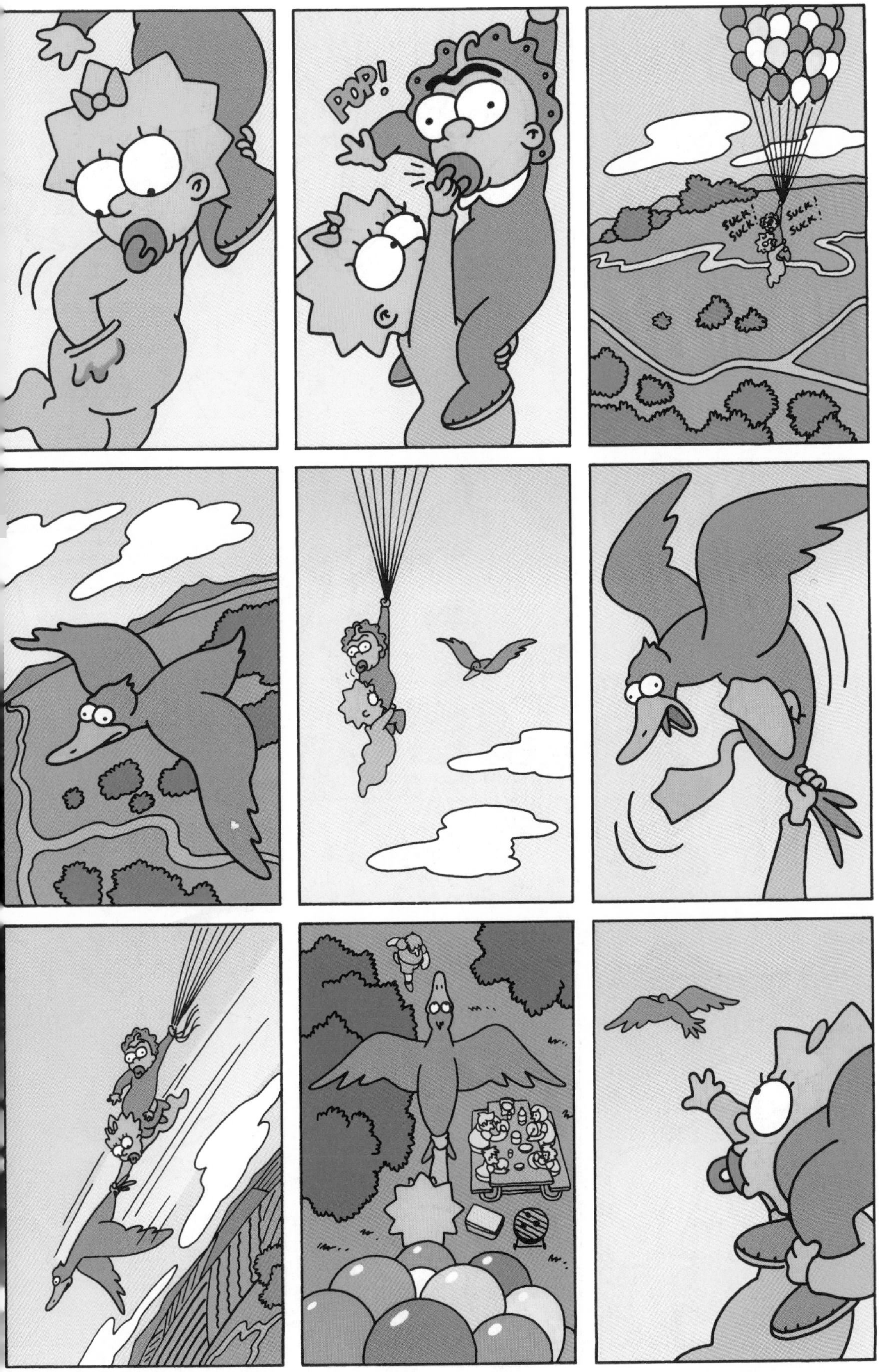
POP!
SUCK! SUCK!
SUCK! SUCK!

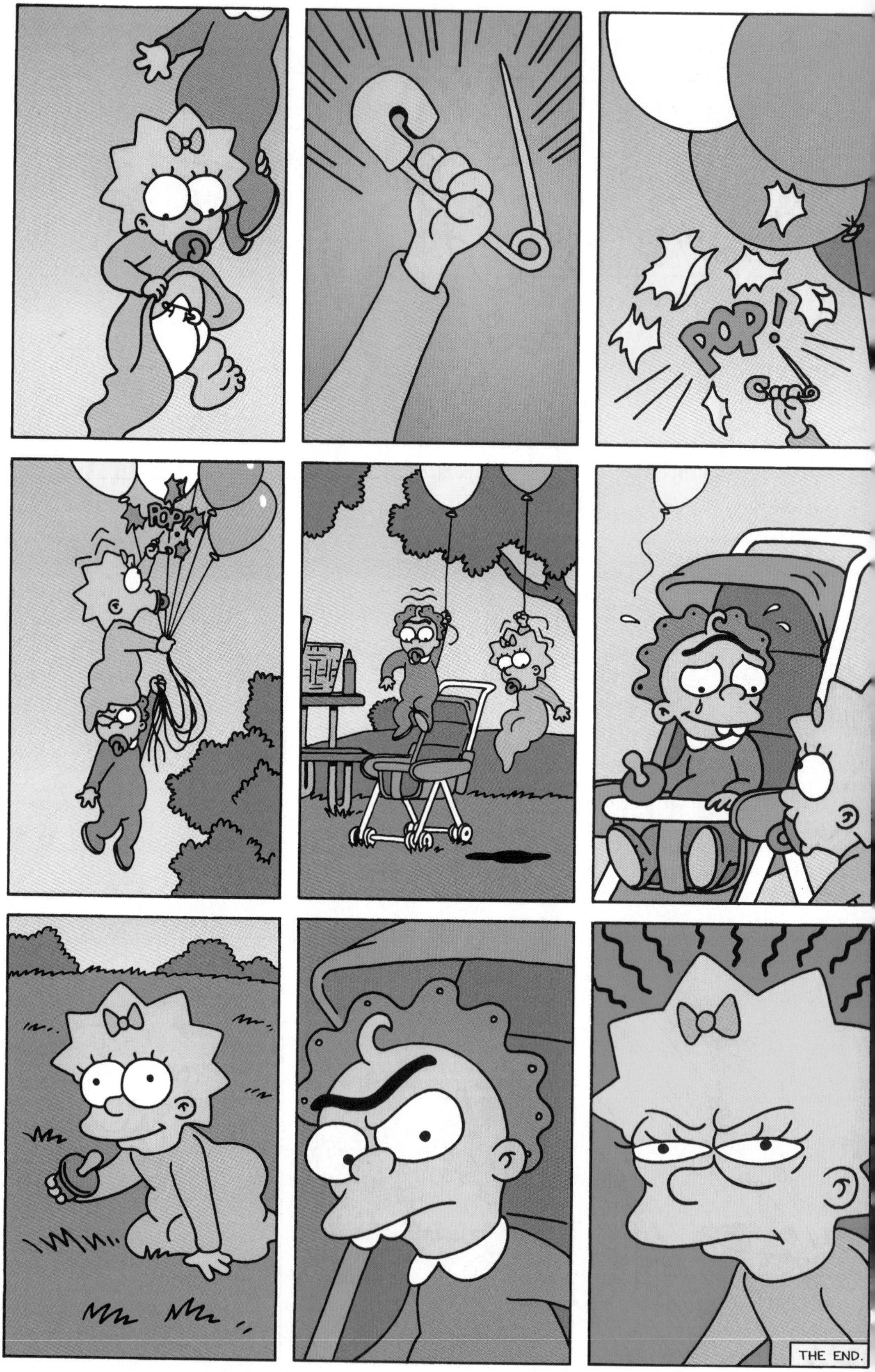
POP!
POP!
THE END.

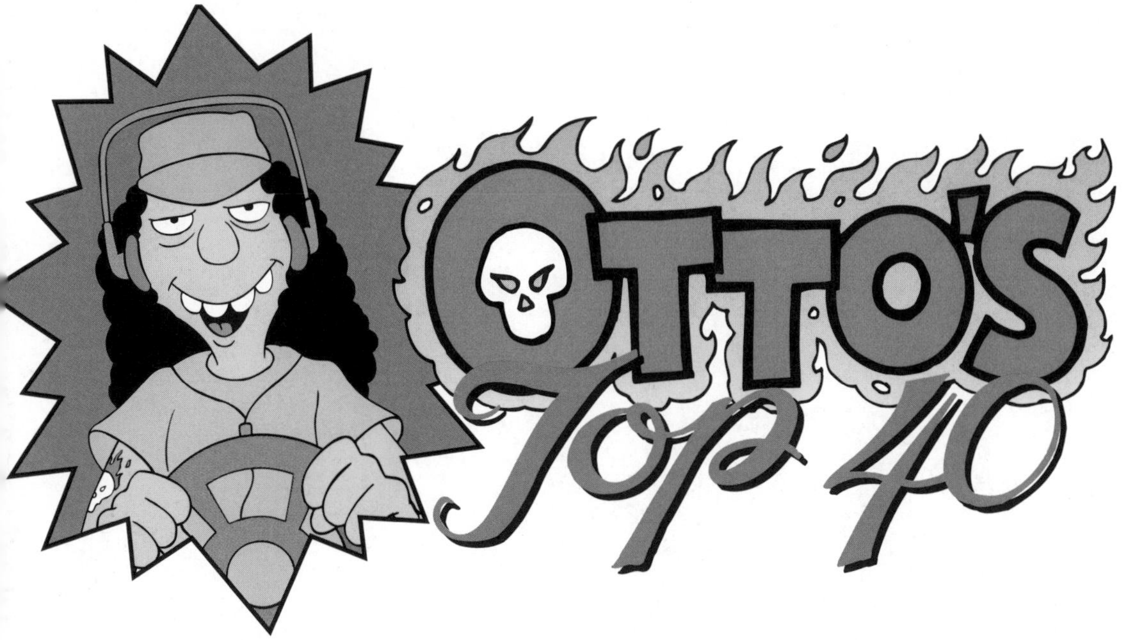
OTTO'S
Top 40

1. Garfield
2. The First Amendment

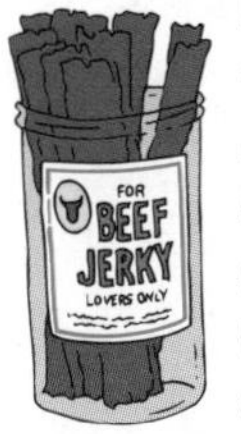
FOR
BEEF
JERKY
LOVERS ONLY

3. Big ol' gnarly tattoos of flaming skulls
4. "Stairway to Heaven"
5. Extra-spicy hickory-smoked beef jerky
6. Erik von Däniken's *Chariots of the Gods*
7. Festival seating
8. Susan Dey
9. Baby humans that have been raised by wolves.
10. The cool way a busload of kids eating corn nuts smells
11. Super-long, intense guitar riffs played with a wah-wah pedal
12. Bandanas on dogs
13. Tape hiss
14. Totally spacing out and forgetting where the bus is parked

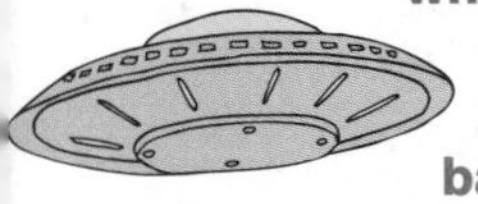

15. Space-age neo-psychedelic head-banger music
16. Grinding all four gears going up a killer incline
17. 20-minute drum solos
18. Bizarre conspiracy theories involving the military and U.F.O.'s
19. Foam rubber
20. Letting your freak flag fly
21. Giving the thumbs-up sign to other bus drivers
22. Politically disenfranchised white male suburban hell-raisers
23. The Miranda Decision
24. 42" woofers
25. Poems about the universe

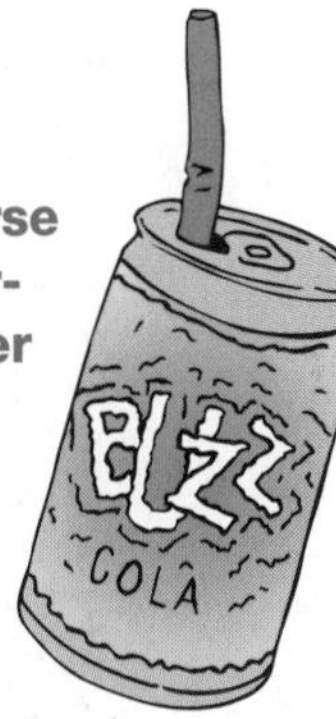
BUZZ
COLA

26. Slowing down to rubber-neck some roadside disaster
27. Pinball
28. Vinyl records
29. Double-dipped, deep-fat-fried corn dogs
30. Underground comix

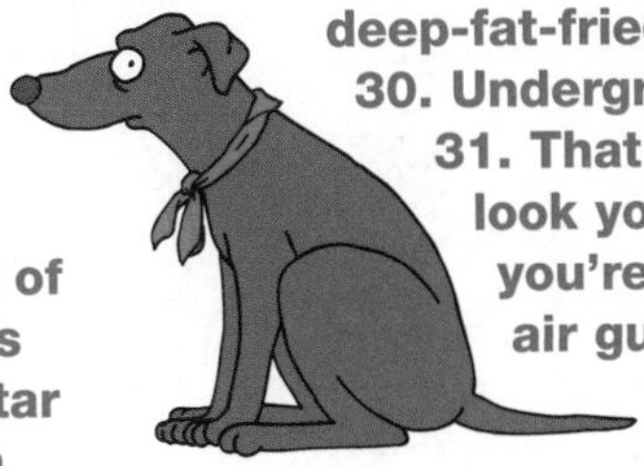

31. That totally intense look you get on your face when you're playing "Wrathchild" on air guitar
32. Passive-aggressive babes of the female persuassion
33. Buzz Cola with twice the sugar, twice the caffeine
34. Air fresheners shaped like trees that really smell like trees
35. Mood rings
36. Onion rings
37. The mesh thing you put on the seat that keeps your butt from getting clammy

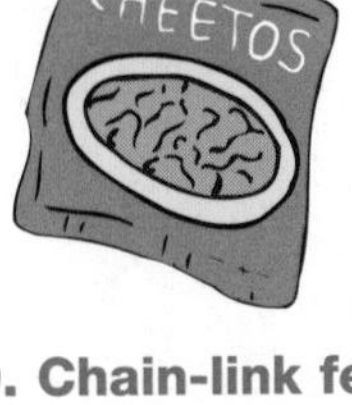
CHEETOS

38. Finding an unopened bag of Chee-tos under a bus seat
39. Chain-link fencing
40. "Inna Gadda Da Vida"

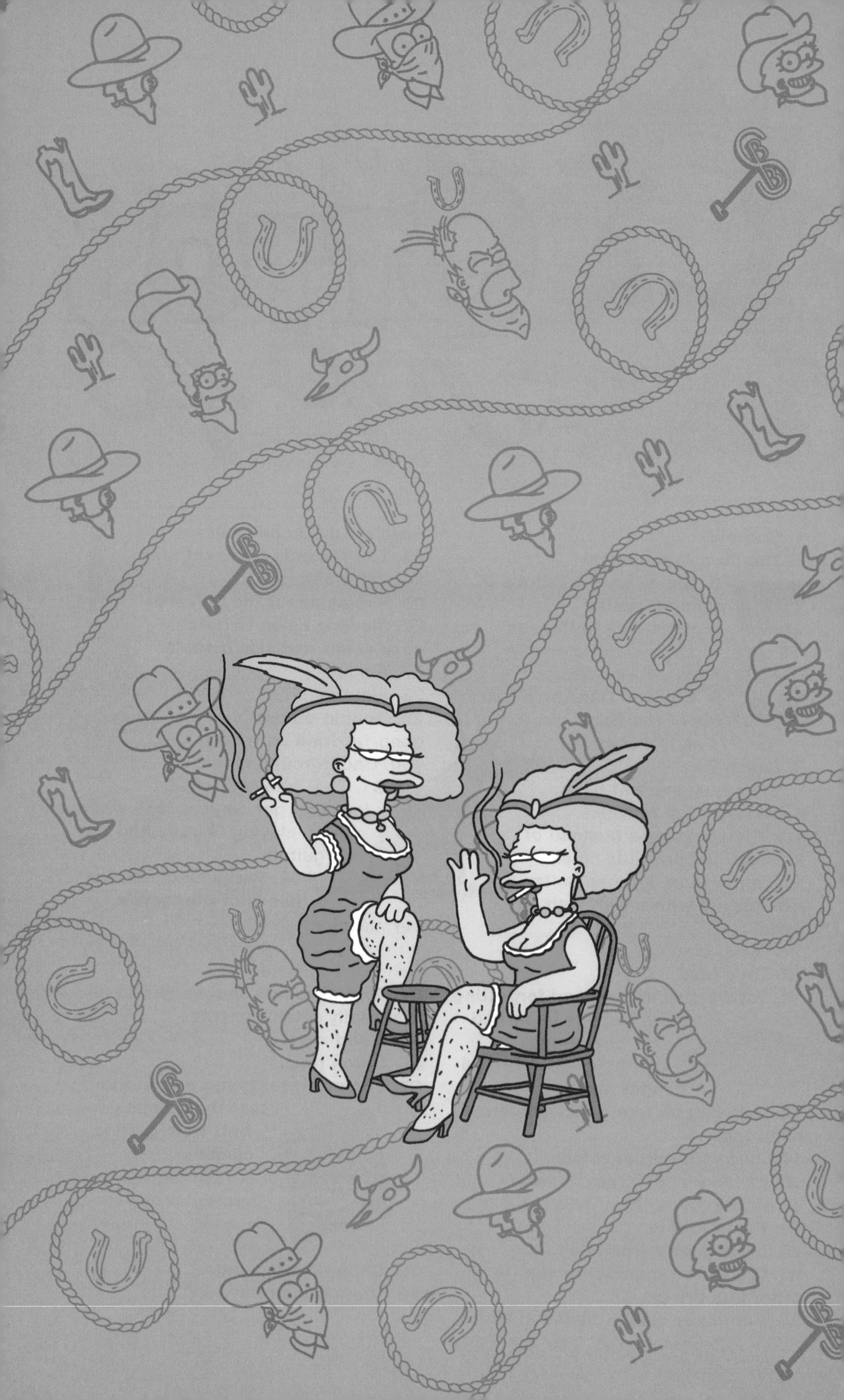

BONGO COMICS GROUP
#30
APPROVED BY THE COMICS CODE AUTHORITY
SIMPSONS COMICS
GROENING
RIPPED FROM TODAY'S SCREAMING HEADLINES...
A CATASTROPHIC CHRONICLE OF CLONING!

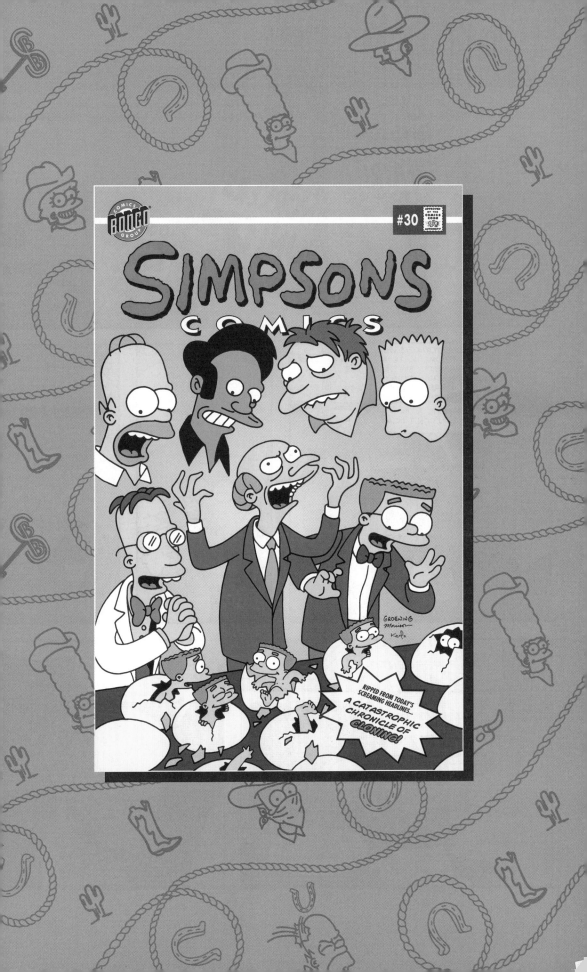

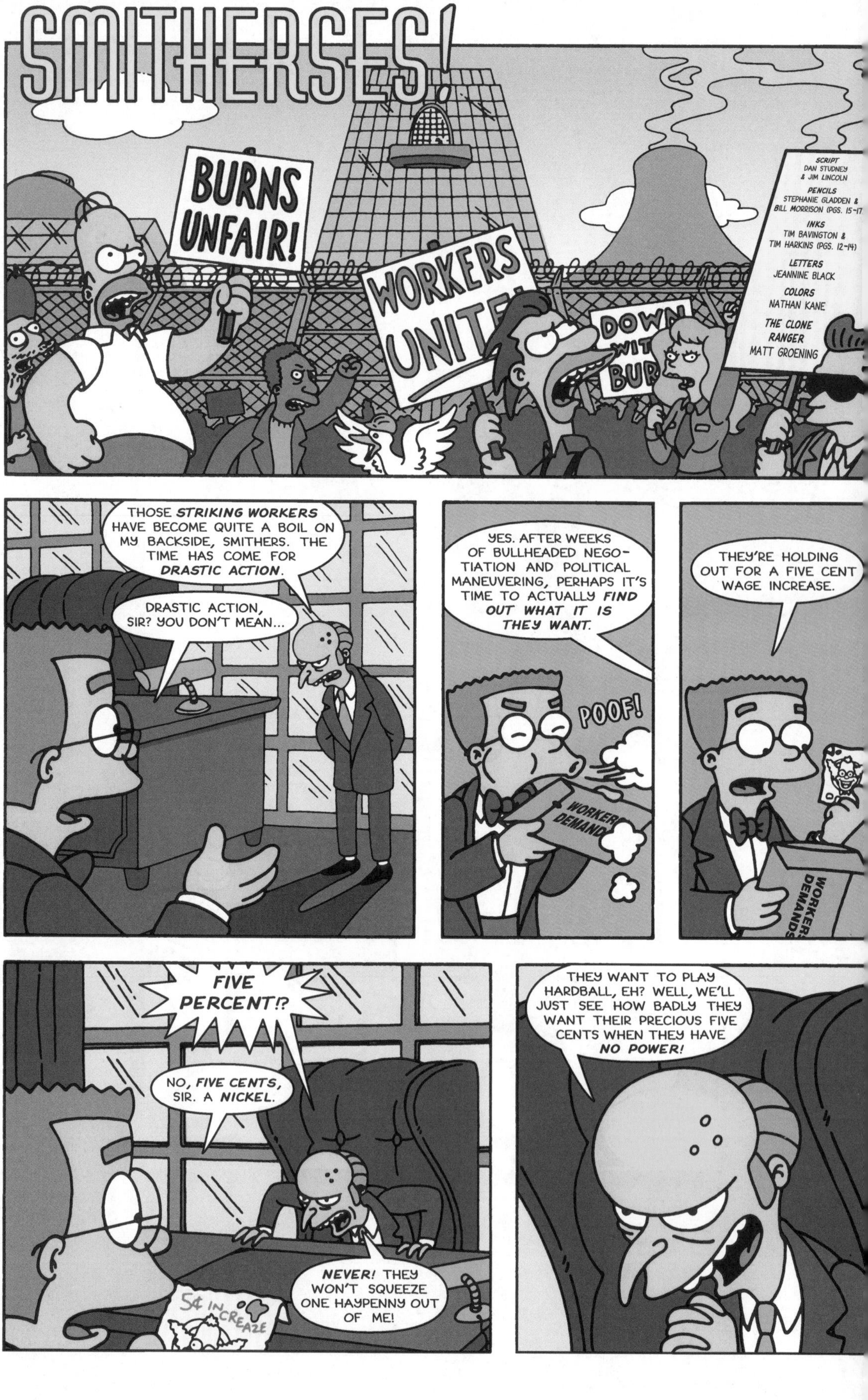
SMITHERSES!
BURNS UNFAIR!
WORKERS UNITE
DOWN WIT BUR
SCRIPT
DAN STUDNEY & JIM LINCOLN
PENCILS
STEPHANIE GLADDEN & BILL MORRISON (PGS. 15-17
INKS
TIM BAVINGTON & TIM HARKINS (PGS. 12-14)
LETTERS
JEANNINE BLACK
COLORS
NATHAN KANE
THE CLONE RANGER
MATT GROENING
THOSE STRIKING WORKERS HAVE BECOME QUITE A BOIL ON MY BACKSIDE, SMITHERS. THE TIME HAS COME FOR DRASTIC ACTION.
DRASTIC ACTION, SIR? YOU DON'T MEAN...
YES. AFTER WEEKS OF BULLHEADED NEGOTIATION AND POLITICAL MANEUVERING, PERHAPS IT'S TIME TO ACTUALLY FIND OUT WHAT IT IS THEY WANT.
POOF!
WORKERS DEMANDS
THEY'RE HOLDING OUT FOR A FIVE CENT WAGE INCREASE.
WORKERS DEMANDS
FIVE PERCENT!?
NO, FIVE CENTS, SIR. A NICKEL.
NEVER! THEY WON'T SQUEEZE ONE HAYPENNY OUT OF ME!
5¢ INCREAZE
THEY WANT TO PLAY HARDBALL, EH? WELL, WE'LL JUST SEE HOW BADLY THEY WANT THEIR PRECIOUS FIVE CENTS WHEN THEY HAVE NO POWER!

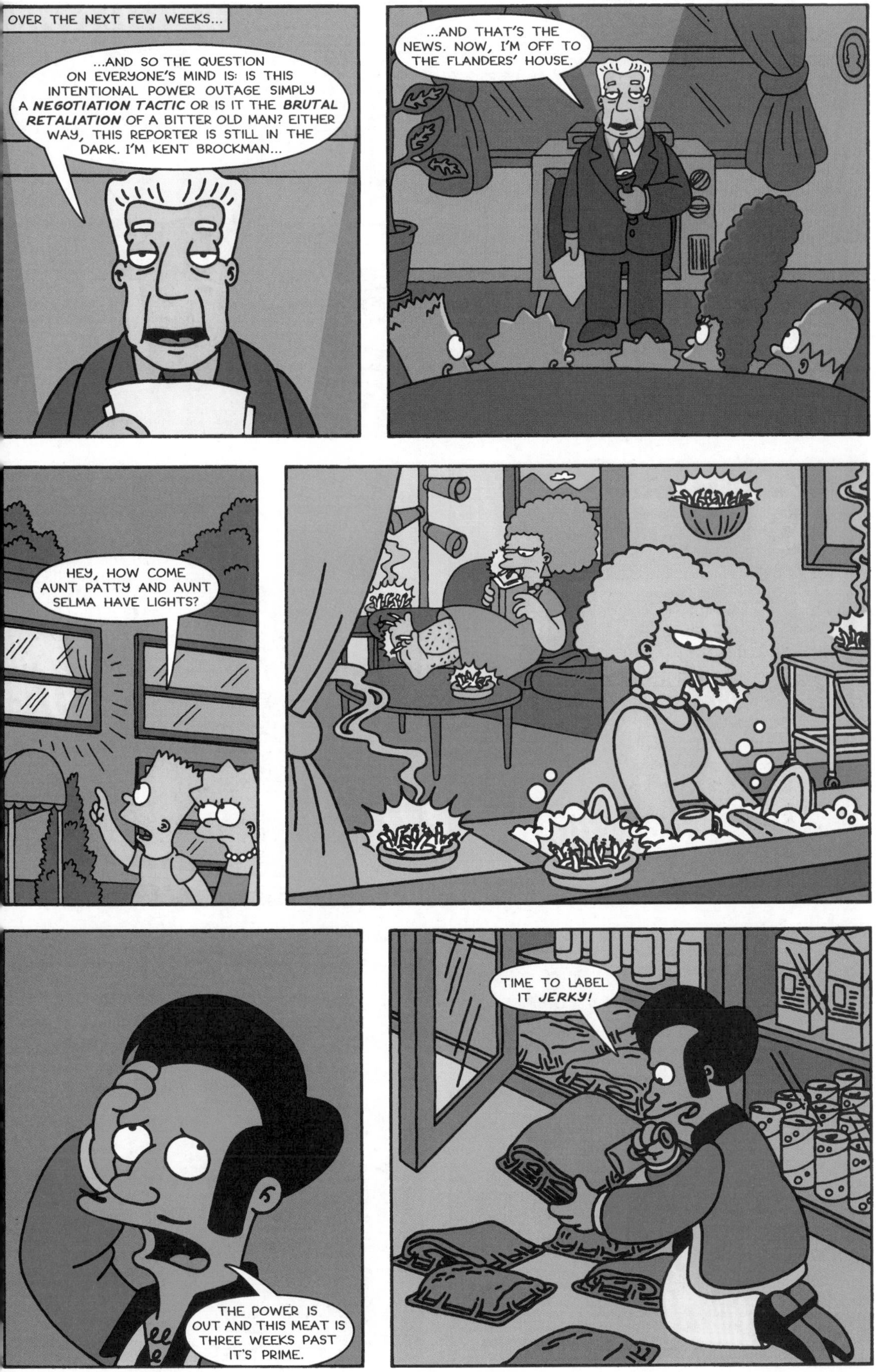
OVER THE NEXT FEW WEEKS...
...AND SO THE QUESTION ON EVERYONE'S MIND IS: IS THIS INTENTIONAL POWER OUTAGE SIMPLY A **NEGOTIATION TACTIC** OR IS IT THE **BRUTAL RETALIATION** OF A BITTER OLD MAN? EITHER WAY, THIS REPORTER IS STILL IN THE DARK. I'M KENT BROCKMAN...
...AND THAT'S THE NEWS. NOW, I'M OFF TO THE FLANDERS' HOUSE.
HEY, HOW COME AUNT PATTY AND AUNT SELMA HAVE LIGHTS?
THE POWER IS OUT AND THIS MEAT IS THREE WEEKS PAST IT'S PRIME.
TIME TO LABEL IT ***JERKY!***

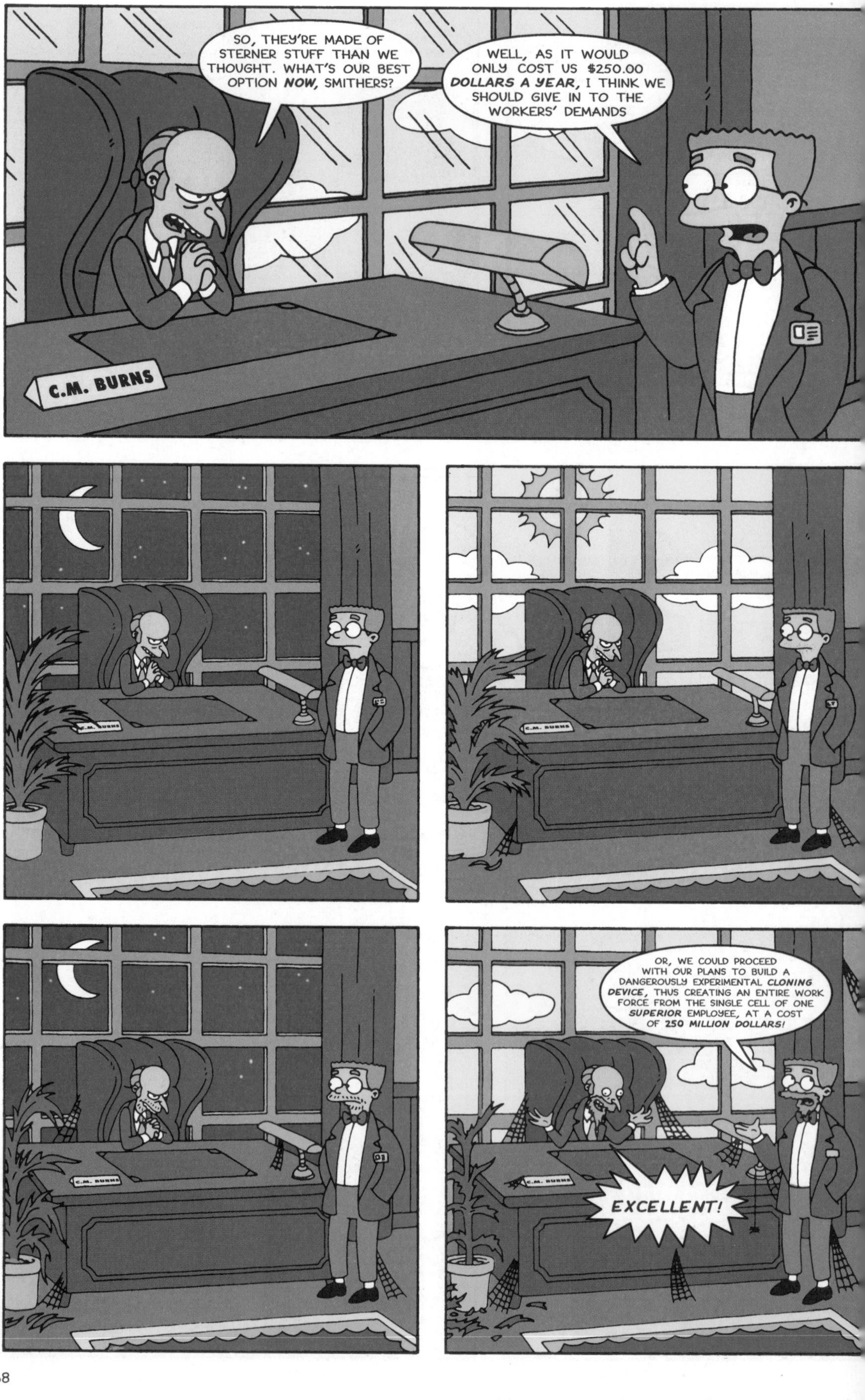
SO, THEY'RE MADE OF STERNER STUFF THAN WE THOUGHT. WHAT'S OUR BEST OPTION **NOW,** SMITHERS?
WELL, AS IT WOULD ONLY COST US $250.00 **DOLLARS A YEAR,** I THINK WE SHOULD GIVE IN TO THE WORKERS' DEMANDS
C.M. BURNS
OR, WE COULD PROCEED WITH OUR PLANS TO BUILD A DANGEROUSLY EXPERIMENTAL **CLONING DEVICE,** THUS CREATING AN ENTIRE WORK FORCE FROM THE SINGLE CELL OF ONE **SUPERIOR** EMPLOYEE, AT A COST OF **250 MILLION DOLLARS!**
EXCELLENT!

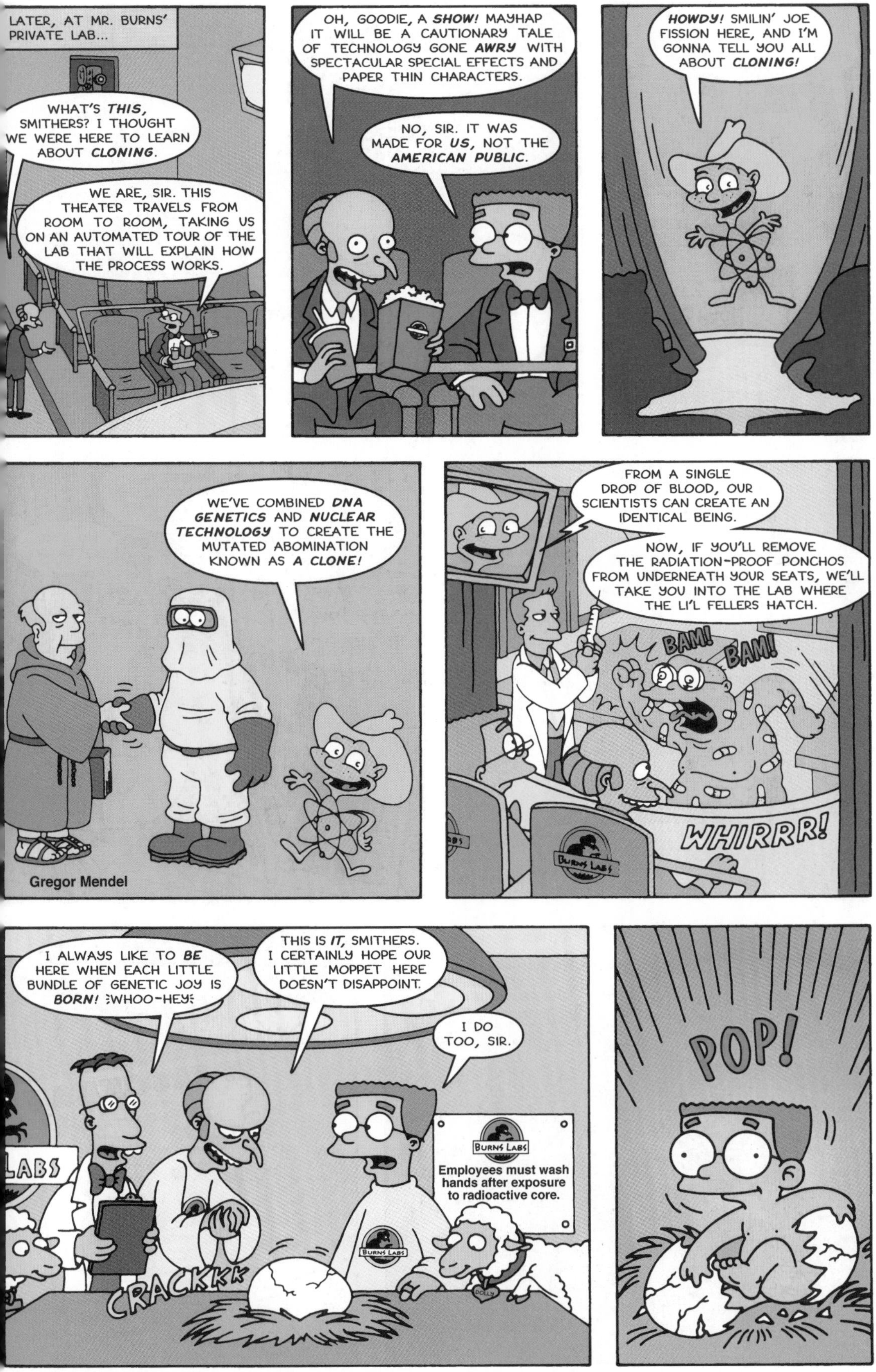

LATER, AT MR. BURNS' PRIVATE LAB...
WHAT'S **THIS,** SMITHERS? I THOUGHT WE WERE HERE TO LEARN ABOUT **CLONING**.
WE ARE, SIR. THIS THEATER TRAVELS FROM ROOM TO ROOM, TAKING US ON AN AUTOMATED TOUR OF THE LAB THAT WILL EXPLAIN HOW THE PROCESS WORKS.
OH, GOODIE, A **SHOW!** MAYHAP IT WILL BE A CAUTIONARY TALE OF TECHNOLOGY GONE **AWRY** WITH SPECTACULAR SPECIAL EFFECTS AND PAPER THIN CHARACTERS.
NO, SIR. IT WAS MADE FOR **US,** NOT THE **AMERICAN PUBLIC**.
HOWDY! SMILIN' JOE FISSION HERE, AND I'M GONNA TELL YOU ALL ABOUT **CLONING!**
WE'VE COMBINED **DNA GENETICS** AND **NUCLEAR TECHNOLOGY** TO CREATE THE MUTATED ABOMINATION KNOWN AS **A CLONE!**
Gregor Mendel
FROM A SINGLE DROP OF BLOOD, OUR SCIENTISTS CAN CREATE AN IDENTICAL BEING.
NOW, IF YOU'LL REMOVE THE RADIATION-PROOF PONCHOS FROM UNDERNEATH YOUR SEATS, WE'LL TAKE YOU INTO THE LAB WHERE THE LI'L FELLERS HATCH.
BAM!
BAM!
WHIRRR!
BURNS LABS
I ALWAYS LIKE TO **BE** HERE WHEN EACH LITTLE BUNDLE OF GENETIC JOY IS **BORN!** ⁐WHOO-HEY⁐
THIS IS **IT,** SMITHERS. I CERTAINLY HOPE OUR LITTLE MOPPET HERE DOESN'T DISAPPOINT.
I DO TOO, SIR.
BURNS LABS
Employees must wash hands after exposure to radioactive core.
LABS
BURNS LABS
CRACKKK
DOLLY
POP!

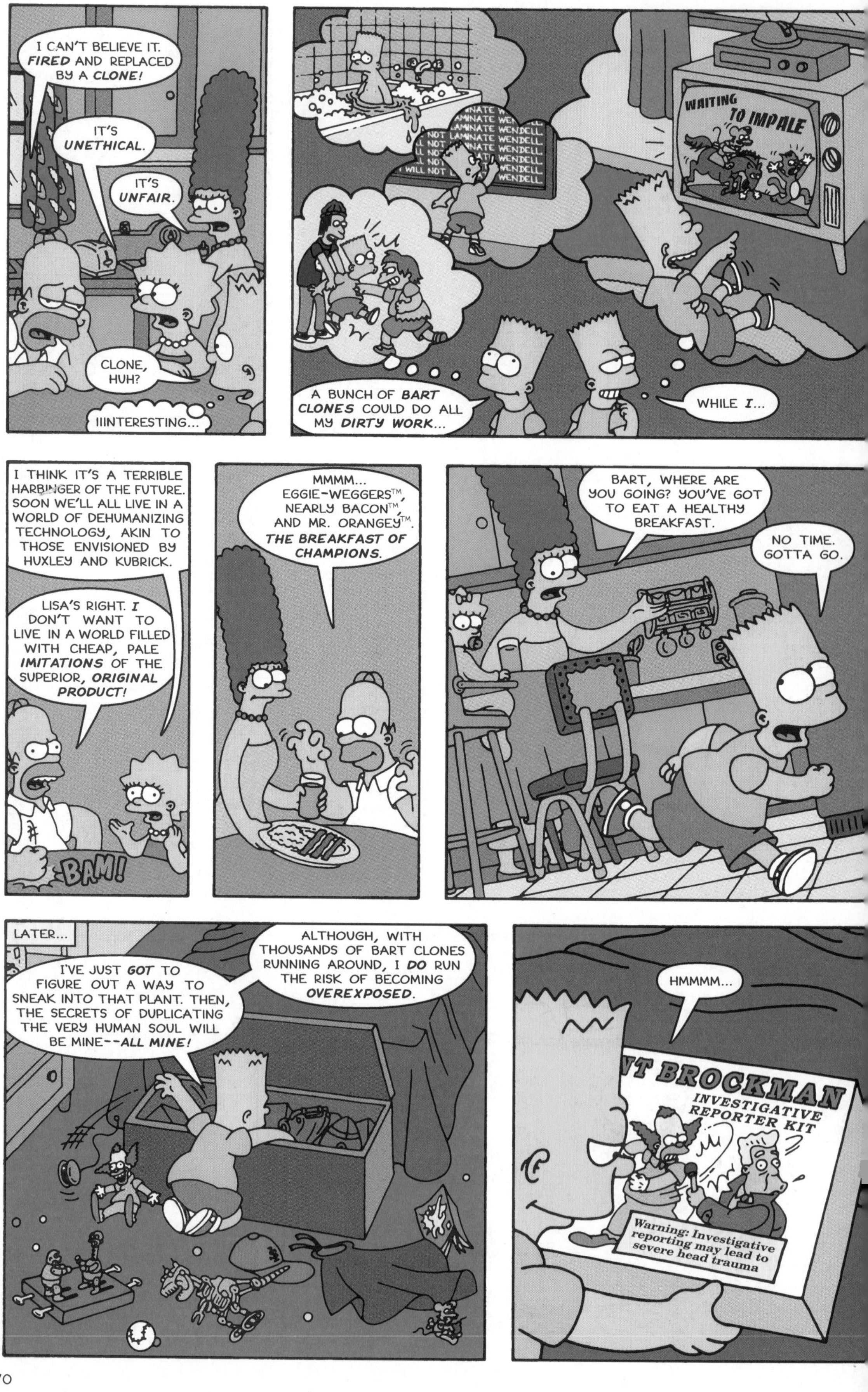
I CAN'T BELIEVE IT. FIRED AND REPLACED BY A CLONE!
IT'S UNETHICAL.
IT'S UNFAIR.
CLONE, HUH?
IIINTERESTING...
I WILL NOT LAMINATE WENDELL.
WAITING TO IMPALE
A BUNCH OF BART CLONES COULD DO ALL MY DIRTY WORK...
WHILE I...
I THINK IT'S A TERRIBLE HARBINGER OF THE FUTURE. SOON WE'LL ALL LIVE IN A WORLD OF DEHUMANIZING TECHNOLOGY, AKIN TO THOSE ENVISIONED BY HUXLEY AND KUBRICK.
LISA'S RIGHT. I DON'T WANT TO LIVE IN A WORLD FILLED WITH CHEAP, PALE IMITATIONS OF THE SUPERIOR, ORIGINAL PRODUCT!
BAM!
MMMM... EGGIE-WEGGERS™, NEARLY BACON™, AND MR. ORANGEY™. THE BREAKFAST OF CHAMPIONS.
BART, WHERE ARE YOU GOING? YOU'VE GOT TO EAT A HEALTHY BREAKFAST.
NO TIME. GOTTA GO.
LATER...
I'VE JUST GOT TO FIGURE OUT A WAY TO SNEAK INTO THAT PLANT. THEN, THE SECRETS OF DUPLICATING THE VERY HUMAN SOUL WILL BE MINE--ALL MINE!
ALTHOUGH, WITH THOUSANDS OF BART CLONES RUNNING AROUND, I DO RUN THE RISK OF BECOMING OVEREXPOSED.
HMMMM...
NT BROCKMAN
INVESTIGATIVE REPORTER KIT
Warning: Investigative reporting may lead to severe head trauma

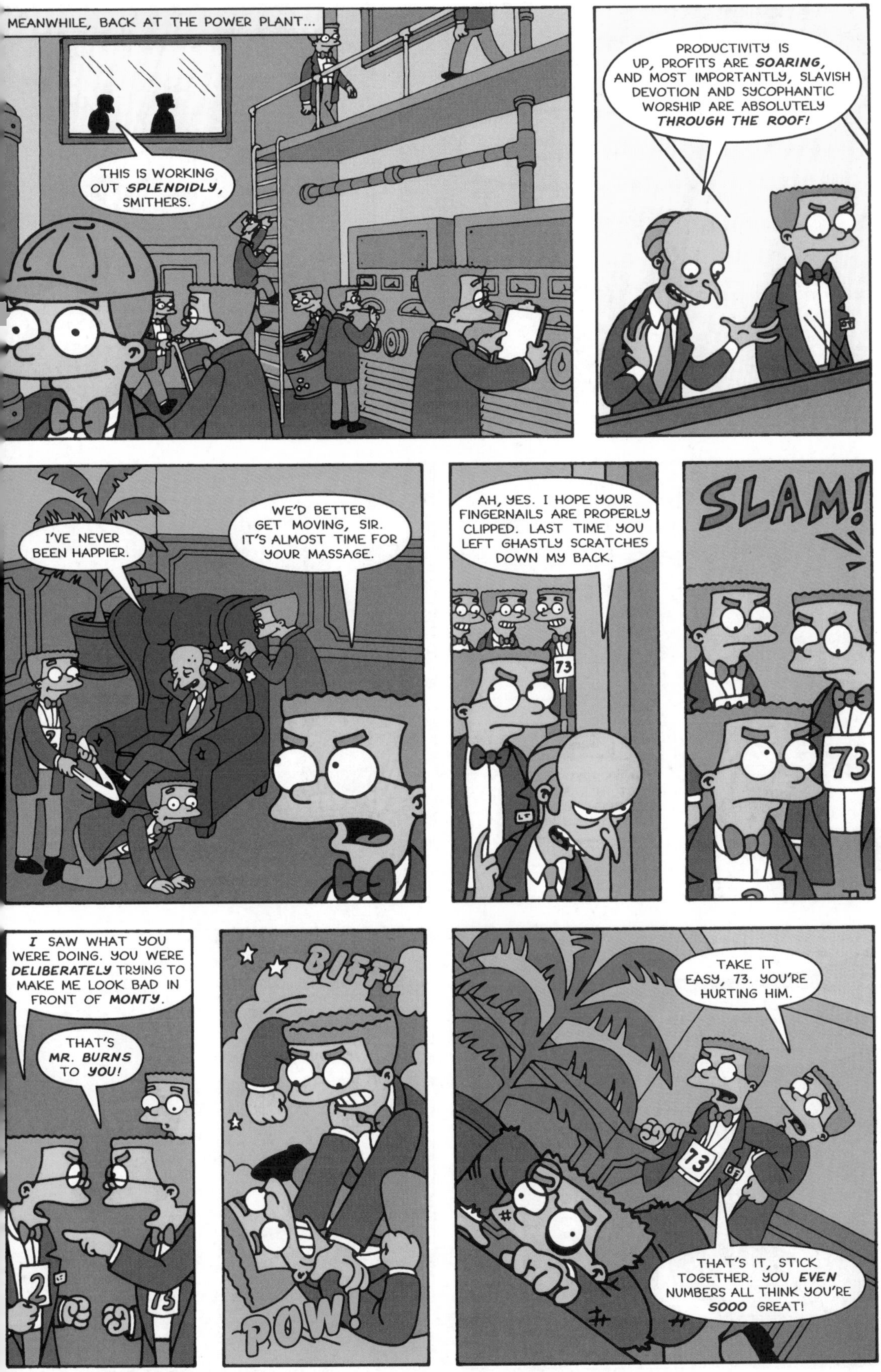
MEANWHILE, BACK AT THE POWER PLANT...
THIS IS WORKING OUT SPLENDIDLY, SMITHERS.
PRODUCTIVITY IS UP, PROFITS ARE SOARING, AND MOST IMPORTANTLY, SLAVISH DEVOTION AND SYCOPHANTIC WORSHIP ARE ABSOLUTELY THROUGH THE ROOF!
I'VE NEVER BEEN HAPPIER.
WE'D BETTER GET MOVING, SIR. IT'S ALMOST TIME FOR YOUR MASSAGE.
AH, YES. I HOPE YOUR FINGERNAILS ARE PROPERLY CLIPPED. LAST TIME YOU LEFT GHASTLY SCRATCHES DOWN MY BACK.
73
SLAM!
73
I SAW WHAT YOU WERE DOING. YOU WERE DELIBERATELY TRYING TO MAKE ME LOOK BAD IN FRONT OF MONTY.
THAT'S MR. BURNS TO YOU!
2
BIFF!
POW!
TAKE IT EASY, 73. YOU'RE HURTING HIM.
73
THAT'S IT, STICK TOGETHER. YOU EVEN NUMBERS ALL THINK YOU'RE SOOO GREAT!

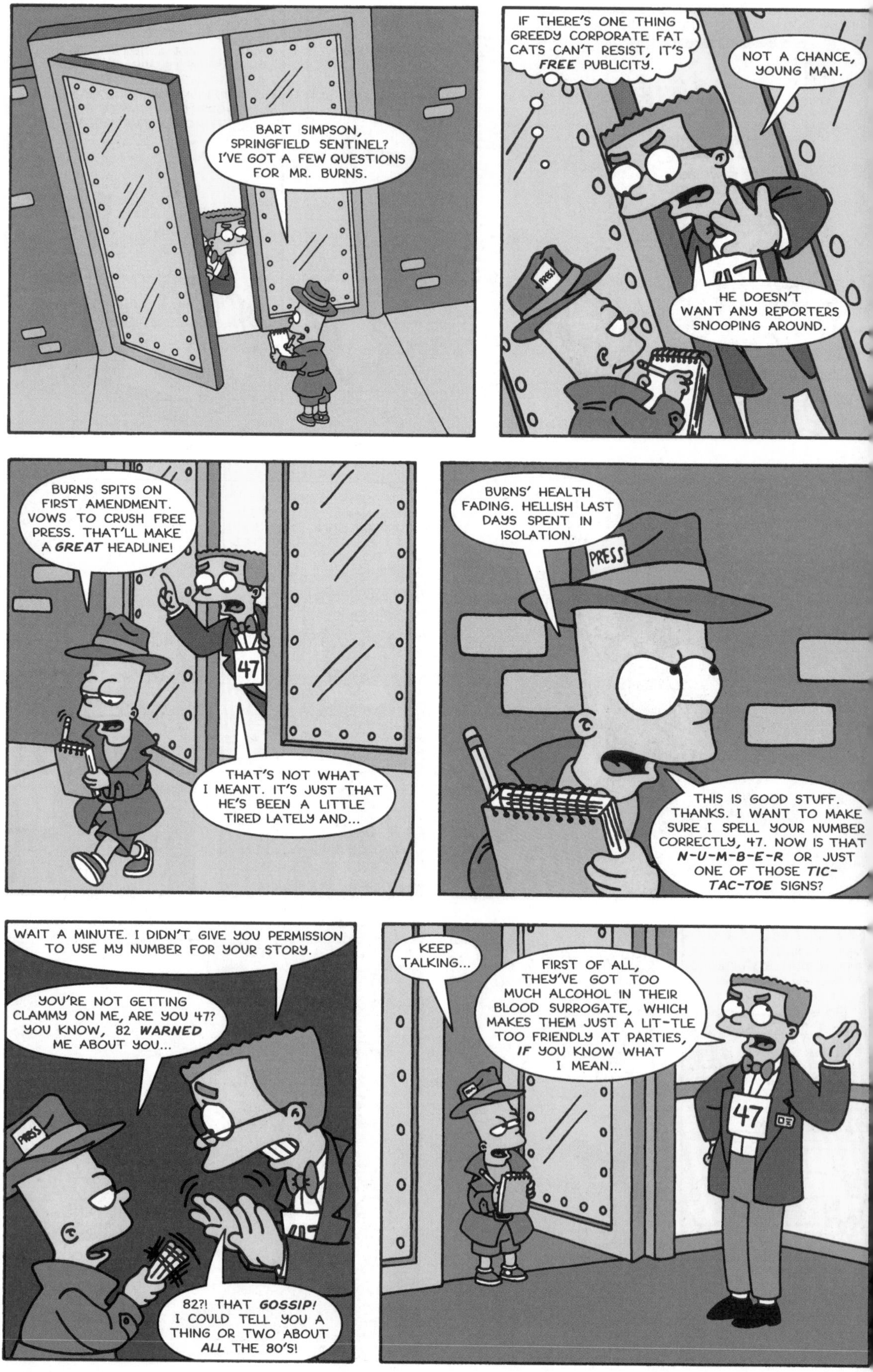
BART SIMPSON, SPRINGFIELD SENTINEL? I'VE GOT A FEW QUESTIONS FOR MR. BURNS.
IF THERE'S ONE THING GREEDY CORPORATE FAT CATS CAN'T RESIST, IT'S FREE PUBLICITY.
NOT A CHANCE, YOUNG MAN.
47
HE DOESN'T WANT ANY REPORTERS SNOOPING AROUND.
PRESS
BURNS SPITS ON FIRST AMENDMENT. VOWS TO CRUSH FREE PRESS. THAT'LL MAKE A GREAT HEADLINE!
47
THAT'S NOT WHAT I MEANT. IT'S JUST THAT HE'S BEEN A LITTLE TIRED LATELY AND...
BURNS' HEALTH FADING. HELLISH LAST DAYS SPENT IN ISOLATION.
PRESS
THIS IS GOOD STUFF. THANKS. I WANT TO MAKE SURE I SPELL YOUR NUMBER CORRECTLY, 47. NOW IS THAT N-U-M-B-E-R OR JUST ONE OF THOSE TIC-TAC-TOE SIGNS?
WAIT A MINUTE. I DIDN'T GIVE YOU PERMISSION TO USE MY NUMBER FOR YOUR STORY.
YOU'RE NOT GETTING CLAMMY ON ME, ARE YOU 47? YOU KNOW, 82 WARNED ME ABOUT YOU...
PRESS
82?! THAT GOSSIP! I COULD TELL YOU A THING OR TWO ABOUT ALL THE 80'S!
KEEP TALKING...
FIRST OF ALL, THEY'VE GOT TOO MUCH ALCOHOL IN THEIR BLOOD SURROGATE, WHICH MAKES THEM JUST A LIT-TLE TOO FRIENDLY AT PARTIES, IF YOU KNOW WHAT I MEAN...
47

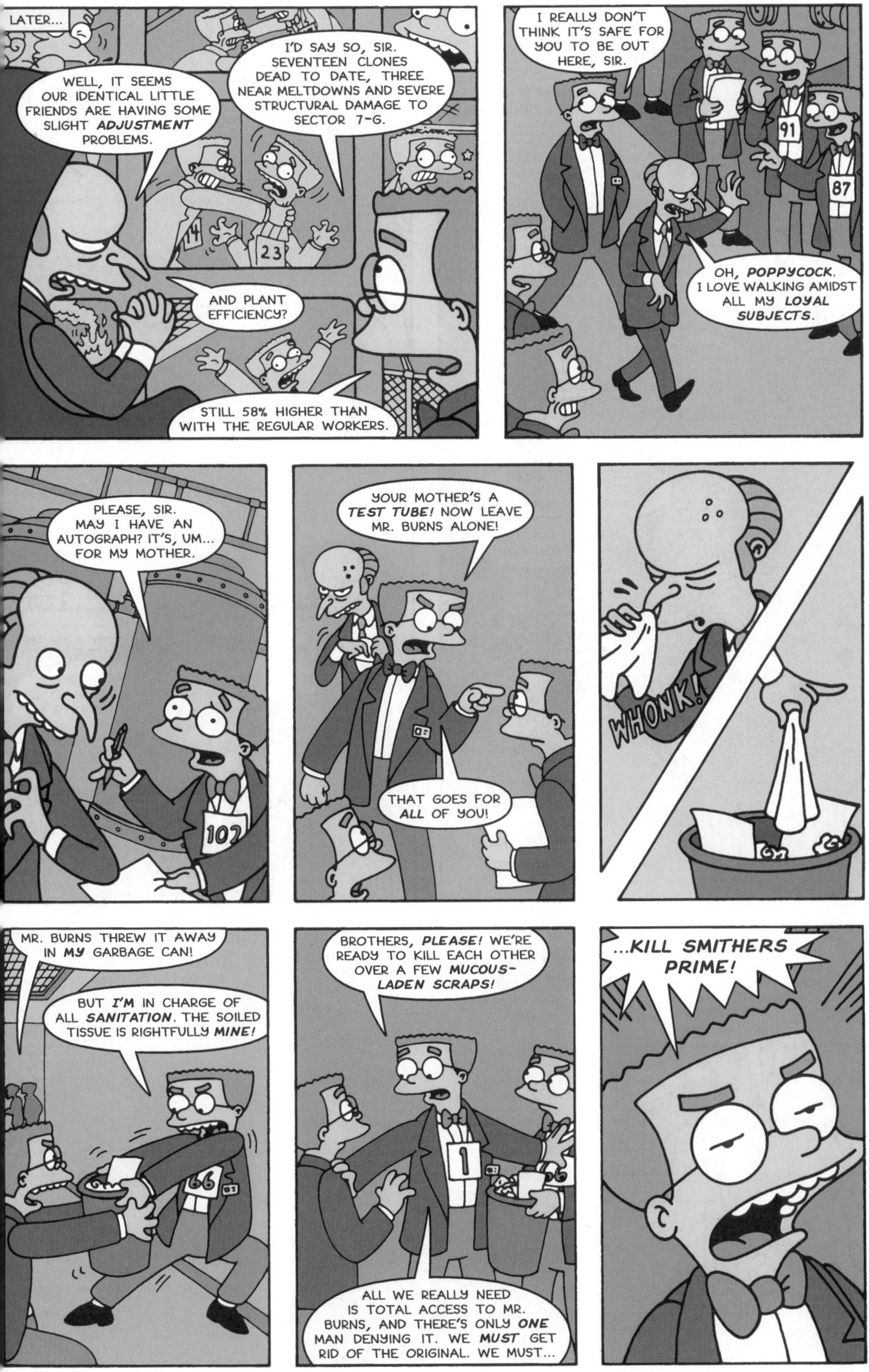
LATER...
WELL, IT SEEMS OUR IDENTICAL LITTLE FRIENDS ARE HAVING SOME SLIGHT ADJUSTMENT PROBLEMS.
I'D SAY SO, SIR. SEVENTEEN CLONES DEAD TO DATE, THREE NEAR MELTDOWNS AND SEVERE STRUCTURAL DAMAGE TO SECTOR 7-G.
AND PLANT EFFICIENCY?
STILL 58% HIGHER THAN WITH THE REGULAR WORKERS.
I REALLY DON'T THINK IT'S SAFE FOR YOU TO BE OUT HERE, SIR.
OH, POPPYCOCK. I LOVE WALKING AMIDST ALL MY LOYAL SUBJECTS.
PLEASE, SIR. MAY I HAVE AN AUTOGRAPH? IT'S, UM... FOR MY MOTHER.
YOUR MOTHER'S A TEST TUBE! NOW LEAVE MR. BURNS ALONE!
THAT GOES FOR ALL OF YOU!
WHONK!
MR. BURNS THREW IT AWAY IN MY GARBAGE CAN!
BUT I'M IN CHARGE OF ALL SANITATION. THE SOILED TISSUE IS RIGHTFULLY MINE!
BROTHERS, PLEASE! WE'RE READY TO KILL EACH OTHER OVER A FEW MUCOUS-LADEN SCRAPS!
ALL WE REALLY NEED IS TOTAL ACCESS TO MR. BURNS, AND THERE'S ONLY ONE MAN DENYING IT. WE MUST GET RID OF THE ORIGINAL. WE MUST...
...KILL SMITHERS PRIME!

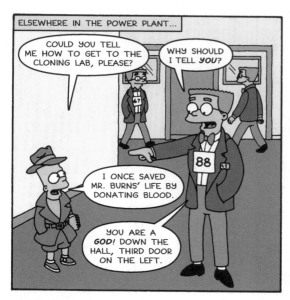

ELSEWHERE IN THE POWER PLANT...

COULD YOU TELL ME HOW TO GET TO THE CLONING LAB, PLEASE?

WHY SHOULD I TELL *YOU*?

I ONCE SAVED MR. BURNS' LIFE BY DONATING BLOOD.

YOU ARE A *GOD*! DOWN THE HALL, THIRD DOOR ON THE LEFT.

MAN, THOSE SMITHERS CLONES ARE CREEPY. AND THERE'S SO MANY OF THEM. I WONDER HOW YOU TELL WHO THE *REAL* ONE IS...

HELP, HELP! THEY'RE GOING TO KILL ME IN A HORRIBLE, VICIOUS...

IS THAT THE SIMPSON BOY?

...NASTY, VIOLENT WAY! *HELP, HELP!*

DON'T PANIC. REMAIN CALM. AS LONG AS THEY DON'T KNOW I'M HERE I'LL BE SAFE.

BESIDES, MR. BURNS IS MONITORING EVERYTHING. *HE'LL* SAVE ME.

THIS THRICE-CURSED CUTICLE IS DRIVING ME MAD. I NEED A BUFF AND I NEED IT *NOW*! WHERE IS SMITHERS AND HIS DANCING EMERY BOARD?

AH, *THERE* YOU ARE, HIDDEN IN SHADOW BEHIND THE PARTICLE ACCELERATOR. COME HERE, SMITHERS. I NEED YOU.

AFTER HIM!!

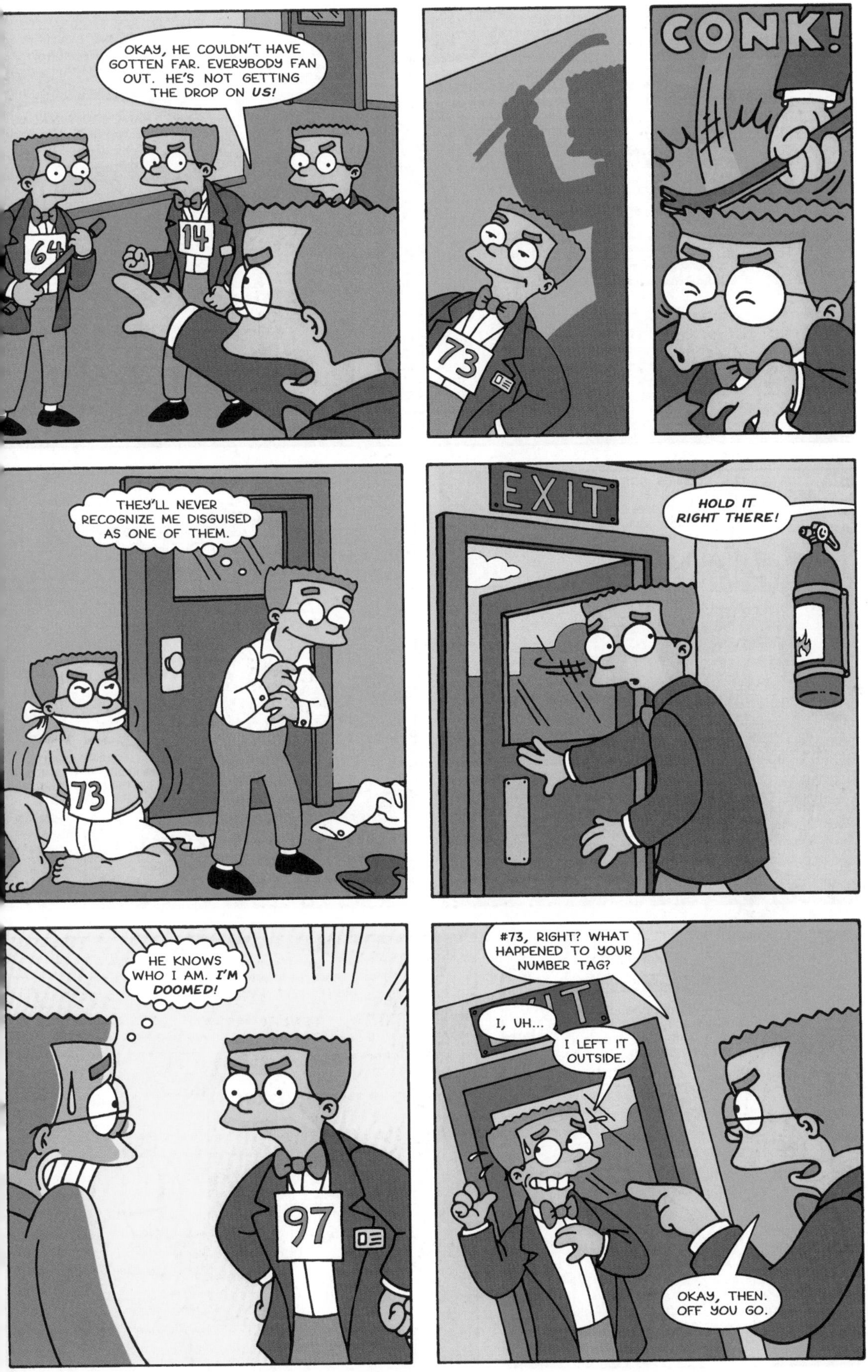
OKAY, HE COULDN'T HAVE GOTTEN FAR. EVERYBODY FAN OUT. HE'S NOT GETTING THE DROP ON *US!*
64
14
73
CONK!
THEY'LL NEVER RECOGNIZE ME DISGUISED AS ONE OF THEM.
73
EXIT
HOLD IT RIGHT THERE!
HE KNOWS WHO I AM. *I'M DOOMED!*
97
#73, RIGHT? WHAT HAPPENED TO YOUR NUMBER TAG?
I, UH...
I LEFT IT OUTSIDE.
OKAY, THEN. OFF YOU GO.

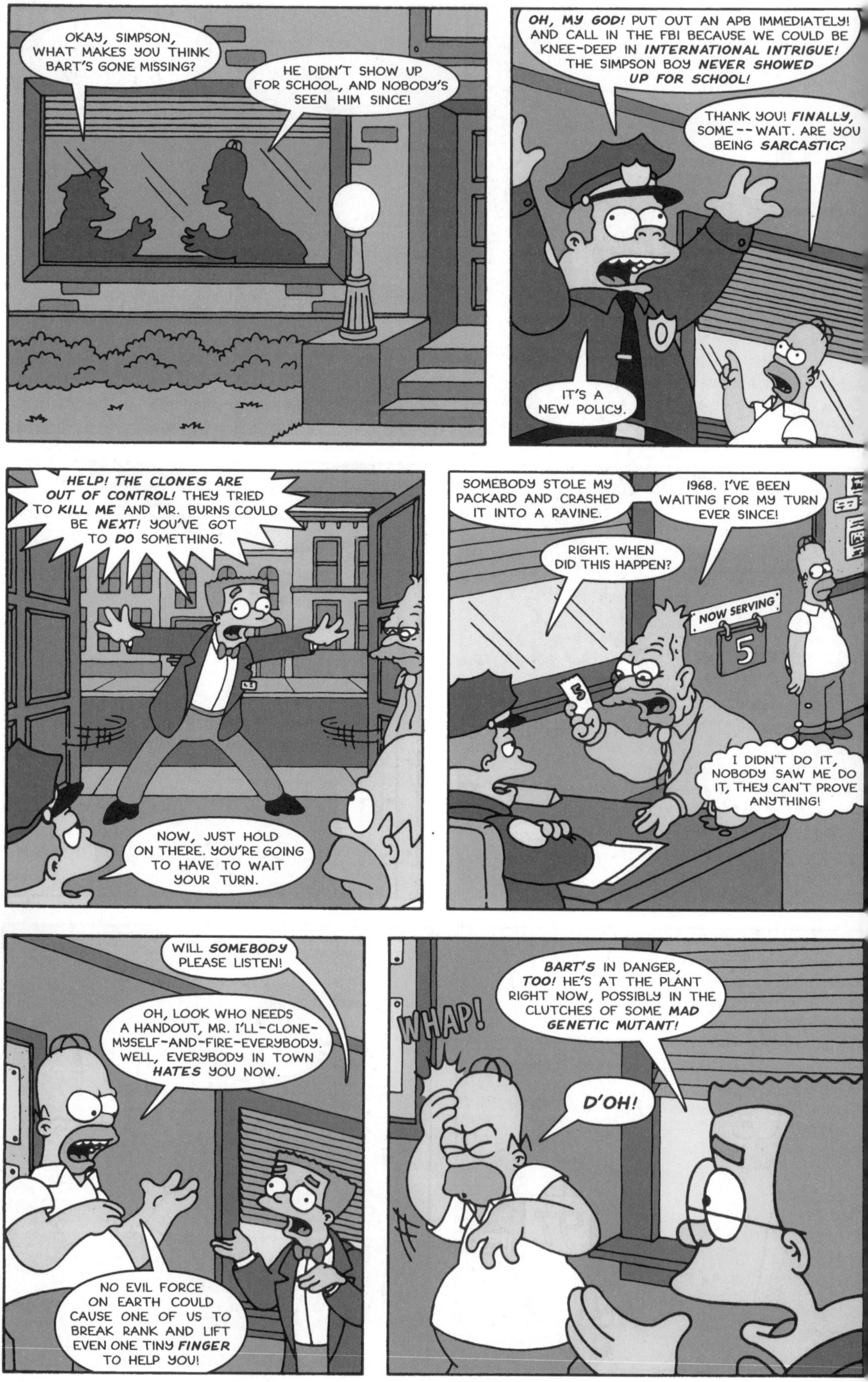
OKAY, SIMPSON, WHAT MAKES YOU THINK BART'S GONE MISSING?
HE DIDN'T SHOW UP FOR SCHOOL, AND NOBODY'S SEEN HIM SINCE!
OH, MY GOD! PUT OUT AN APB IMMEDIATELY! AND CALL IN THE FBI BECAUSE WE COULD BE KNEE-DEEP IN INTERNATIONAL INTRIGUE! THE SIMPSON BOY NEVER SHOWED UP FOR SCHOOL!
THANK YOU! FINALLY, SOME--WAIT. ARE YOU BEING SARCASTIC?
IT'S A NEW POLICY.
HELP! THE CLONES ARE OUT OF CONTROL! THEY TRIED TO KILL ME AND MR. BURNS COULD BE NEXT! YOU'VE GOT TO DO SOMETHING.
NOW, JUST HOLD ON THERE. YOU'RE GOING TO HAVE TO WAIT YOUR TURN.
SOMEBODY STOLE MY PACKARD AND CRASHED IT INTO A RAVINE.
RIGHT. WHEN DID THIS HAPPEN?
1968. I'VE BEEN WAITING FOR MY TURN EVER SINCE!
NOW SERVING
5
I DIDN'T DO IT, NOBODY SAW ME DO IT, THEY CAN'T PROVE ANYTHING!
WILL SOMEBODY PLEASE LISTEN!
OH, LOOK WHO NEEDS A HANDOUT, MR. I'LL-CLONE-MYSELF-AND-FIRE-EVERYBODY. WELL, EVERYBODY IN TOWN HATES YOU NOW.
NO EVIL FORCE ON EARTH COULD CAUSE ONE OF US TO BREAK RANK AND LIFT EVEN ONE TINY FINGER TO HELP YOU!
BART'S IN DANGER, TOO! HE'S AT THE PLANT RIGHT NOW, POSSIBLY IN THE CLUTCHES OF SOME MAD GENETIC MUTANT!
WHAP!
D'OH!

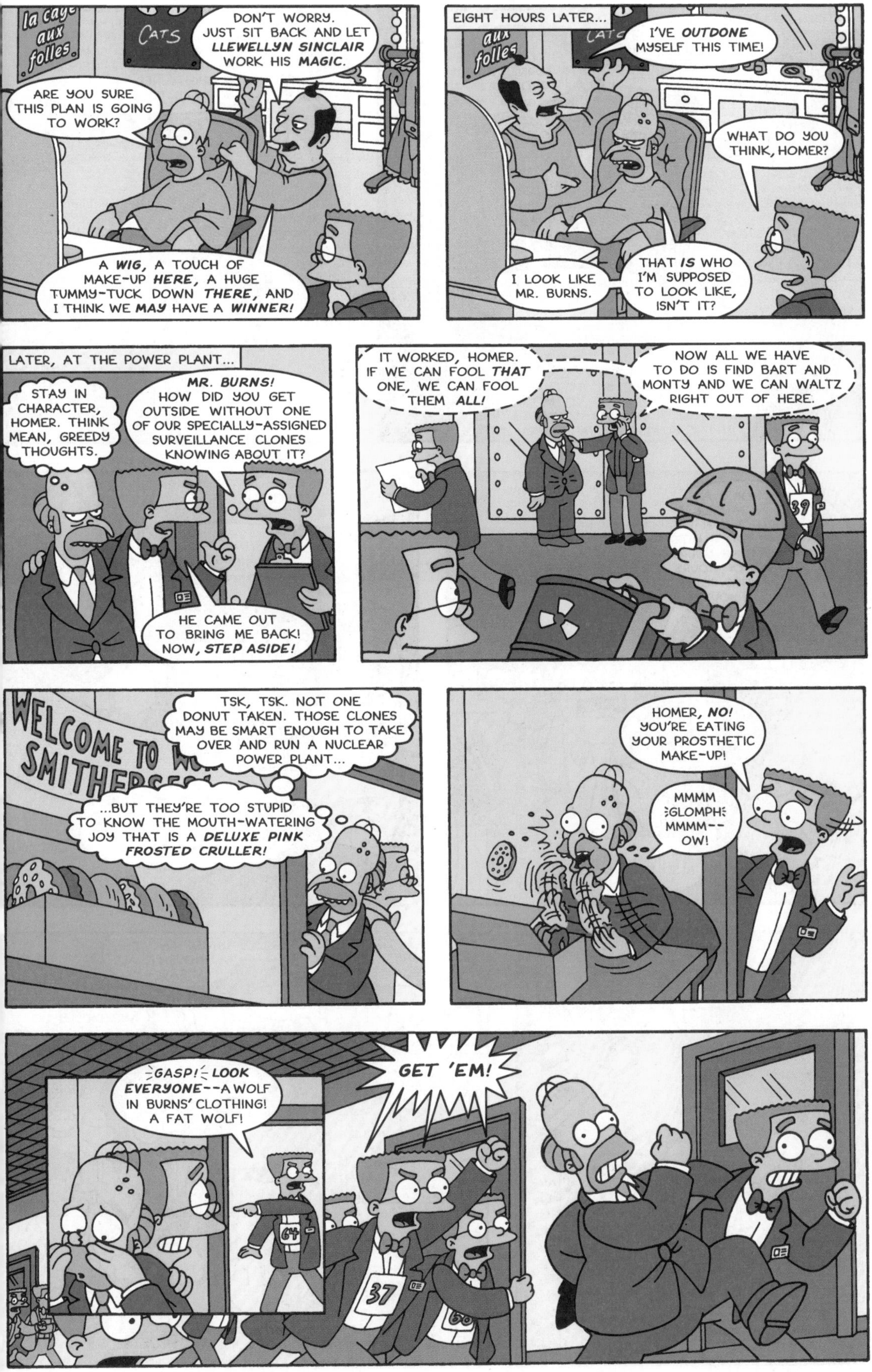
la cage aux folles
CATS
ARE YOU SURE THIS PLAN IS GOING TO WORK?
DON'T WORRY. JUST SIT BACK AND LET LLEWELLYN SINCLAIR WORK HIS MAGIC.
A WIG, A TOUCH OF MAKE-UP HERE, A HUGE TUMMY-TUCK DOWN THERE, AND I THINK WE MAY HAVE A WINNER!
EIGHT HOURS LATER...
I'VE OUTDONE MYSELF THIS TIME!
WHAT DO YOU THINK, HOMER?
I LOOK LIKE MR. BURNS.
THAT IS WHO I'M SUPPOSED TO LOOK LIKE, ISN'T IT?
LATER, AT THE POWER PLANT...
STAY IN CHARACTER, HOMER. THINK MEAN, GREEDY THOUGHTS.
MR. BURNS! HOW DID YOU GET OUTSIDE WITHOUT ONE OF OUR SPECIALLY-ASSIGNED SURVEILLANCE CLONES KNOWING ABOUT IT?
HE CAME OUT TO BRING ME BACK! NOW, STEP ASIDE!
IT WORKED, HOMER. IF WE CAN FOOL THAT ONE, WE CAN FOOL THEM ALL!
NOW ALL WE HAVE TO DO IS FIND BART AND MONTY AND WE CAN WALTZ RIGHT OUT OF HERE.
39
WELCOME TO WO SMITHERS
TSK, TSK. NOT ONE DONUT TAKEN. THOSE CLONES MAY BE SMART ENOUGH TO TAKE OVER AND RUN A NUCLEAR POWER PLANT...
...BUT THEY'RE TOO STUPID TO KNOW THE MOUTH-WATERING JOY THAT IS A DELUXE PINK FROSTED CRULLER!
HOMER, NO! YOU'RE EATING YOUR PROSTHETIC MAKE-UP!
MMMM GLOMPH MMMM-- OW!
GASP! LOOK EVERYONE--A WOLF IN BURNS' CLOTHING! A FAT WOLF!
GET 'EM!
64
37
68

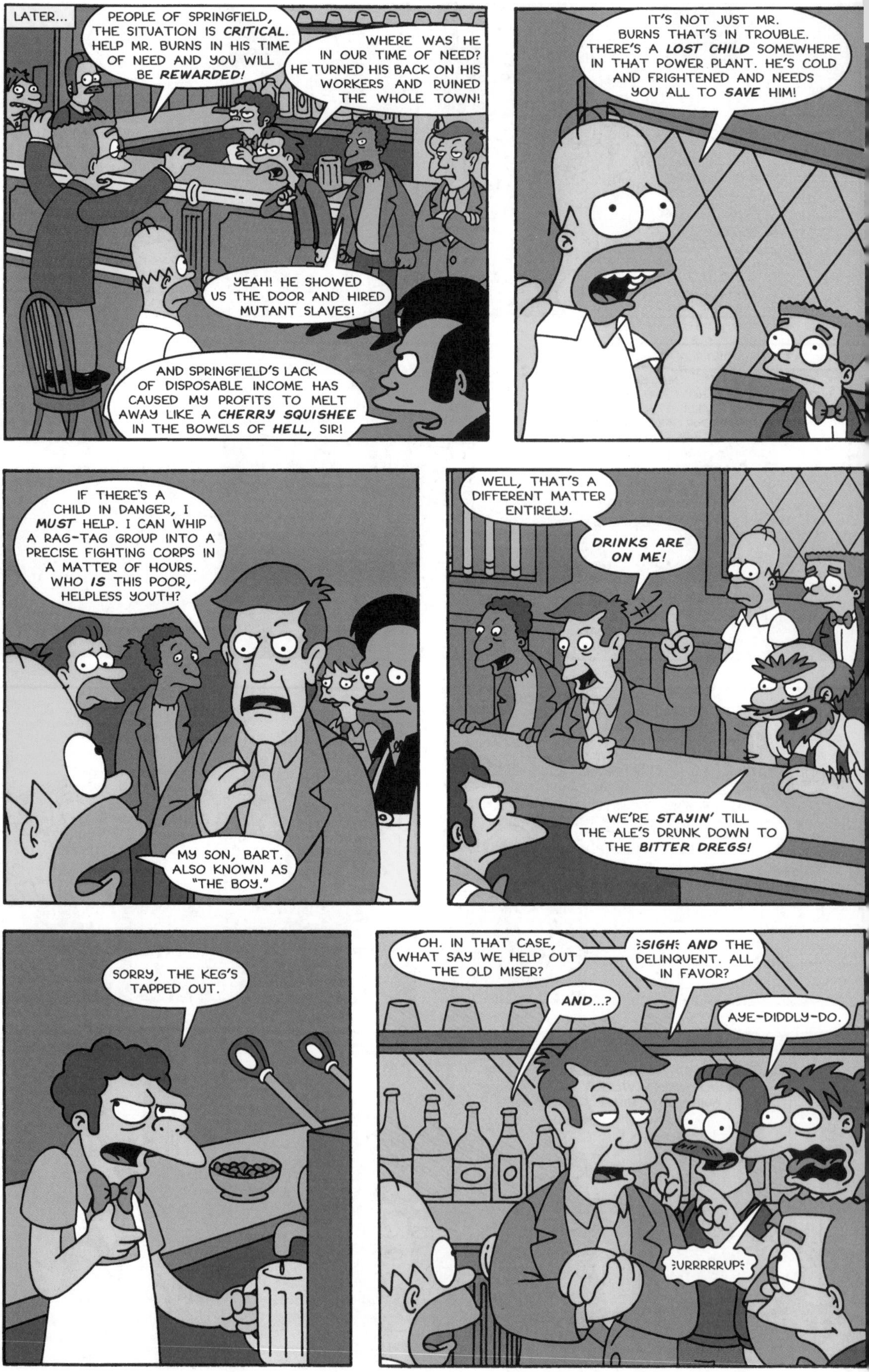
LATER...
PEOPLE OF SPRINGFIELD, THE SITUATION IS *CRITICAL*. HELP MR. BURNS IN HIS TIME OF NEED AND YOU WILL BE *REWARDED!*
WHERE WAS HE IN OUR TIME OF NEED? HE TURNED HIS BACK ON HIS WORKERS AND RUINED THE WHOLE TOWN!
YEAH! HE SHOWED US THE DOOR AND HIRED MUTANT SLAVES!
AND SPRINGFIELD'S LACK OF DISPOSABLE INCOME HAS CAUSED MY PROFITS TO MELT AWAY LIKE A *CHERRY SQUISHEE* IN THE BOWELS OF *HELL,* SIR!
IT'S NOT JUST MR. BURNS THAT'S IN TROUBLE. THERE'S A *LOST CHILD* SOMEWHERE IN THAT POWER PLANT. HE'S COLD AND FRIGHTENED AND NEEDS YOU ALL TO *SAVE* HIM!
IF THERE'S A CHILD IN DANGER, I *MUST* HELP. I CAN WHIP A RAG-TAG GROUP INTO A PRECISE FIGHTING CORPS IN A MATTER OF HOURS. WHO *IS* THIS POOR, HELPLESS YOUTH?
MY SON, BART. ALSO KNOWN AS "THE BOY."
WELL, THAT'S A DIFFERENT MATTER ENTIRELY.
DRINKS ARE ON ME!
WE'RE *STAYIN'* TILL THE ALE'S DRUNK DOWN TO THE *BITTER DREGS!*
SORRY, THE KEG'S TAPPED OUT.
OH. IN THAT CASE, WHAT SAY WE HELP OUT THE OLD MISER?
AND...?
SIGH *AND* THE DELINQUENT. ALL IN FAVOR?
AYE-DIDDLY-DO.
URRRRRUP

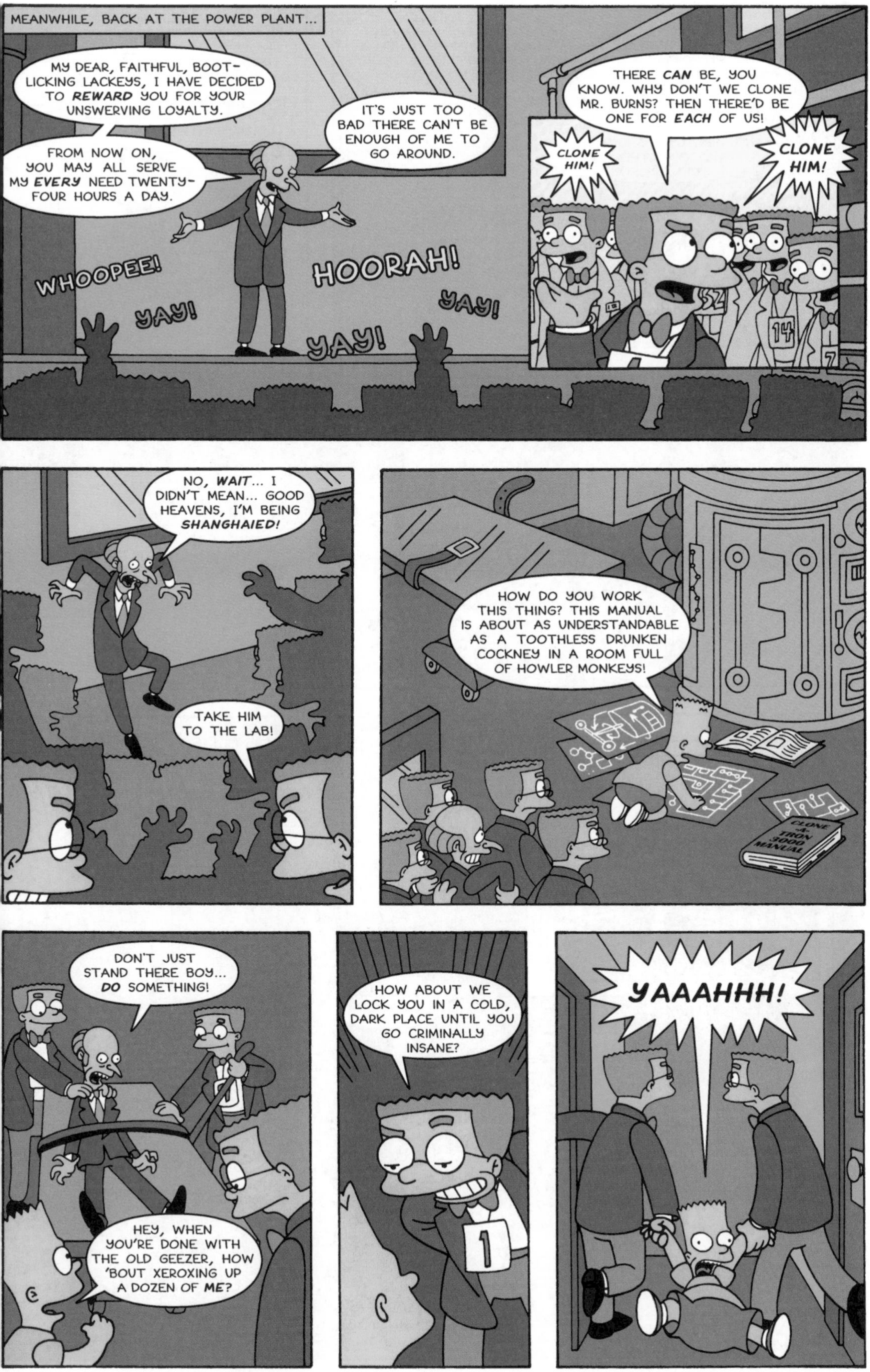
MEANWHILE, BACK AT THE POWER PLANT...
MY DEAR, FAITHFUL, BOOT-LICKING LACKEYS, I HAVE DECIDED TO *REWARD* YOU FOR YOUR UNSWERVING LOYALTY.
FROM NOW ON, YOU MAY ALL SERVE MY *EVERY* NEED TWENTY-FOUR HOURS A DAY.
IT'S JUST TOO BAD THERE CAN'T BE ENOUGH OF ME TO GO AROUND.
WHOOPEE!
YAY!
HOORAH!
YAY!
YAY!
THERE *CAN* BE, YOU KNOW. WHY DON'T WE CLONE MR. BURNS? THEN THERE'D BE ONE FOR *EACH* OF US!
CLONE HIM!
CLONE HIM!
NO, *WAIT*... I DIDN'T MEAN... GOOD HEAVENS, I'M BEING *SHANGHAIED!*
TAKE HIM TO THE LAB!
HOW DO YOU WORK THIS THING? THIS MANUAL IS ABOUT AS UNDERSTANDABLE AS A TOOTHLESS DRUNKEN COCKNEY IN A ROOM FULL OF HOWLER MONKEYS!
CLONE-A-TRON 3000 MANUAL
DON'T JUST STAND THERE BOY... *DO* SOMETHING!
HEY, WHEN YOU'RE DONE WITH THE OLD GEEZER, HOW 'BOUT XEROXING UP A DOZEN OF *ME*?
HOW ABOUT WE LOCK YOU IN A COLD, DARK PLACE UNTIL YOU GO CRIMINALLY INSANE?
YAAAHHH!

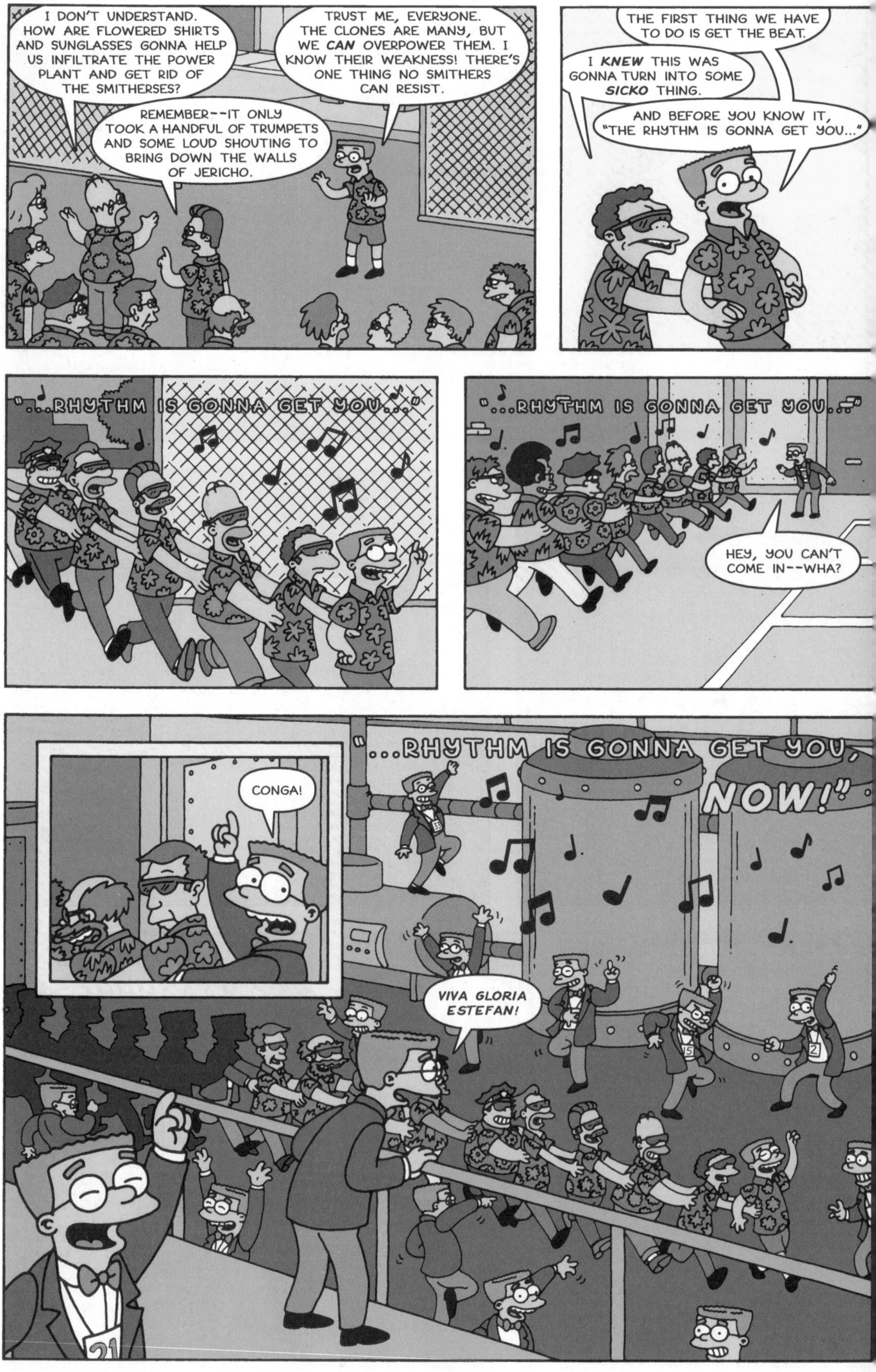
I DON'T UNDERSTAND. HOW ARE FLOWERED SHIRTS AND SUNGLASSES GONNA HELP US INFILTRATE THE POWER PLANT AND GET RID OF THE SMITHERSES?
TRUST ME, EVERYONE. THE CLONES ARE MANY, BUT WE CAN OVERPOWER THEM. I KNOW THEIR WEAKNESS! THERE'S ONE THING NO SMITHERS CAN RESIST.
REMEMBER--IT ONLY TOOK A HANDFUL OF TRUMPETS AND SOME LOUD SHOUTING TO BRING DOWN THE WALLS OF JERICHO.
THE FIRST THING WE HAVE TO DO IS GET THE BEAT.
I KNEW THIS WAS GONNA TURN INTO SOME SICKO THING.
AND BEFORE YOU KNOW IT, "THE RHYTHM IS GONNA GET YOU..."
"...RHYTHM IS GONNA GET YOU..."
"...RHYTHM IS GONNA GET YOU..."
HEY, YOU CAN'T COME IN--WHA?
"...RHYTHM IS GONNA GET YOU, NOW!"
CONGA!
VIVA GLORIA ESTEFAN!

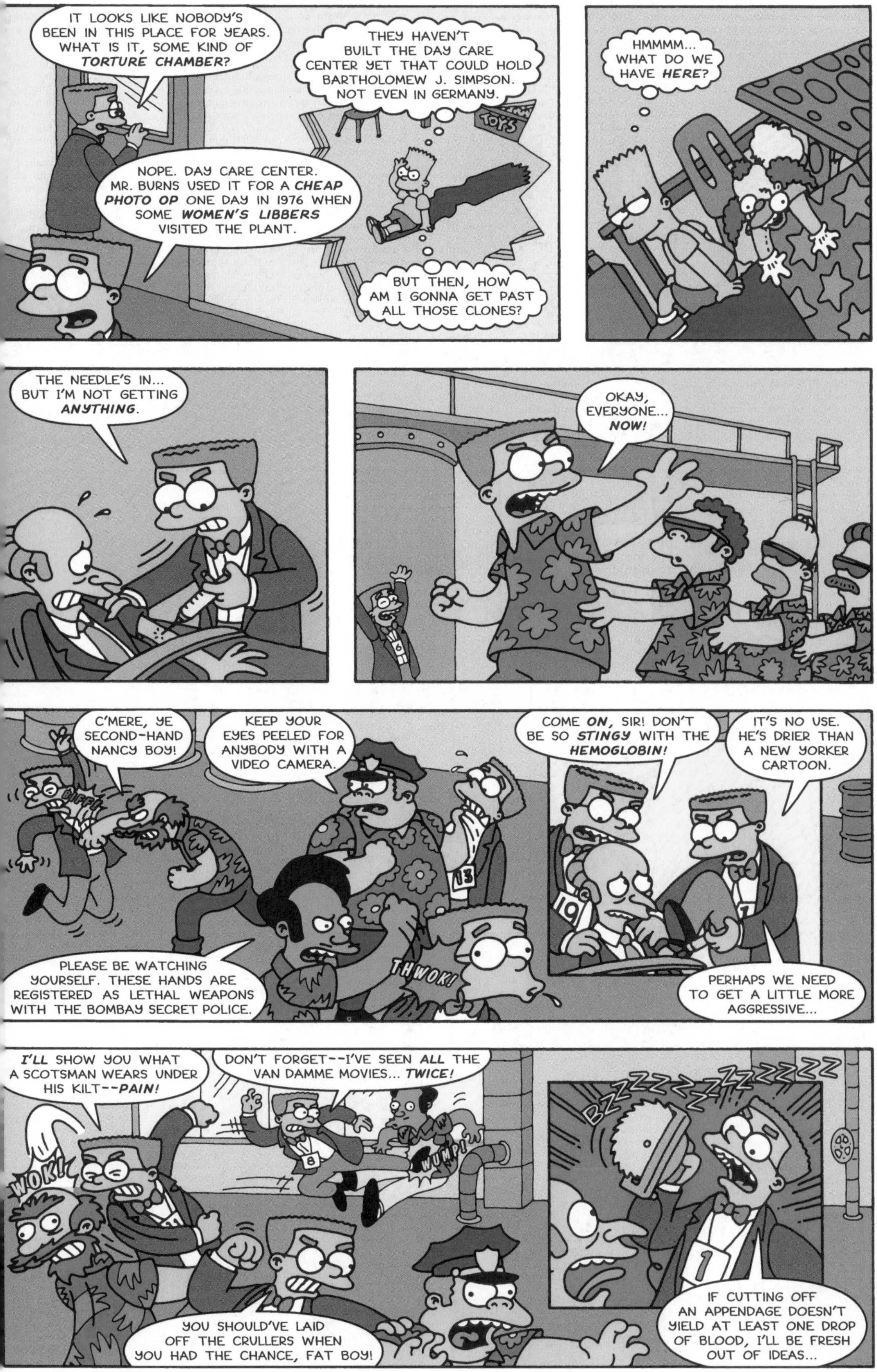

IT LOOKS LIKE NOBODY'S BEEN IN THIS PLACE FOR YEARS. WHAT IS IT, SOME KIND OF TORTURE CHAMBER?
NOPE. DAY CARE CENTER. MR. BURNS USED IT FOR A CHEAP PHOTO OP ONE DAY IN 1976 WHEN SOME WOMEN'S LIBBERS VISITED THE PLANT.
THEY HAVEN'T BUILT THE DAY CARE CENTER YET THAT COULD HOLD BARTHOLOMEW J. SIMPSON. NOT EVEN IN GERMANY.
TOYS
BUT THEN, HOW AM I GONNA GET PAST ALL THOSE CLONES?
HMMMM... WHAT DO WE HAVE HERE?
THE NEEDLE'S IN... BUT I'M NOT GETTING ANYTHING.
OKAY, EVERYONE... NOW!
C'MERE, YE SECOND-HAND NANCY BOY!
BIFF!
KEEP YOUR EYES PEELED FOR ANYBODY WITH A VIDEO CAMERA.
PLEASE BE WATCHING YOURSELF. THESE HANDS ARE REGISTERED AS LETHAL WEAPONS WITH THE BOMBAY SECRET POLICE.
THWOK!
COME ON, SIR! DON'T BE SO STINGY WITH THE HEMOGLOBIN!
IT'S NO USE. HE'S DRIER THAN A NEW YORKER CARTOON.
PERHAPS WE NEED TO GET A LITTLE MORE AGGRESSIVE...
I'LL SHOW YOU WHAT A SCOTSMAN WEARS UNDER HIS KILT--PAIN!
WOK!
DON'T FORGET--I'VE SEEN ALL THE VAN DAMME MOVIES... TWICE!
WUMP!
YOU SHOULD'VE LAID OFF THE CRULLERS WHEN YOU HAD THE CHANCE, FAT BOY!
BZZZZZZZZZZZZZ
IF CUTTING OFF AN APPENDAGE DOESN'T YIELD AT LEAST ONE DROP OF BLOOD, I'LL BE FRESH OUT OF IDEAS...

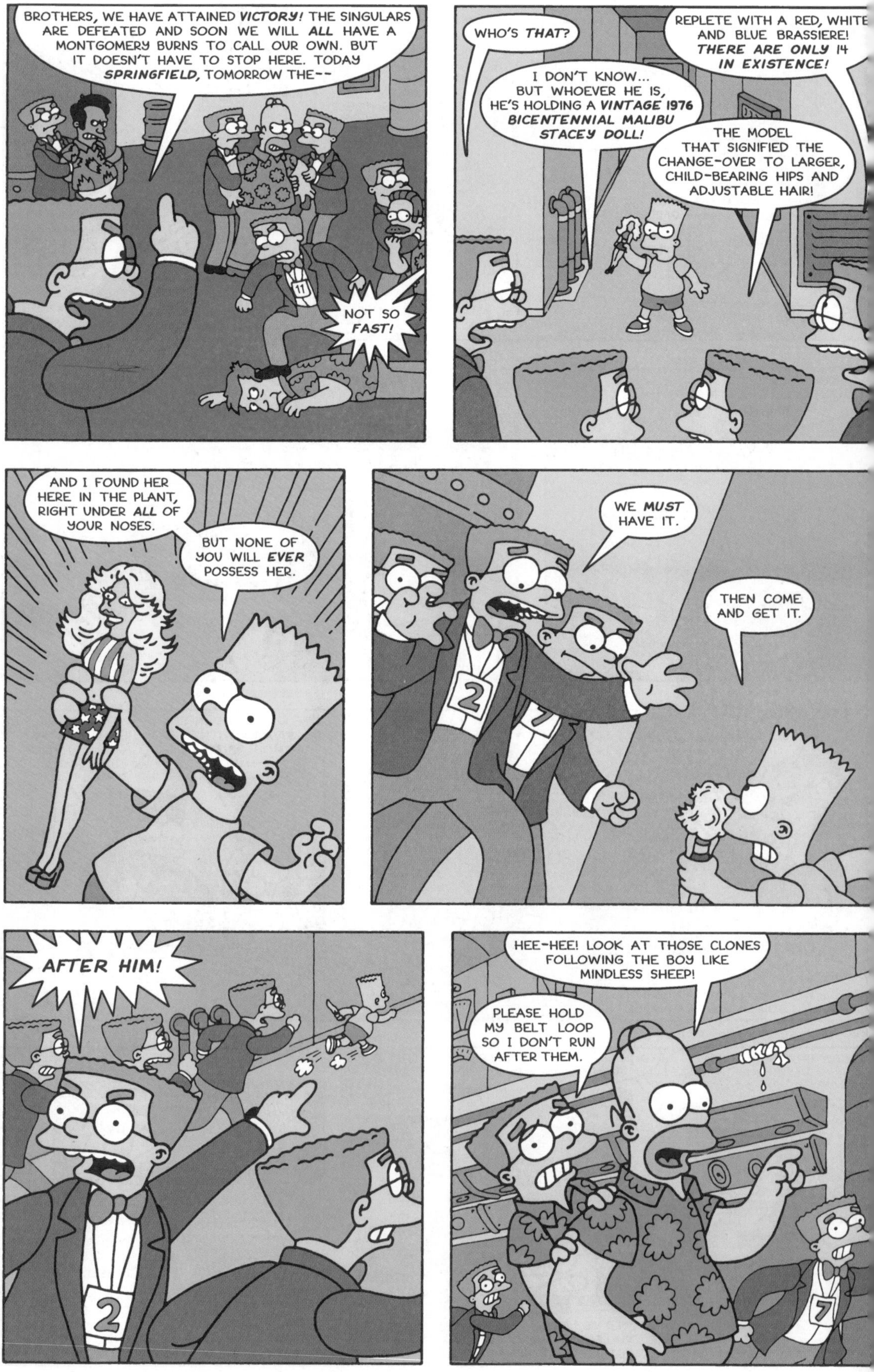
BROTHERS, WE HAVE ATTAINED VICTORY! THE SINGULARS ARE DEFEATED AND SOON WE WILL ALL HAVE A MONTGOMERY BURNS TO CALL OUR OWN. BUT IT DOESN'T HAVE TO STOP HERE. TODAY SPRINGFIELD, TOMORROW THE--
NOT SO FAST!
WHO'S THAT?
I DON'T KNOW... BUT WHOEVER HE IS, HE'S HOLDING A VINTAGE 1976 BICENTENNIAL MALIBU STACEY DOLL!
REPLETE WITH A RED, WHITE AND BLUE BRASSIERE! THERE ARE ONLY 14 IN EXISTENCE!
THE MODEL THAT SIGNIFIED THE CHANGE-OVER TO LARGER, CHILD-BEARING HIPS AND ADJUSTABLE HAIR!
AND I FOUND HER HERE IN THE PLANT, RIGHT UNDER ALL OF YOUR NOSES.
BUT NONE OF YOU WILL EVER POSSESS HER.
WE MUST HAVE IT.
THEN COME AND GET IT.
AFTER HIM!
HEE-HEE! LOOK AT THOSE CLONES FOLLOWING THE BOY LIKE MINDLESS SHEEP!
PLEASE HOLD MY BELT LOOP SO I DON'T RUN AFTER THEM.

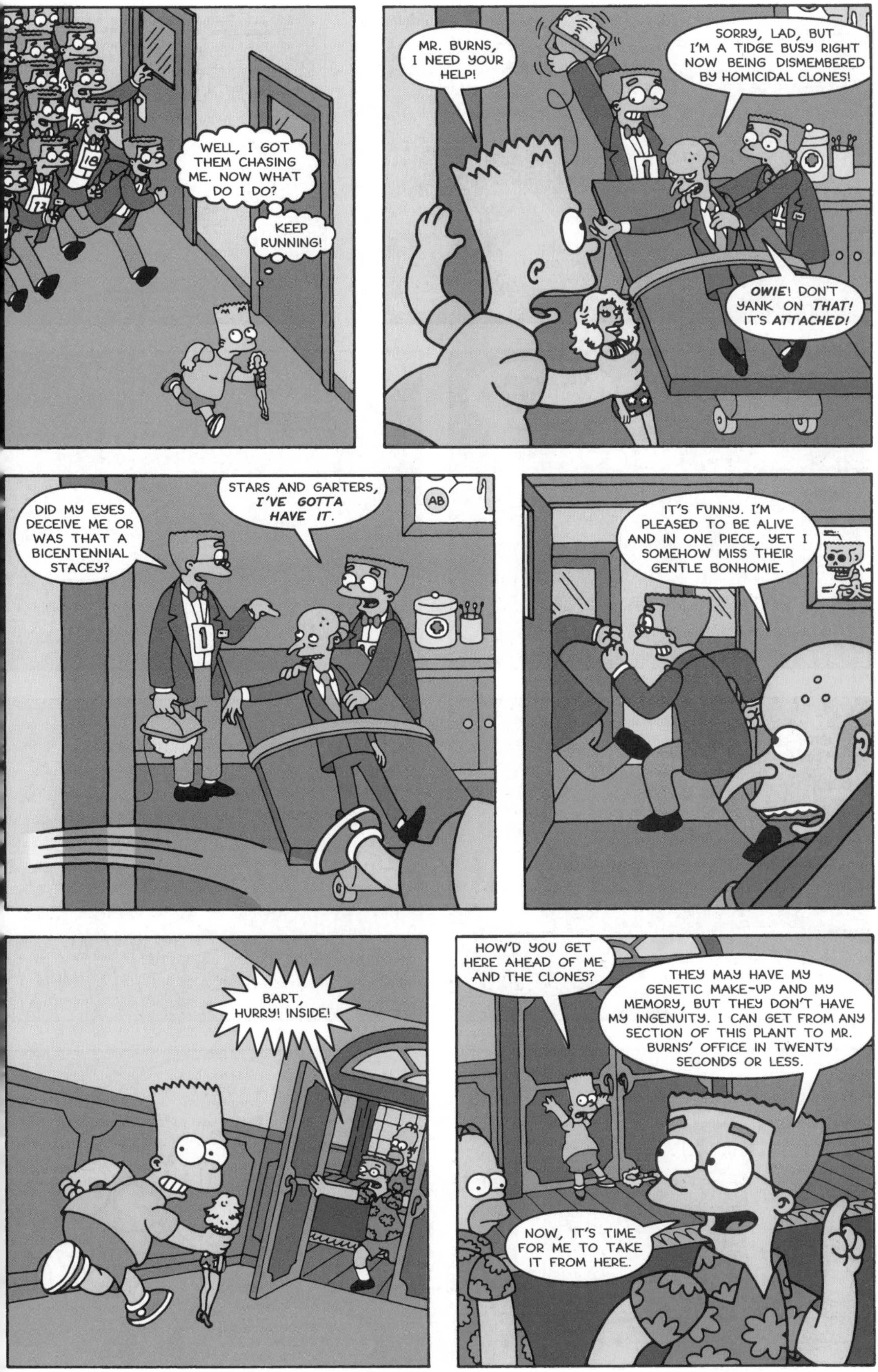
WELL, I GOT THEM CHASING ME. NOW WHAT DO I DO?
KEEP RUNNING!
MR. BURNS, I NEED YOUR HELP!
SORRY, LAD, BUT I'M A TIDGE BUSY RIGHT NOW BEING DISMEMBERED BY HOMICIDAL CLONES!
OWIE! DON'T YANK ON THAT! IT'S ATTACHED!
DID MY EYES DECEIVE ME OR WAS THAT A BICENTENNIAL STACEY?
STARS AND GARTERS, I'VE GOTTA HAVE IT.
IT'S FUNNY. I'M PLEASED TO BE ALIVE AND IN ONE PIECE, YET I SOMEHOW MISS THEIR GENTLE BONHOMIE.
BART, HURRY! INSIDE!
HOW'D YOU GET HERE AHEAD OF ME AND THE CLONES?
THEY MAY HAVE MY GENETIC MAKE-UP AND MY MEMORY, BUT THEY DON'T HAVE MY INGENUITY. I CAN GET FROM ANY SECTION OF THIS PLANT TO MR. BURNS' OFFICE IN TWENTY SECONDS OR LESS.
NOW, IT'S TIME FOR ME TO TAKE IT FROM HERE.

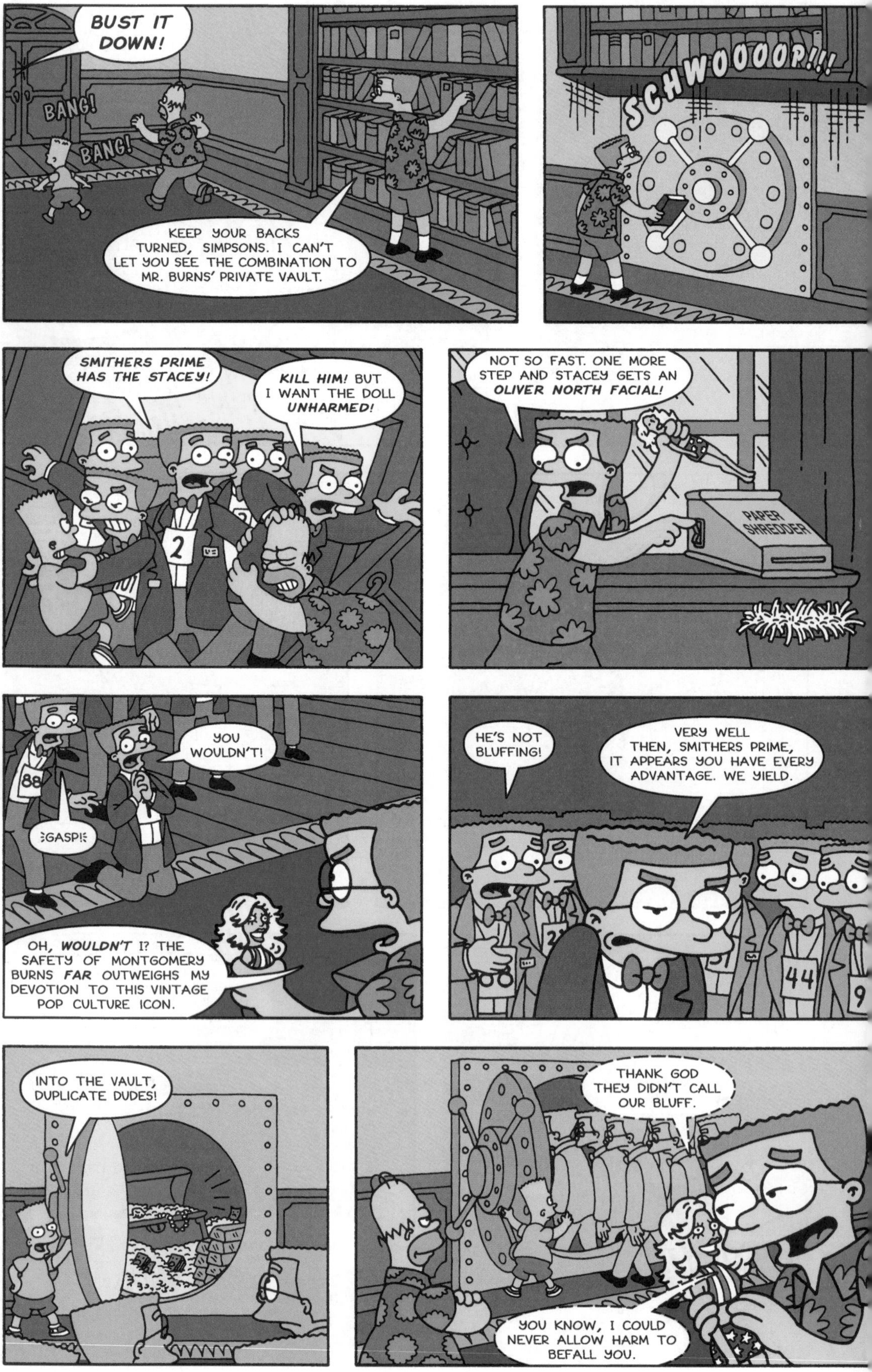
BUST IT DOWN!
BANG!
BANG!
KEEP YOUR BACKS TURNED, SIMPSONS. I CAN'T LET YOU SEE THE COMBINATION TO MR. BURNS' PRIVATE VAULT.
SCHWOOOOP!!!
SMITHERS PRIME HAS THE STACEY!
KILL HIM! BUT I WANT THE DOLL UNHARMED!
NOT SO FAST. ONE MORE STEP AND STACEY GETS AN OLIVER NORTH FACIAL!
PAPER SHREDDER
YOU WOULDN'T!
GASP!
OH, WOULDN'T I? THE SAFETY OF MONTGOMERY BURNS FAR OUTWEIGHS MY DEVOTION TO THIS VINTAGE POP CULTURE ICON.
HE'S NOT BLUFFING!
VERY WELL THEN, SMITHERS PRIME, IT APPEARS YOU HAVE EVERY ADVANTAGE. WE YIELD.
INTO THE VAULT, DUPLICATE DUDES!
THANK GOD THEY DIDN'T CALL OUR BLUFF.
YOU KNOW, I COULD NEVER ALLOW HARM TO BEFALL YOU.

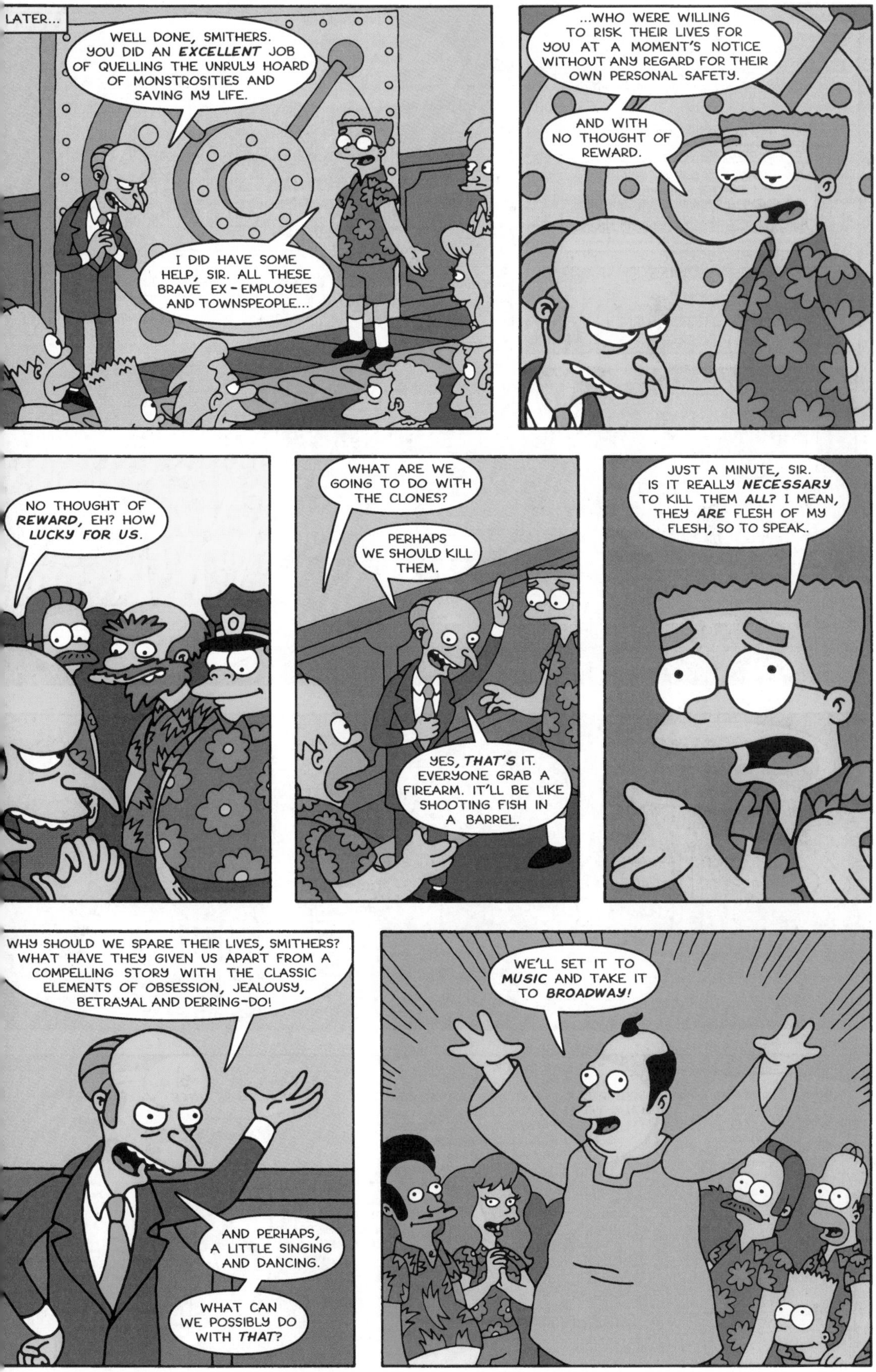
LATER...
WELL DONE, SMITHERS. YOU DID AN EXCELLENT JOB OF QUELLING THE UNRULY HOARD OF MONSTROSITIES AND SAVING MY LIFE.
I DID HAVE SOME HELP, SIR. ALL THESE BRAVE EX-EMPLOYEES AND TOWNSPEOPLE...
...WHO WERE WILLING TO RISK THEIR LIVES FOR YOU AT A MOMENT'S NOTICE WITHOUT ANY REGARD FOR THEIR OWN PERSONAL SAFETY.
AND WITH NO THOUGHT OF REWARD.
NO THOUGHT OF REWARD, EH? HOW LUCKY FOR US.
WHAT ARE WE GOING TO DO WITH THE CLONES?
PERHAPS WE SHOULD KILL THEM.
YES, THAT'S IT. EVERYONE GRAB A FIREARM. IT'LL BE LIKE SHOOTING FISH IN A BARREL.
JUST A MINUTE, SIR. IS IT REALLY NECESSARY TO KILL THEM ALL? I MEAN, THEY ARE FLESH OF MY FLESH, SO TO SPEAK.
WHY SHOULD WE SPARE THEIR LIVES, SMITHERS? WHAT HAVE THEY GIVEN US APART FROM A COMPELLING STORY WITH THE CLASSIC ELEMENTS OF OBSESSION, JEALOUSY, BETRAYAL AND DERRING-DO!
AND PERHAPS, A LITTLE SINGING AND DANCING.
WHAT CAN WE POSSIBLY DO WITH THAT?
WE'LL SET IT TO MUSIC AND TAKE IT TO BROADWAY!

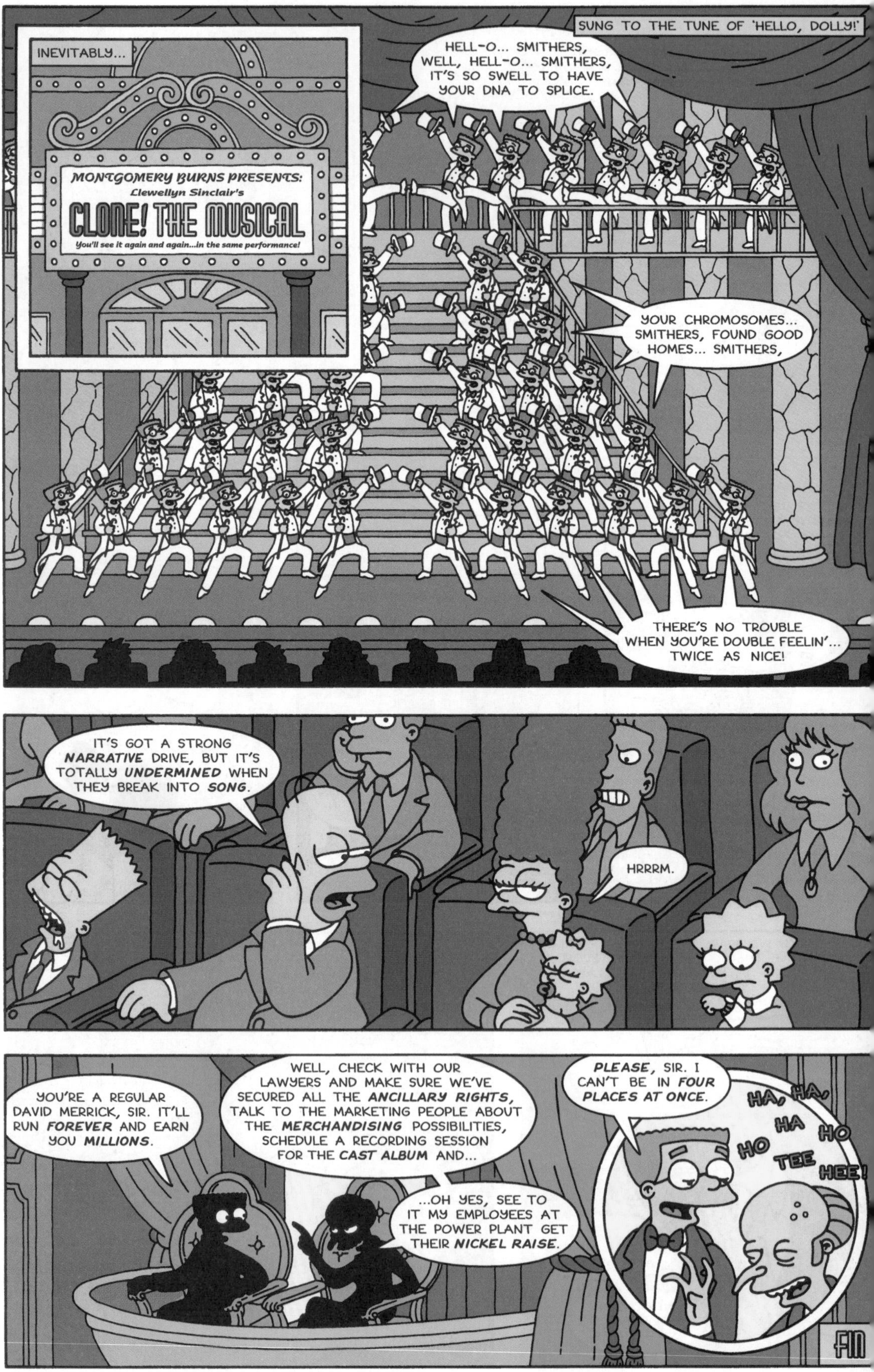

INEVITABLY...
MONTGOMERY BURNS PRESENTS:
Llewellyn Sinclair's
CLONE! THE MUSICAL
You'll see it again and again...in the same performance!
SUNG TO THE TUNE OF 'HELLO, DOLLY!'
HELL-O... SMITHERS, WELL, HELL-O... SMITHERS, IT'S SO SWELL TO HAVE YOUR DNA TO SPLICE.
YOUR CHROMOSOMES... SMITHERS, FOUND GOOD HOMES... SMITHERS,
THERE'S NO TROUBLE WHEN YOU'RE DOUBLE FEELIN'... TWICE AS NICE!
IT'S GOT A STRONG NARRATIVE DRIVE, BUT IT'S TOTALLY UNDERMINED WHEN THEY BREAK INTO SONG.
HRRRM.
YOU'RE A REGULAR DAVID MERRICK, SIR. IT'LL RUN FOREVER AND EARN YOU MILLIONS.
WELL, CHECK WITH OUR LAWYERS AND MAKE SURE WE'VE SECURED ALL THE ANCILLARY RIGHTS, TALK TO THE MARKETING PEOPLE ABOUT THE MERCHANDISING POSSIBILITIES, SCHEDULE A RECORDING SESSION FOR THE CAST ALBUM AND...
...OH YES, SEE TO IT MY EMPLOYEES AT THE POWER PLANT GET THEIR NICKEL RAISE.
PLEASE, SIR. I CAN'T BE IN FOUR PLACES AT ONCE.
HA, HA, HA HO HO TEE HEE!
FIN

BART & MILHOUSE IN "BORE US THE MOVIE GRUEL"

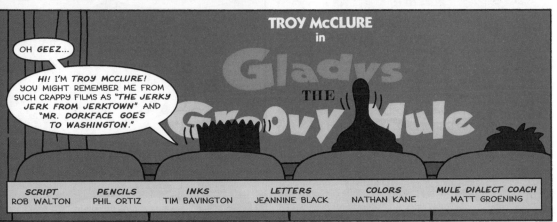

SCRIPT	PENCILS	INKS	LETTERS	COLORS	MULE DIALECT COACH
ROB WALTON	PHIL ORTIZ	TIM BAVINGTON	JEANNINE BLACK	NATHAN KANE	MATT GROENING

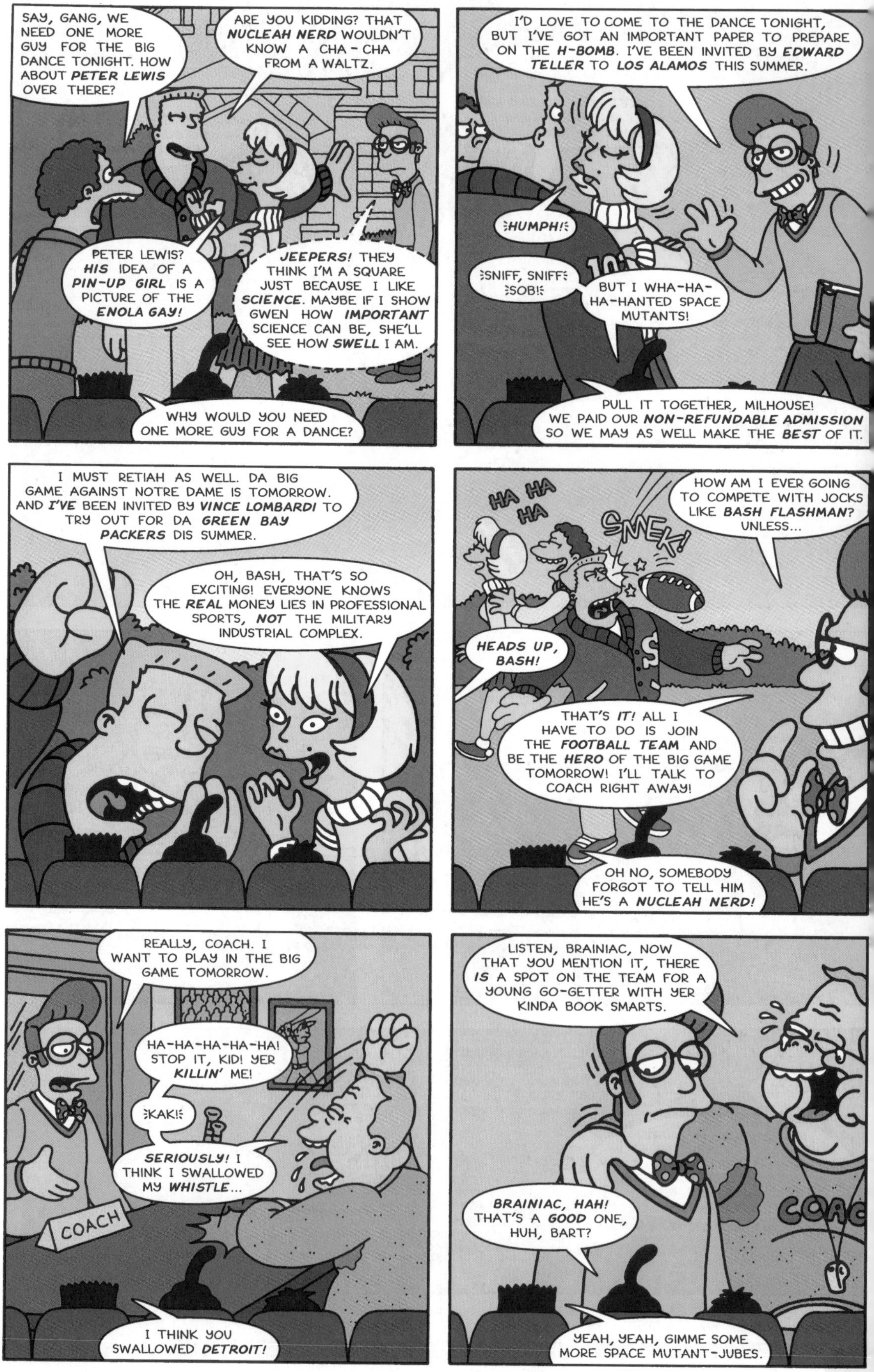
SAY, GANG, WE NEED ONE MORE GUY FOR THE BIG DANCE TONIGHT. HOW ABOUT PETER LEWIS OVER THERE?
ARE YOU KIDDING? THAT NUCLEAH NERD WOULDN'T KNOW A CHA-CHA FROM A WALTZ.
PETER LEWIS? HIS IDEA OF A PIN-UP GIRL IS A PICTURE OF THE ENOLA GAY!
JEEPERS! THEY THINK I'M A SQUARE JUST BECAUSE I LIKE SCIENCE. MAYBE IF I SHOW GWEN HOW IMPORTANT SCIENCE CAN BE, SHE'LL SEE HOW SWELL I AM.
WHY WOULD YOU NEED ONE MORE GUY FOR A DANCE?
I'D LOVE TO COME TO THE DANCE TONIGHT, BUT I'VE GOT AN IMPORTANT PAPER TO PREPARE ON THE H-BOMB. I'VE BEEN INVITED BY EDWARD TELLER TO LOS ALAMOS THIS SUMMER.
HUMPH!
SNIFF, SNIFF SOB!
BUT I WHA-HA-HA-HANTED SPACE MUTANTS!
PULL IT TOGETHER, MILHOUSE! WE PAID OUR NON-REFUNDABLE ADMISSION SO WE MAY AS WELL MAKE THE BEST OF IT.
I MUST RETIAH AS WELL. DA BIG GAME AGAINST NOTRE DAME IS TOMORROW. AND I'VE BEEN INVITED BY VINCE LOMBARDI TO TRY OUT FOR DA GREEN BAY PACKERS DIS SUMMER.
OH, BASH, THAT'S SO EXCITING! EVERYONE KNOWS THE REAL MONEY LIES IN PROFESSIONAL SPORTS, NOT THE MILITARY INDUSTRIAL COMPLEX.
HA HA HA
SMEK!
HOW AM I EVER GOING TO COMPETE WITH JOCKS LIKE BASH FLASHMAN? UNLESS...
HEADS UP, BASH!
THAT'S IT! ALL I HAVE TO DO IS JOIN THE FOOTBALL TEAM AND BE THE HERO OF THE BIG GAME TOMORROW! I'LL TALK TO COACH RIGHT AWAY!
OH NO, SOMEBODY FORGOT TO TELL HIM HE'S A NUCLEAH NERD!
REALLY, COACH. I WANT TO PLAY IN THE BIG GAME TOMORROW.
HA-HA-HA-HA-HA! STOP IT, KID! YER KILLIN' ME!
KAK!
SERIOUSLY! I THINK I SWALLOWED MY WHISTLE...
COACH
I THINK YOU SWALLOWED DETROIT!
LISTEN, BRAINIAC, NOW THAT YOU MENTION IT, THERE IS A SPOT ON THE TEAM FOR A YOUNG GO-GETTER WITH YER KINDA BOOK SMARTS.
BRAINIAC, HAH! THAT'S A GOOD ONE, HUH, BART?
YEAH, YEAH, GIMME SOME MORE SPACE MUTANT-JUBES.

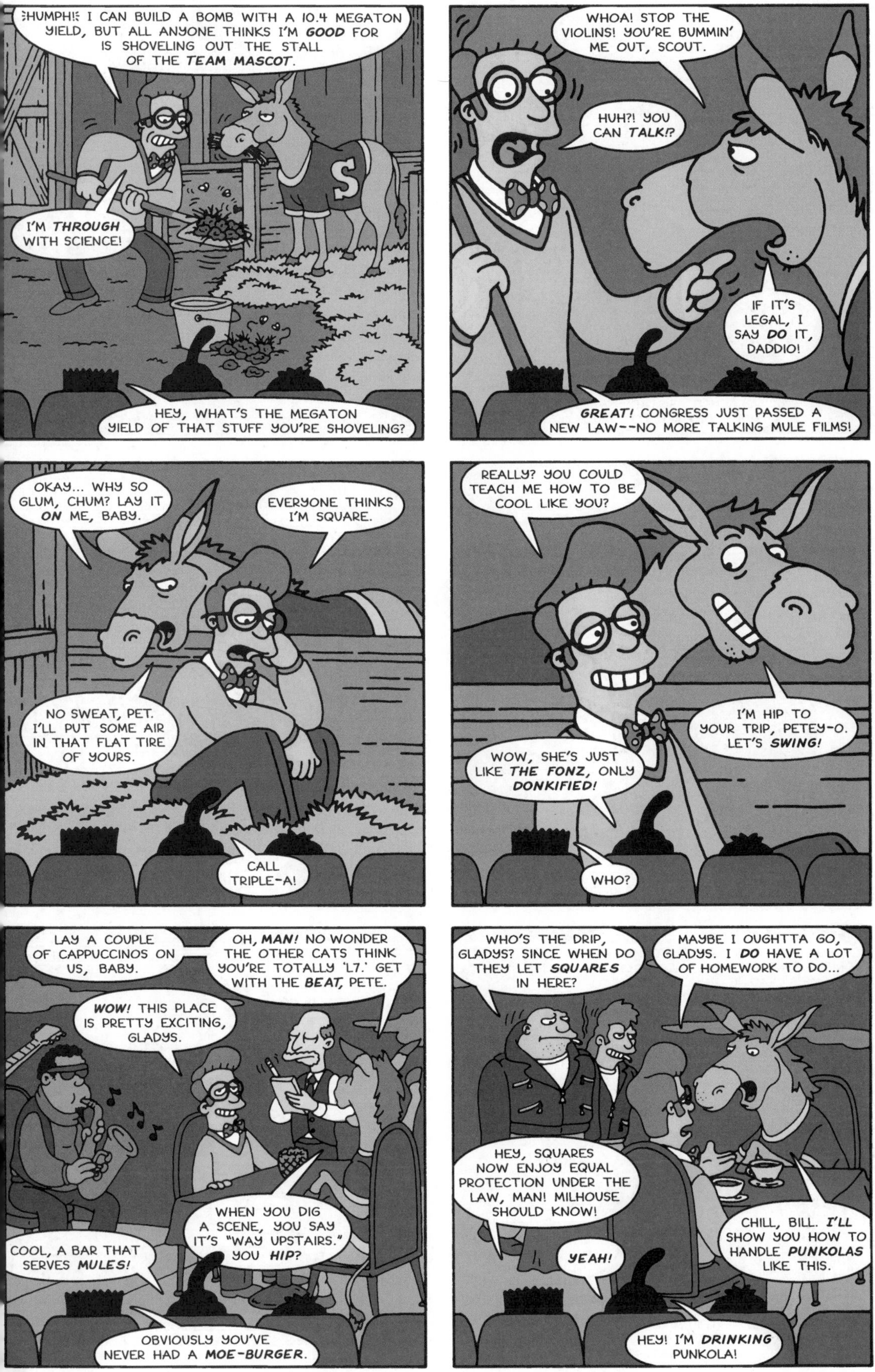

¡HUMPH!¡ I CAN BUILD A BOMB WITH A 10.4 MEGATON YIELD, BUT ALL ANYONE THINKS I'M GOOD FOR IS SHOVELING OUT THE STALL OF THE TEAM MASCOT.
S
I'M THROUGH WITH SCIENCE!
HEY, WHAT'S THE MEGATON YIELD OF THAT STUFF YOU'RE SHOVELING?
WHOA! STOP THE VIOLINS! YOU'RE BUMMIN' ME OUT, SCOUT.
HUH?! YOU CAN TALK!?
IF IT'S LEGAL, I SAY DO IT, DADDIO!
GREAT! CONGRESS JUST PASSED A NEW LAW--NO MORE TALKING MULE FILMS!
OKAY... WHY SO GLUM, CHUM? LAY IT ON ME, BABY.
EVERYONE THINKS I'M SQUARE.
NO SWEAT, PET. I'LL PUT SOME AIR IN THAT FLAT TIRE OF YOURS.
CALL TRIPLE-A!
REALLY? YOU COULD TEACH ME HOW TO BE COOL LIKE YOU?
I'M HIP TO YOUR TRIP, PETEY-O. LET'S SWING!
WOW, SHE'S JUST LIKE THE FONZ, ONLY DONKIFIED!
WHO?
LAY A COUPLE OF CAPPUCCINOS ON US, BABY.
OH, MAN! NO WONDER THE OTHER CATS THINK YOU'RE TOTALLY 'L7.' GET WITH THE BEAT, PETE.
WOW! THIS PLACE IS PRETTY EXCITING, GLADYS.
WHEN YOU DIG A SCENE, YOU SAY IT'S "WAY UPSTAIRS." YOU HIP?
COOL, A BAR THAT SERVES MULES!
OBVIOUSLY YOU'VE NEVER HAD A MOE-BURGER.
WHO'S THE DRIP, GLADYS? SINCE WHEN DO THEY LET SQUARES IN HERE?
MAYBE I OUGHTTA GO, GLADYS. I DO HAVE A LOT OF HOMEWORK TO DO...
HEY, SQUARES NOW ENJOY EQUAL PROTECTION UNDER THE LAW, MAN! MILHOUSE SHOULD KNOW!
YEAH!
CHILL, BILL. I'LL SHOW YOU HOW TO HANDLE PUNKOLAS LIKE THIS.
HEY! I'M DRINKING PUNKOLA!

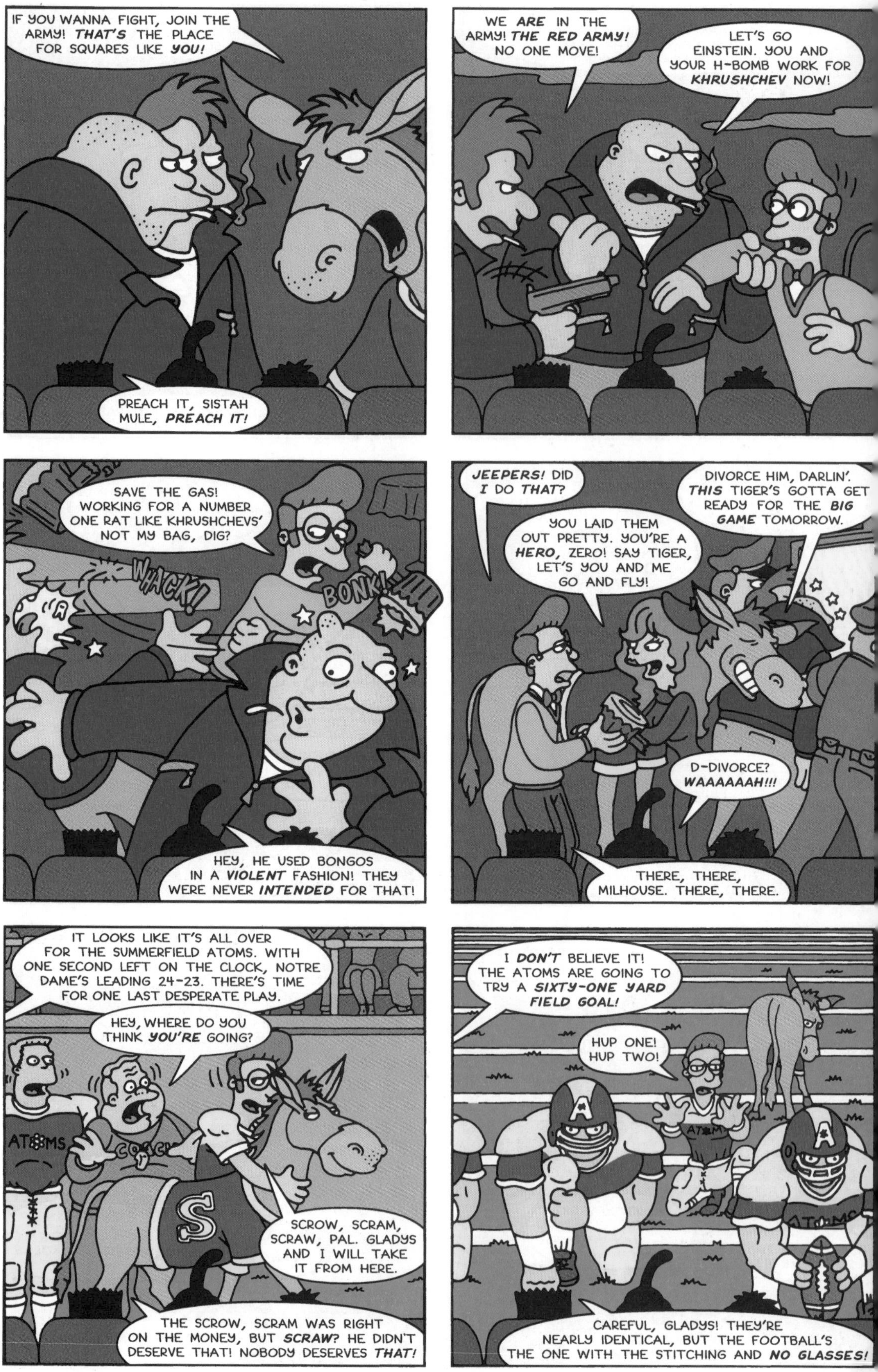
IF YOU WANNA FIGHT, JOIN THE ARMY! *THAT'S* THE PLACE FOR SQUARES LIKE *YOU!*
PREACH IT, SISTAH MULE, *PREACH IT!*
WE *ARE* IN THE ARMY! *THE RED ARMY!* NO ONE MOVE!
LET'S GO EINSTEIN. YOU AND YOUR H-BOMB WORK FOR *KHRUSHCHEV* NOW!
SAVE THE GAS! WORKING FOR A NUMBER ONE RAT LIKE KHRUSHCHEVS' NOT MY BAG, DIG?
WHACK!
BONK!
HEY, HE USED BONGOS IN A *VIOLENT* FASHION! THEY WERE NEVER *INTENDED* FOR THAT!
JEEPERS! DID *I* DO *THAT?*
YOU LAID THEM OUT PRETTY. YOU'RE A *HERO,* ZERO! SAY TIGER, LET'S YOU AND ME GO AND FLY!
DIVORCE HIM, DARLIN'. *THIS* TIGER'S GOTTA GET READY FOR THE *BIG GAME* TOMORROW.
D-DIVORCE? *WAAAAAAH!!!*
THERE, THERE, MILHOUSE. THERE, THERE.
IT LOOKS LIKE IT'S ALL OVER FOR THE SUMMERFIELD ATOMS. WITH ONE SECOND LEFT ON THE CLOCK, NOTRE DAME'S LEADING 24-23. THERE'S TIME FOR ONE LAST DESPERATE PLAY.
HEY, WHERE DO YOU THINK *YOU'RE* GOING?
ATOMS
SCROW, SCRAM, SCRAW, PAL. GLADYS AND I WILL TAKE IT FROM HERE.
THE SCROW, SCRAM WAS RIGHT ON THE MONEY, BUT *SCRAW?* HE DIDN'T DESERVE THAT! NOBODY DESERVES *THAT!*
I *DON'T* BELIEVE IT! THE ATOMS ARE GOING TO TRY A *SIXTY-ONE YARD FIELD GOAL!*
HUP ONE! HUP TWO!
CAREFUL, GLADYS! THEY'RE NEARLY IDENTICAL, BUT THE FOOTBALL'S THE ONE WITH THE STITCHING AND *NO GLASSES!*

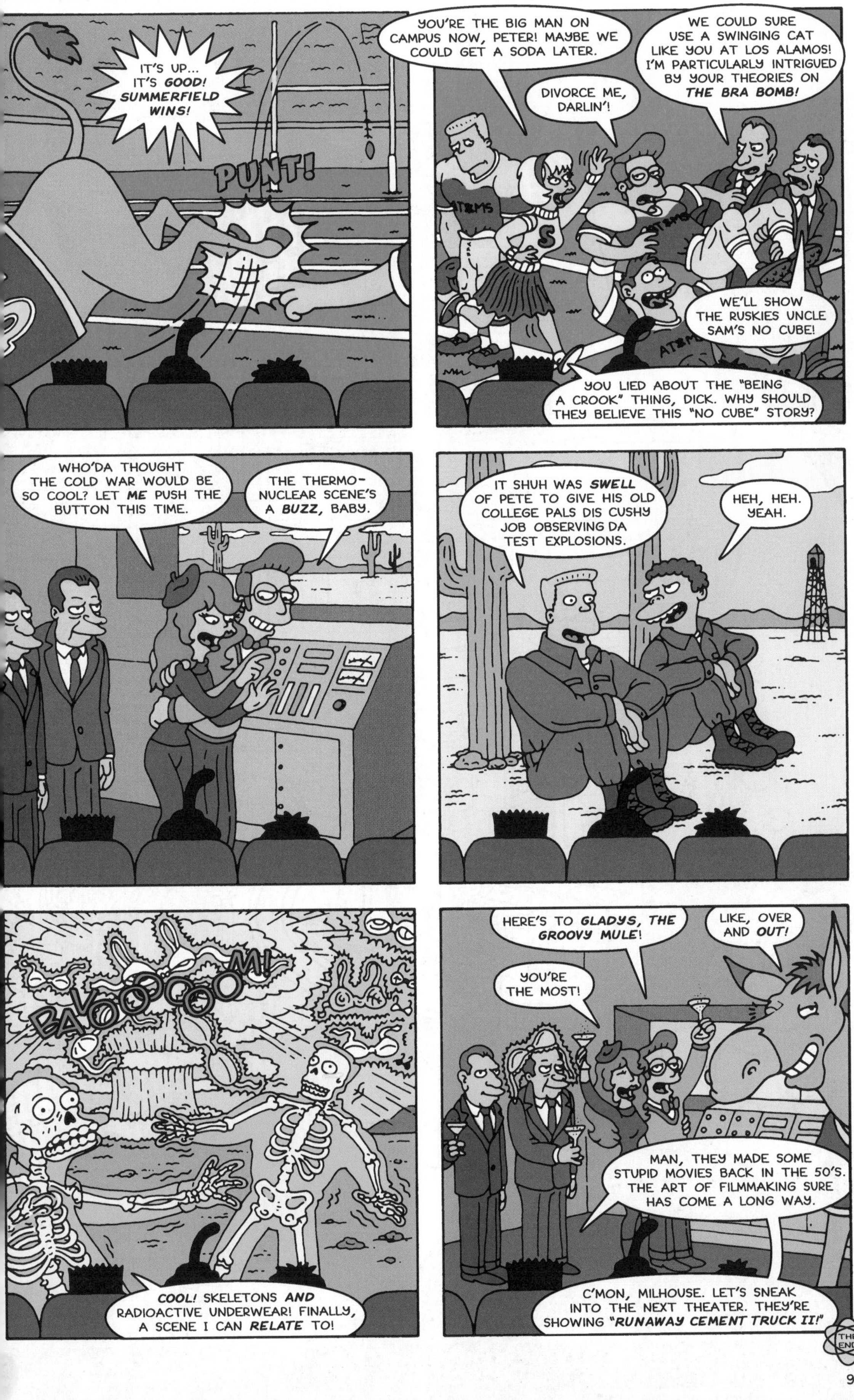

IT'S UP... IT'S *GOOD!* *SUMMERFIELD WINS!*
PUNT!
YOU'RE THE BIG MAN ON CAMPUS NOW, PETER! MAYBE WE COULD GET A SODA LATER.
DIVORCE ME, DARLIN'!
WE COULD SURE USE A SWINGING CAT LIKE YOU AT LOS ALAMOS! I'M PARTICULARLY INTRIGUED BY YOUR THEORIES ON *THE BRA BOMB!*
WE'LL SHOW THE RUSKIES UNCLE SAM'S NO CUBE!
YOU LIED ABOUT THE "BEING A CROOK" THING, DICK. WHY SHOULD THEY BELIEVE THIS "NO CUBE" STORY?
WHO'DA THOUGHT THE COLD WAR WOULD BE SO COOL? LET *ME* PUSH THE BUTTON THIS TIME.
THE THERMO-NUCLEAR SCENE'S A *BUZZ*, BABY.
IT SHUH WAS *SWELL* OF PETE TO GIVE HIS OLD COLLEGE PALS DIS CUSHY JOB OBSERVING DA TEST EXPLOSIONS.
HEH, HEH. YEAH.
BAVOOOOOOM!
COOL! SKELETONS *AND* RADIOACTIVE UNDERWEAR! FINALLY, A SCENE I CAN *RELATE* TO!
HERE'S TO *GLADYS, THE GROOVY MULE*!
LIKE, OVER AND *OUT!*
YOU'RE THE MOST!
MAN, THEY MADE SOME STUPID MOVIES BACK IN THE 50'S. THE ART OF FILMMAKING SURE HAS COME A LONG WAY.
C'MON, MILHOUSE. LET'S SNEAK INTO THE NEXT THEATER. THEY'RE SHOWING *"RUNAWAY CEMENT TRUCK II!"*
THE END

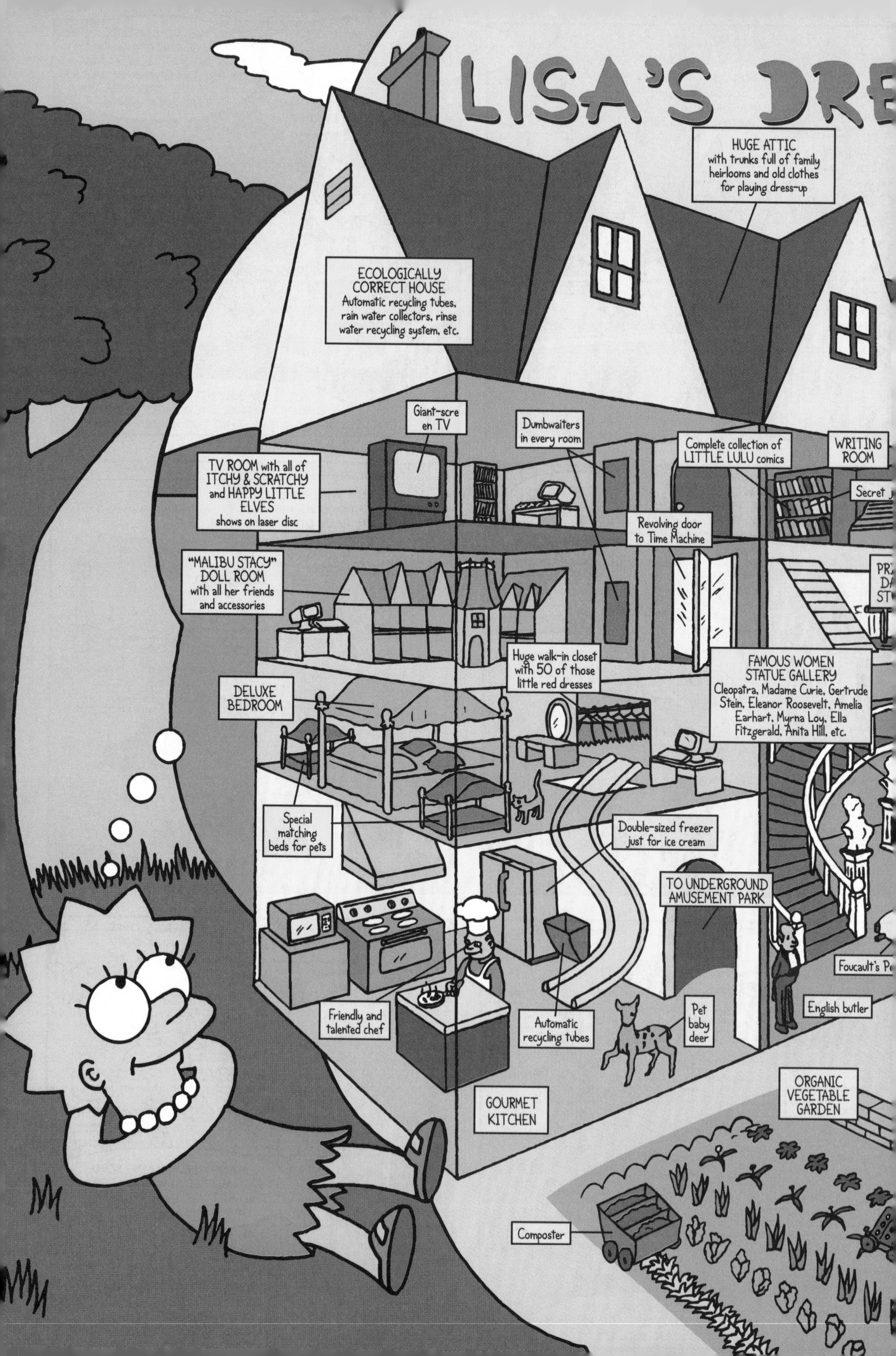
LISA'S
HUGE ATTIC
with trunks full of family heirlooms and old clothes for playing dress-up
ECOLOGICALLY CORRECT HOUSE
Automatic recycling tubes, rain water collectors, rinse water recycling system, etc.
Giant-scre en TV
Dumbwaiters in every room
Complete collection of LITTLE LULU comics
WRITING ROOM
TV ROOM with all of ITCHY & SCRATCHY and HAPPY LITTLE ELVES shows on laser disc
Revolving door to Time Machine
"MALIBU STACY" DOLL ROOM
with all her friends and accessories
Huge walk-in closet with 50 of those little red dresses
FAMOUS WOMEN STATUE GALLERY
Cleopatra, Madame Curie, Gertrude Stein, Eleanor Roosevelt, Amelia Earhart, Myrna Loy, Ella Fitzgerald, Anita Hill, etc.
DELUXE BEDROOM
Special matching beds for pets
Double-sized freezer just for ice cream
TO UNDERGROUND AMUSEMENT PARK
English butler
Friendly and talented chef
Automatic recycling tubes
Pet baby deer
GOURMET KITCHEN
ORGANIC VEGETABLE GARDEN
Composter

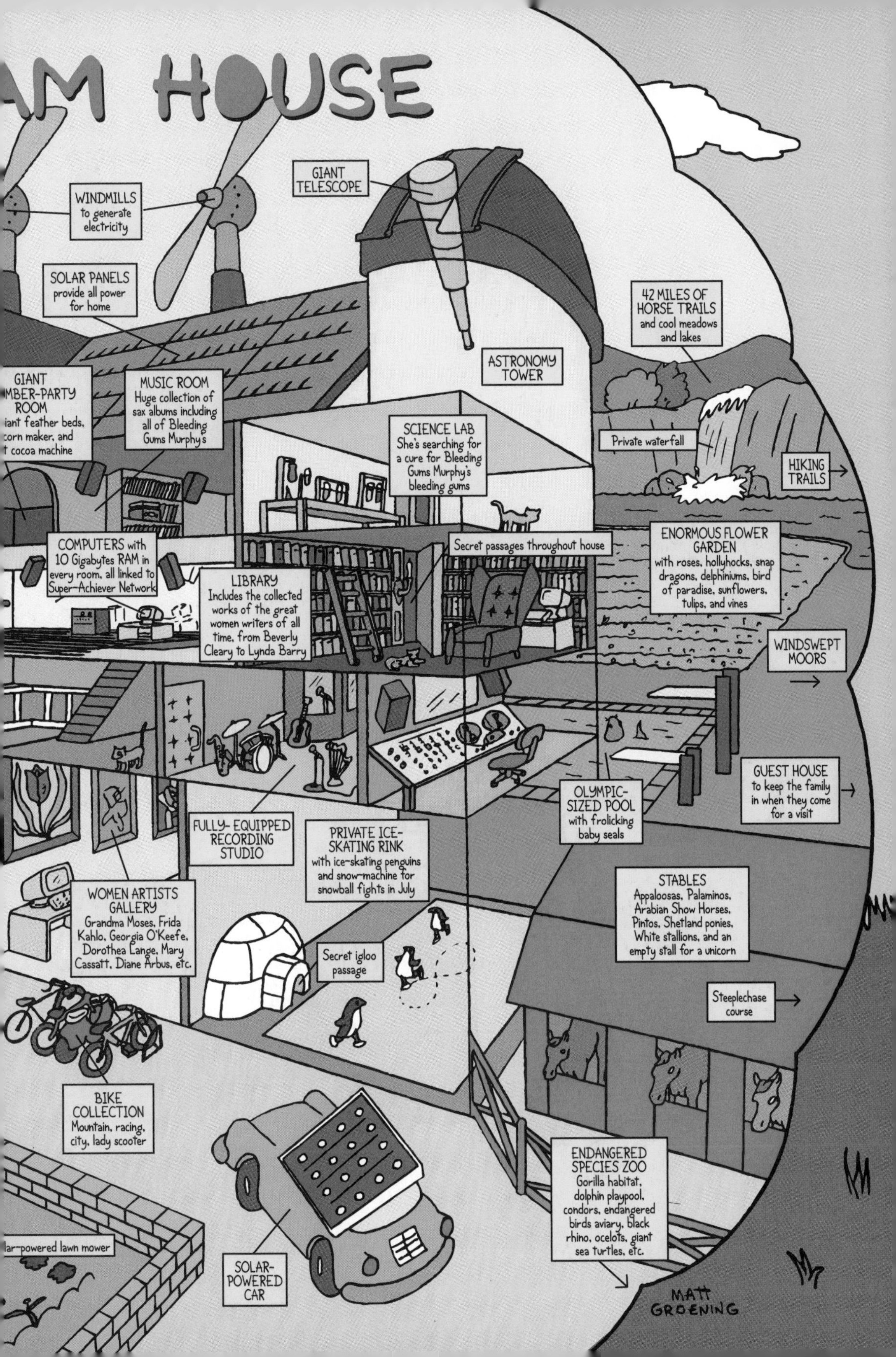
AM HOUSE
WINDMILLS to generate electricity
SOLAR PANELS provide all power for home
GIANT TELESCOPE
ASTRONOMY TOWER
42 MILES OF HORSE TRAILS and cool meadows and lakes
GIANT
MBER-PARTY
ROOM
iant feather beds,
corn maker, and
t cocoa machine
MUSIC ROOM Huge collection of sax albums including all of Bleeding Gums Murphy's
SCIENCE LAB She's searching for a cure for Bleeding Gums Murphy's bleeding gums
Private waterfall
HIKING TRAILS
Secret passages throughout house
ENORMOUS FLOWER GARDEN with roses, hollyhocks, snap dragons, delphiniums, bird of paradise, sunflowers, tulips, and vines
COMPUTERS with 10 Gigabytes RAM in every room, all linked to Super-Achiever Network
LIBRARY Includes the collected works of the great women writers of all time, from Beverly Cleary to Lynda Barry
WINDSWEPT MOORS
GUEST HOUSE to keep the family in when they come for a visit
OLYMPIC-SIZED POOL with frolicking baby seals
FULLY-EQUIPPED RECORDING STUDIO
PRIVATE ICE-SKATING RINK with ice-skating penguins and snow-machine for snowball fights in July
STABLES Appaloosas, Palaminos, Arabian Show Horses, Pintos, Shetland ponies, White stallions, and an empty stall for a unicorn
WOMEN ARTISTS GALLERY Grandma Moses, Frida Kahlo, Georgia O'Keefe, Dorothea Lange, Mary Cassatt, Diane Arbus, etc.
Secret igloo passage
Steeplechase course
BIKE COLLECTION Mountain, racing, city, lady scooter
ENDANGERED SPECIES ZOO Gorilla habitat, dolphin playpool, condors, endangered birds aviary, black rhino, ocelots, giant sea turtles, etc.
lar-powered lawn mower
SOLAR-POWERED CAR
MATT GROENING

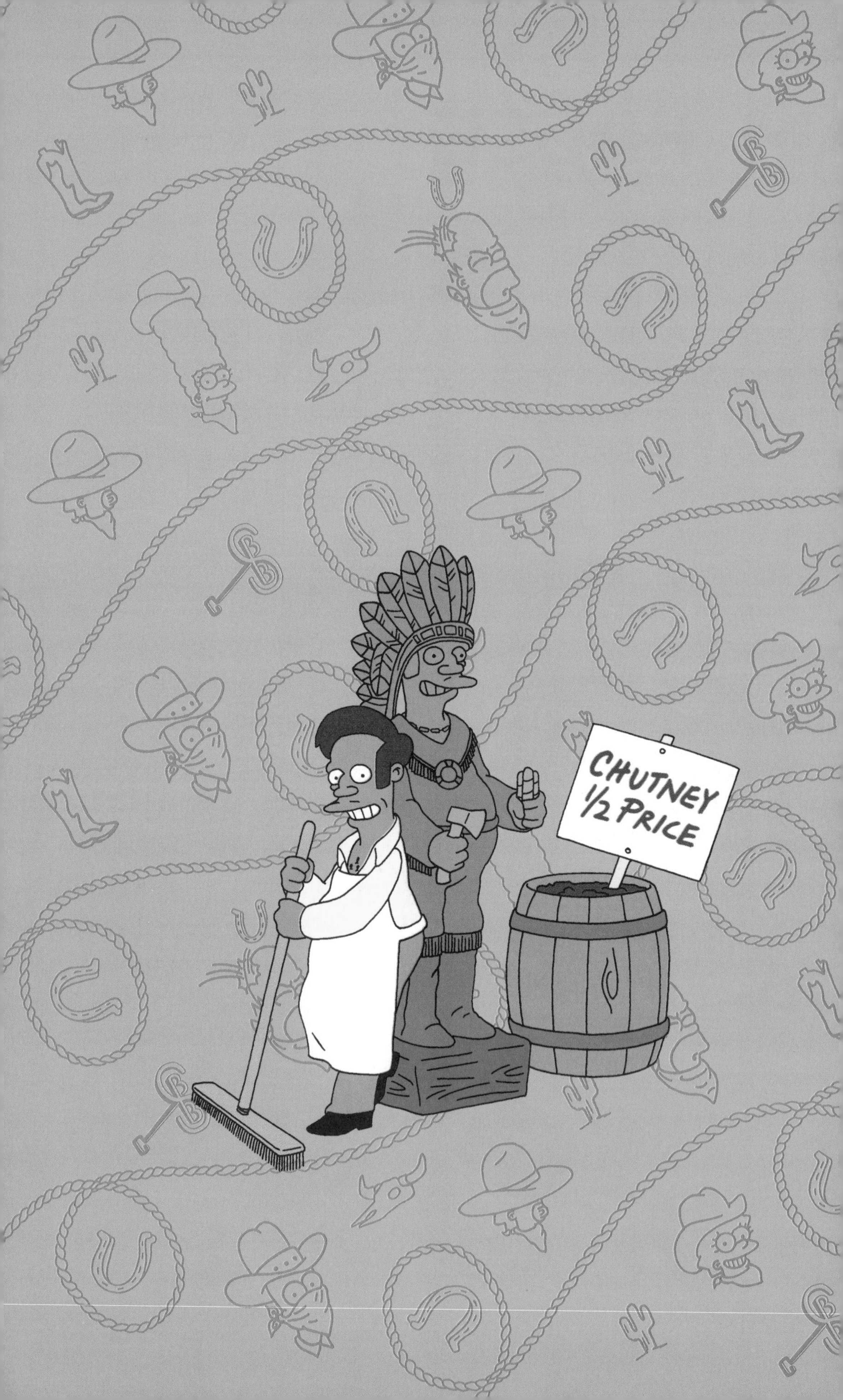
CHUTNEY
1/2 PRICE

BONGO COMICS GROUP
#31
APPROVED BY THE COMICS CODE AUTHORITY
SIMPSONS COMICS
GROENING

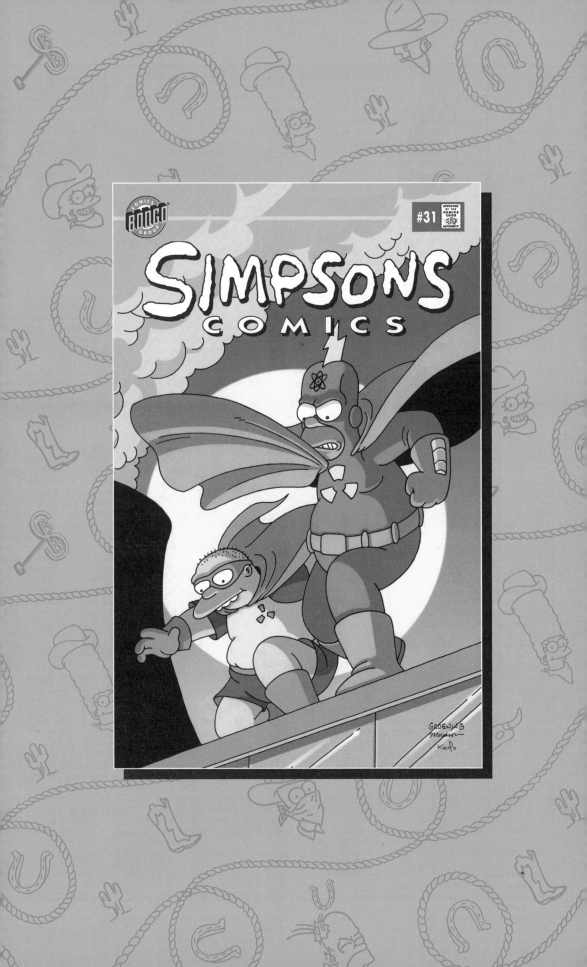

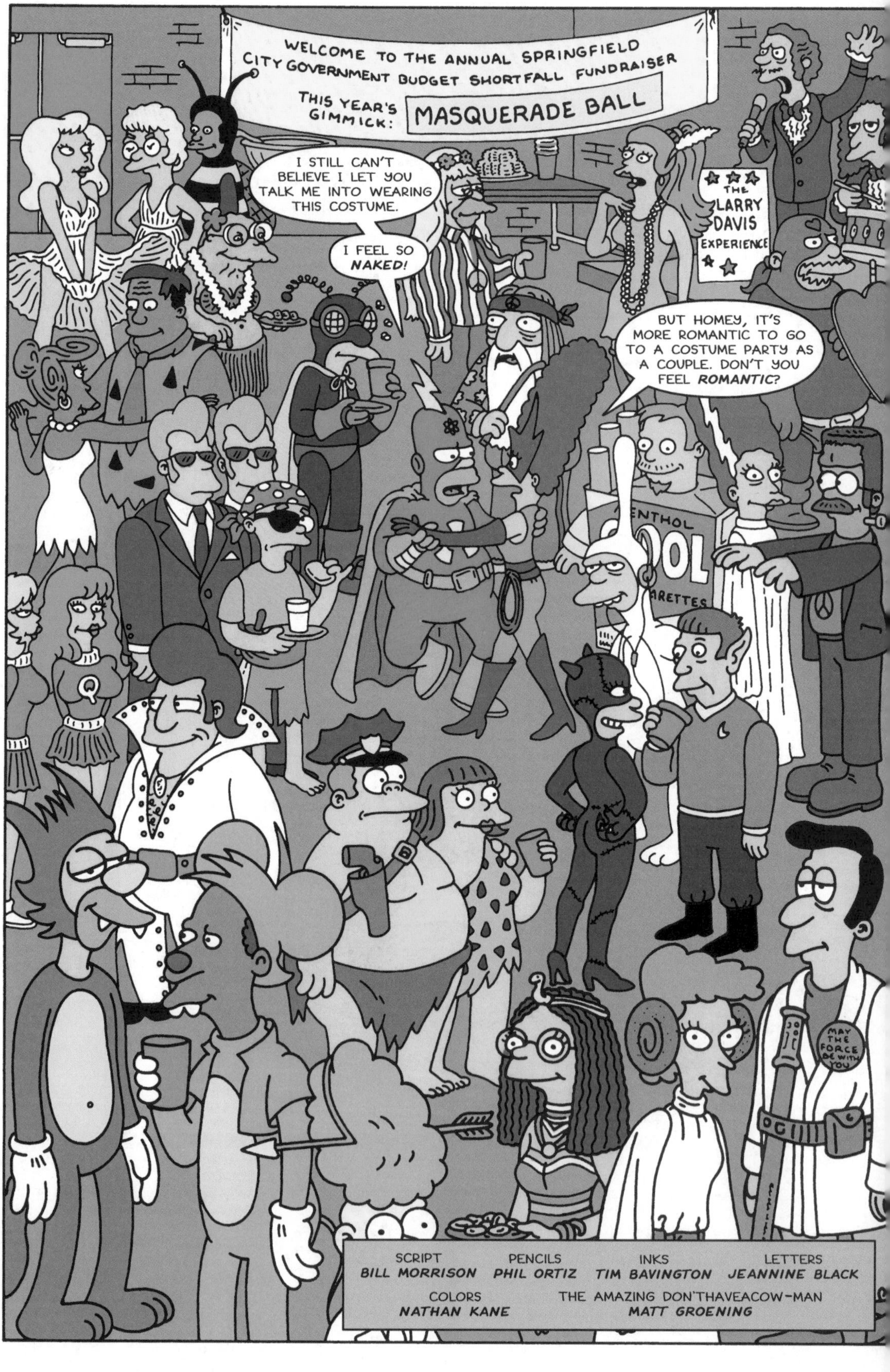
WELCOME TO THE ANNUAL SPRINGFIELD CITY GOVERNMENT BUDGET SHORTFALL FUNDRAISER
THIS YEAR'S GIMMICK: MASQUERADE BALL
THE LARRY DAVIS EXPERIENCE
I STILL CAN'T BELIEVE I LET YOU TALK ME INTO WEARING THIS COSTUME.
I FEEL SO *NAKED!*
BUT HOMEY, IT'S MORE ROMANTIC TO GO TO A COSTUME PARTY AS A COUPLE. DON'T YOU FEEL *ROMANTIC*?
ENTHOL
OOL
ARETTES
MAY THE FORCE BE WITH YOU
SCRIPT *BILL MORRISON*
PENCILS *PHIL ORTIZ*
INKS *TIM BAVINGTON*
LETTERS *JEANNINE BLACK*
COLORS *NATHAN KANE*
THE AMAZING DON'THAVEACOW-MAN *MATT GROENING*

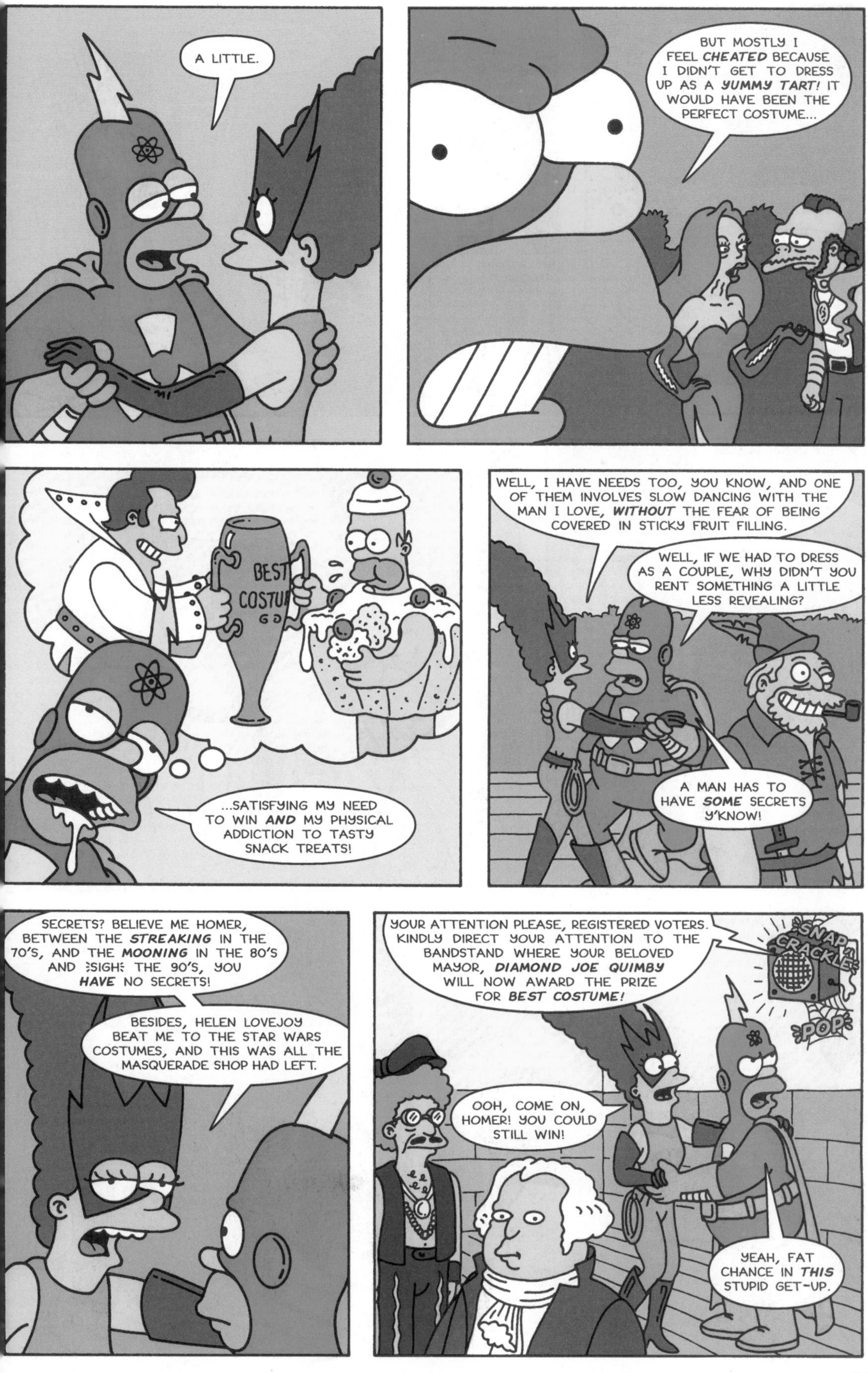
A LITTLE.
BUT MOSTLY I FEEL CHEATED BECAUSE I DIDN'T GET TO DRESS UP AS A YUMMY TART! IT WOULD HAVE BEEN THE PERFECT COSTUME...
BEST COSTU
...SATISFYING MY NEED TO WIN AND MY PHYSICAL ADDICTION TO TASTY SNACK TREATS!
WELL, I HAVE NEEDS TOO, YOU KNOW, AND ONE OF THEM INVOLVES SLOW DANCING WITH THE MAN I LOVE, WITHOUT THE FEAR OF BEING COVERED IN STICKY FRUIT FILLING.
WELL, IF WE HAD TO DRESS AS A COUPLE, WHY DIDN'T YOU RENT SOMETHING A LITTLE LESS REVEALING?
A MAN HAS TO HAVE SOME SECRETS Y'KNOW!
SECRETS? BELIEVE ME HOMER, BETWEEN THE STREAKING IN THE 70'S, AND THE MOONING IN THE 80'S AND :SIGH: THE 90'S, YOU HAVE NO SECRETS!
BESIDES, HELEN LOVEJOY BEAT ME TO THE STAR WARS COSTUMES, AND THIS WAS ALL THE MASQUERADE SHOP HAD LEFT.
YOUR ATTENTION PLEASE, REGISTERED VOTERS. KINDLY DIRECT YOUR ATTENTION TO THE BANDSTAND WHERE YOUR BELOVED MAYOR, DIAMOND JOE QUIMBY WILL NOW AWARD THE PRIZE FOR BEST COSTUME!
SNAP
CRACKLE
POP
OOH, COME ON, HOMER! YOU COULD STILL WIN!
YEAH, FAT CHANCE IN THIS STUPID GET-UP.

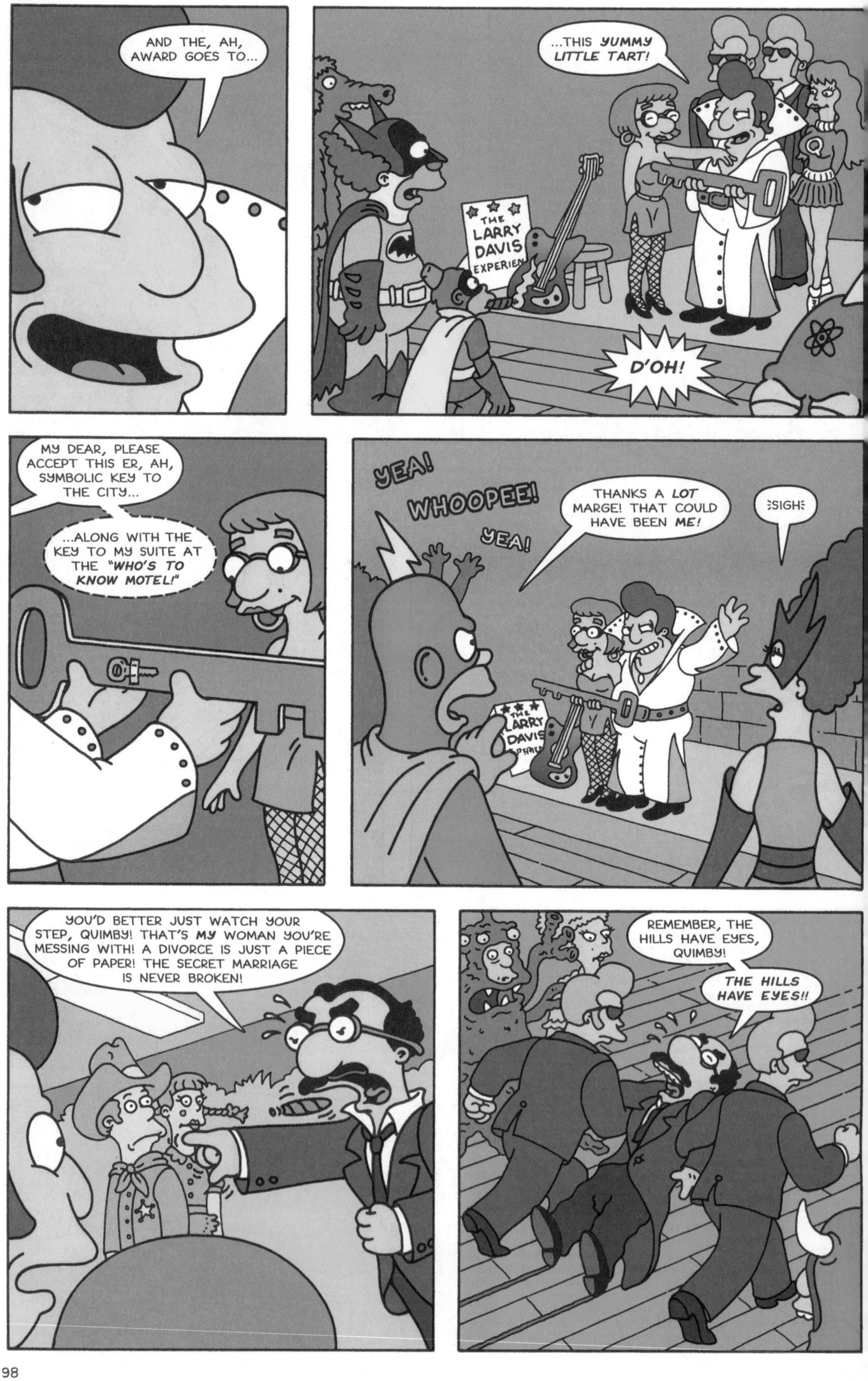
AND THE, AH, AWARD GOES TO...
...THIS YUMMY LITTLE TART!
THE LARRY DAVIS EXPERIEN
D'OH!
MY DEAR, PLEASE ACCEPT THIS ER, AH, SYMBOLIC KEY TO THE CITY...
...ALONG WITH THE KEY TO MY SUITE AT THE "WHO'S TO KNOW MOTEL!"
YEA!
WHOOPEE!
YEA!
THANKS A LOT MARGE! THAT COULD HAVE BEEN ME!
SIGH
YOU'D BETTER JUST WATCH YOUR STEP, QUIMBY! THAT'S MY WOMAN YOU'RE MESSING WITH! A DIVORCE IS JUST A PIECE OF PAPER! THE SECRET MARRIAGE IS NEVER BROKEN!
REMEMBER, THE HILLS HAVE EYES, QUIMBY!
THE HILLS HAVE EYES!!

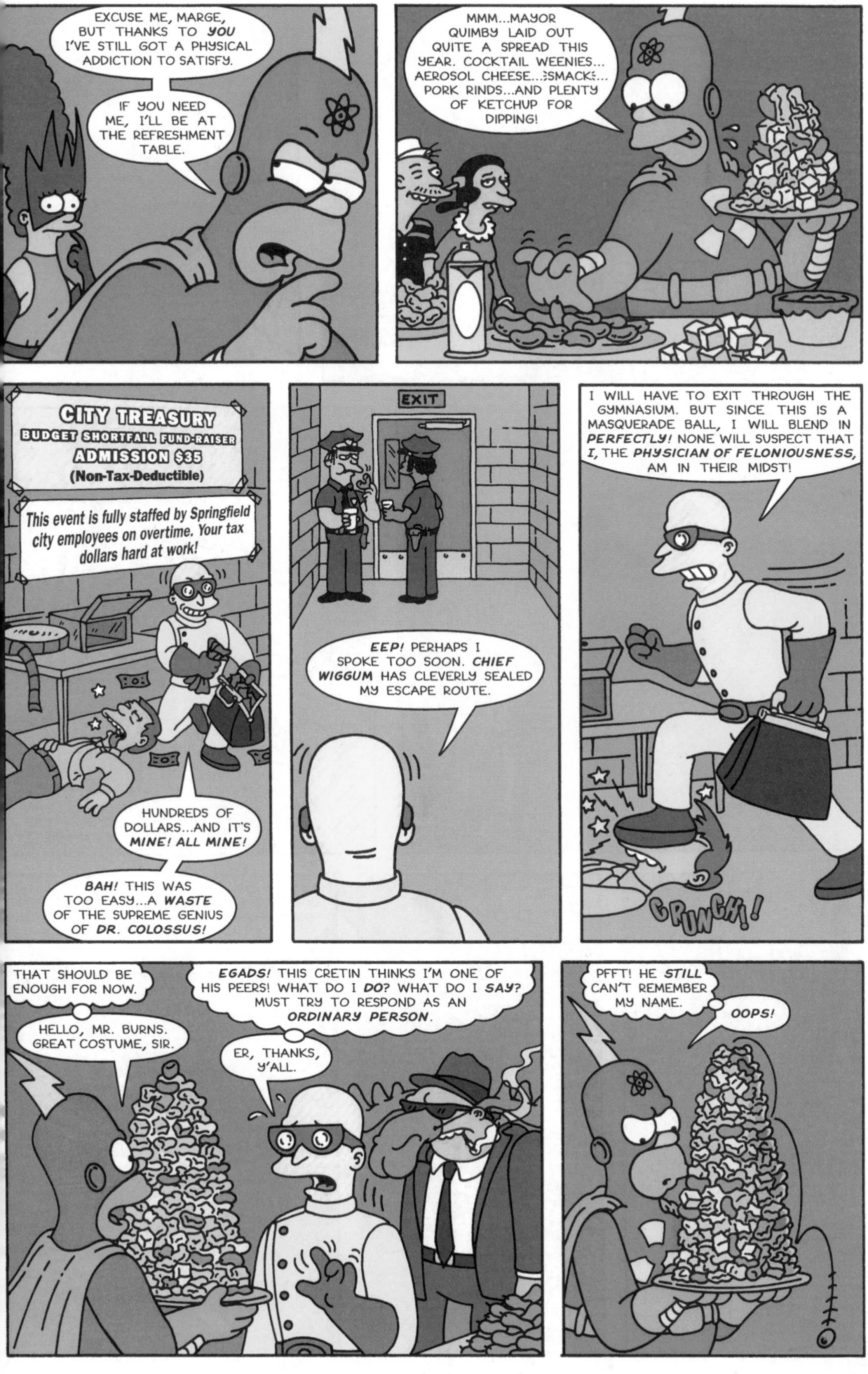
EXCUSE ME, MARGE, BUT THANKS TO *YOU* I'VE STILL GOT A PHYSICAL ADDICTION TO SATISFY.
IF YOU NEED ME, I'LL BE AT THE REFRESHMENT TABLE.
MMM...MAYOR QUIMBY LAID OUT QUITE A SPREAD THIS YEAR. COCKTAIL WEENIES... AEROSOL CHEESE...SMACK...PORK RINDS...AND PLENTY OF KETCHUP FOR DIPPING!
CITY TREASURY
BUDGET SHORTFALL FUND-RAISER
ADMISSION $35
(Non-Tax-Deductible)
This event is fully staffed by Springfield city employees on overtime. Your tax dollars hard at work!
HUNDREDS OF DOLLARS...AND IT'S *MINE! ALL MINE!*
BAH! THIS WAS TOO EASY...A *WASTE* OF THE SUPREME GENIUS OF *DR. COLOSSUS!*
EXIT
EEP! PERHAPS I SPOKE TOO SOON. *CHIEF WIGGUM* HAS CLEVERLY SEALED MY ESCAPE ROUTE.
I WILL HAVE TO EXIT THROUGH THE GYMNASIUM. BUT SINCE THIS IS A MASQUERADE BALL, I WILL BLEND IN *PERFECTLY!* NONE WILL SUSPECT THAT *I*, THE *PHYSICIAN OF FELONIOUSNESS*, AM IN THEIR MIDST!
CRUNCH!
THAT SHOULD BE ENOUGH FOR NOW.
HELLO, MR. BURNS. GREAT COSTUME, SIR.
EGADS! THIS CRETIN THINKS I'M ONE OF HIS PEERS! WHAT DO I *DO*? WHAT DO I *SAY*? MUST TRY TO RESPOND AS AN *ORDINARY PERSON*.
ER, THANKS, Y'ALL.
PFFT! HE *STILL* CAN'T REMEMBER MY NAME.
OOPS!

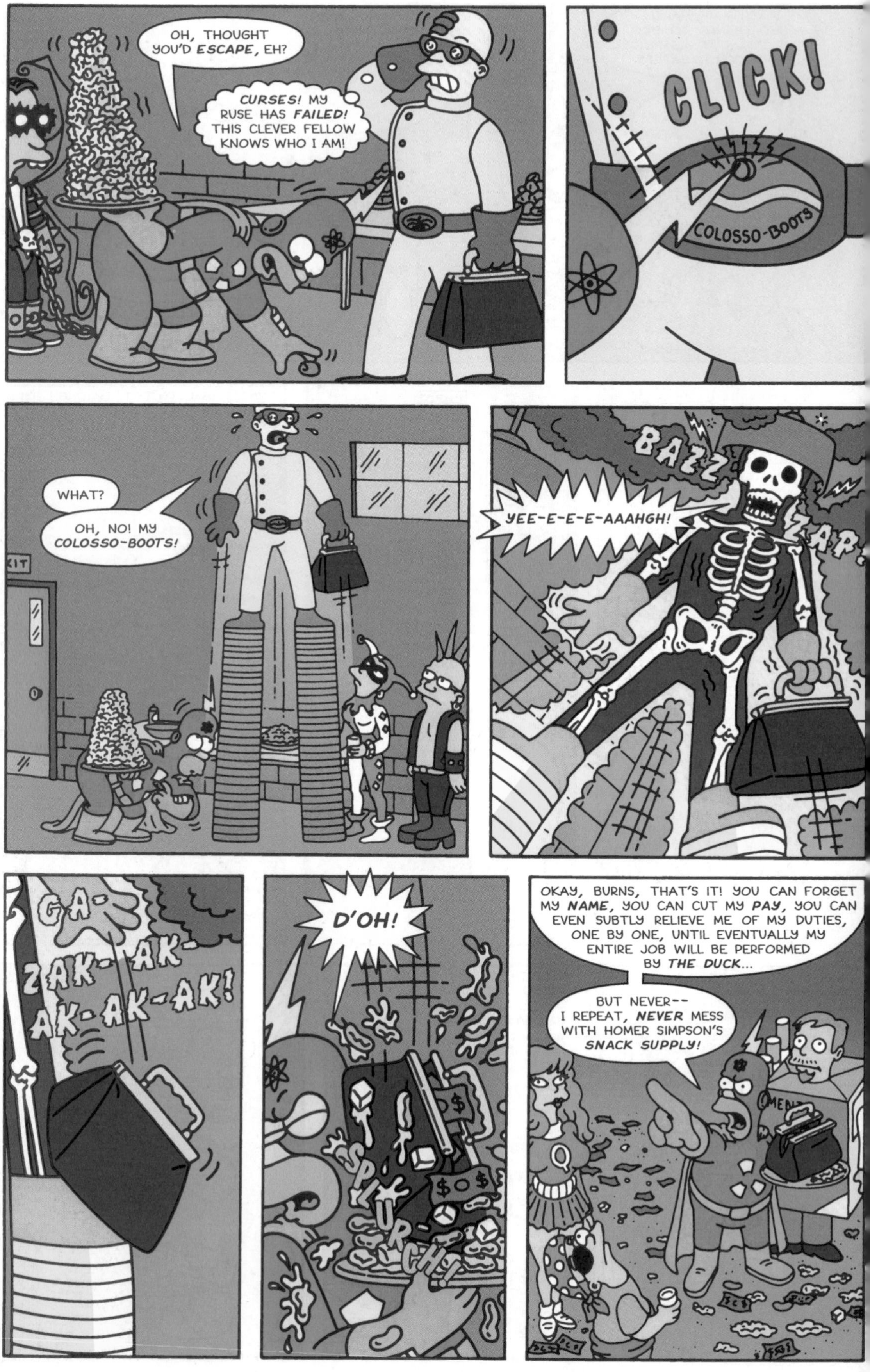

OH, THOUGHT YOU'D ESCAPE, EH?
CURSES! MY RUSE HAS FAILED! THIS CLEVER FELLOW KNOWS WHO I AM!
CLICK!
COLOSSO-BOOTS
WHAT?
OH, NO! MY COLOSSO-BOOTS!
EXIT
BAZZ
YEE-E-E-E-AAAHGH!
ZAP.
GA-ZAK-AK-AK-AK-AK!
D'OH!
SPLURCH!
OKAY, BURNS, THAT'S IT! YOU CAN FORGET MY NAME, YOU CAN CUT MY PAY, YOU CAN EVEN SUBTLY RELIEVE ME OF MY DUTIES, ONE BY ONE, UNTIL EVENTUALLY MY ENTIRE JOB WILL BE PERFORMED BY THE DUCK...
BUT NEVER-- I REPEAT, NEVER MESS WITH HOMER SIMPSON'S SNACK SUPPLY!

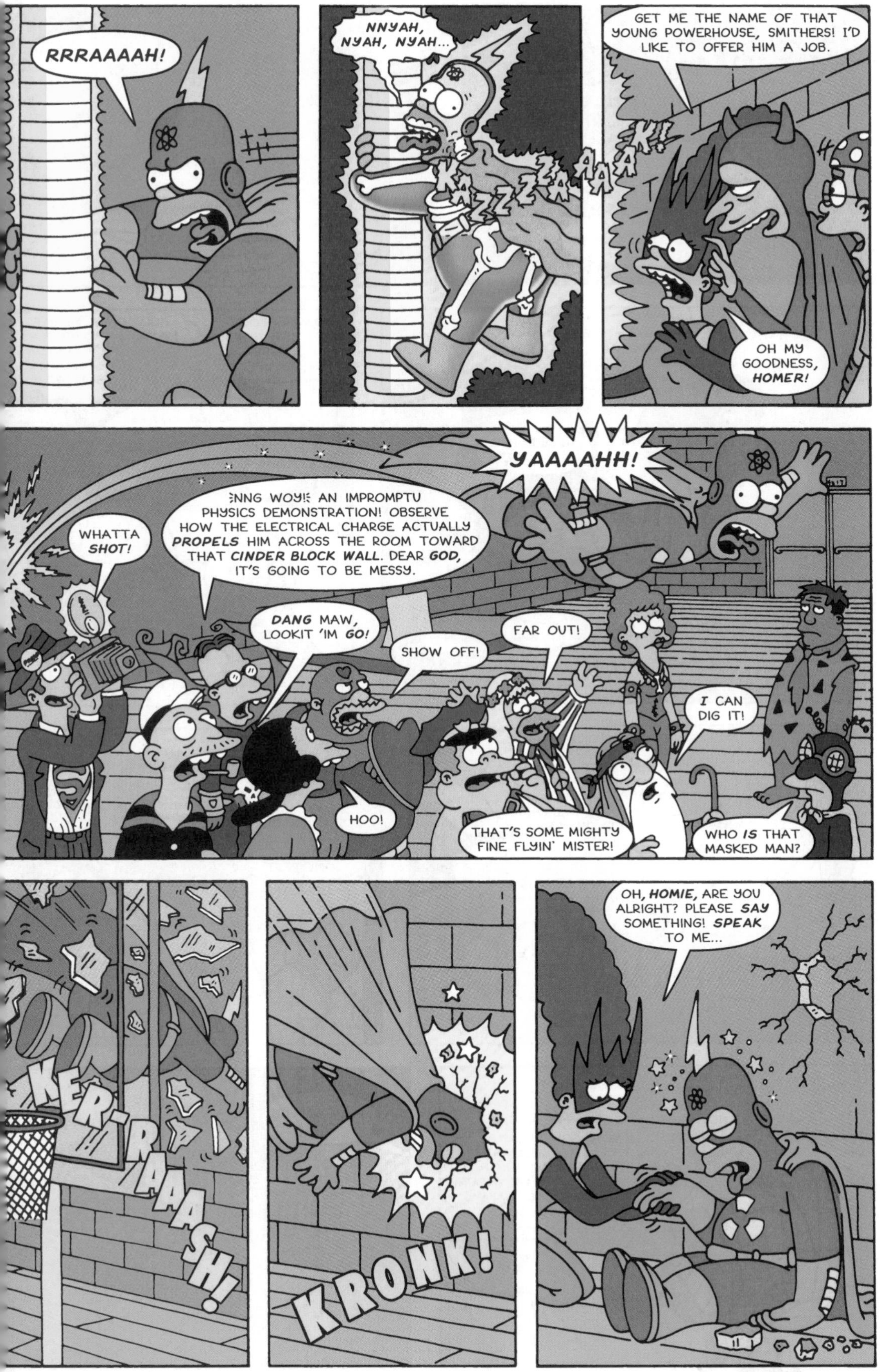
RRRAAAAH!
NNYAH, NYAH, NYAH...
KAZZZZAAAAK!
GET ME THE NAME OF THAT YOUNG POWERHOUSE, SMITHERS! I'D LIKE TO OFFER HIM A JOB.
OH MY GOODNESS, HOMER!
YAAAAHH!
NNG WOY! AN IMPROMPTU PHYSICS DEMONSTRATION! OBSERVE HOW THE ELECTRICAL CHARGE ACTUALLY PROPELS HIM ACROSS THE ROOM TOWARD THAT CINDER BLOCK WALL. DEAR GOD, IT'S GOING TO BE MESSY.
WHATTA SHOT!
DANG MAW, LOOKIT 'IM GO!
SHOW OFF!
FAR OUT!
I CAN DIG IT!
HOO!
THAT'S SOME MIGHTY FINE FLYIN' MISTER!
WHO IS THAT MASKED MAN?
KER-RAAASH!
KRONK!
OH, HOMIE, ARE YOU ALRIGHT? PLEASE SAY SOMETHING! SPEAK TO ME...

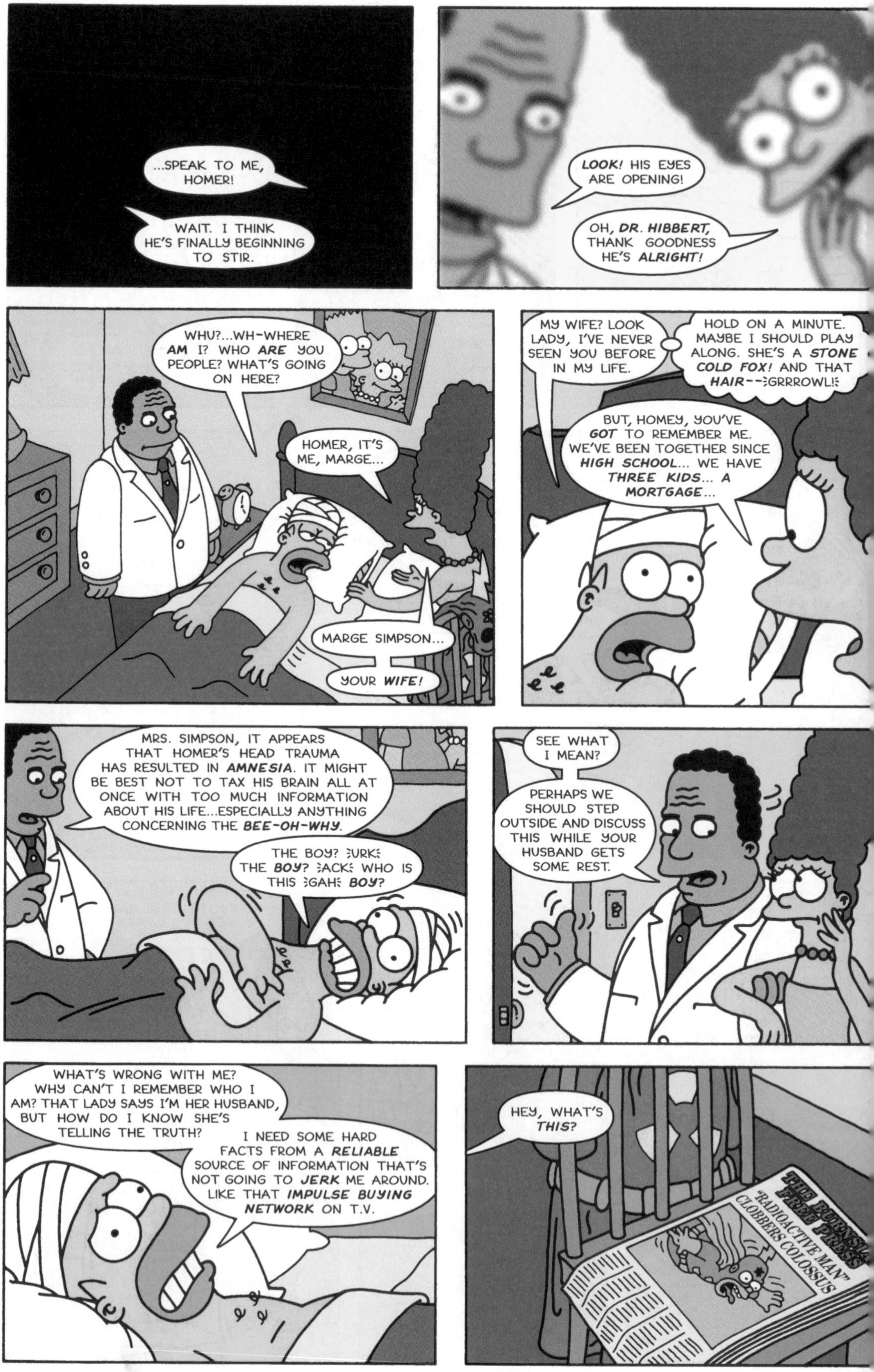
...SPEAK TO ME, HOMER!
WAIT. I THINK HE'S FINALLY BEGINNING TO STIR.
LOOK! HIS EYES ARE OPENING!
OH, DR. HIBBERT, THANK GOODNESS HE'S ALRIGHT!
WHU?...WH-WHERE AM I? WHO ARE YOU PEOPLE? WHAT'S GOING ON HERE?
HOMER, IT'S ME, MARGE...
MARGE SIMPSON...
YOUR WIFE!
MY WIFE? LOOK LADY, I'VE NEVER SEEN YOU BEFORE IN MY LIFE.
HOLD ON A MINUTE. MAYBE I SHOULD PLAY ALONG. SHE'S A STONE COLD FOX! AND THAT HAIR--GRRROWL!
BUT, HOMEY, YOU'VE GOT TO REMEMBER ME. WE'VE BEEN TOGETHER SINCE HIGH SCHOOL... WE HAVE THREE KIDS... A MORTGAGE...
MRS. SIMPSON, IT APPEARS THAT HOMER'S HEAD TRAUMA HAS RESULTED IN AMNESIA. IT MIGHT BE BEST NOT TO TAX HIS BRAIN ALL AT ONCE WITH TOO MUCH INFORMATION ABOUT HIS LIFE...ESPECIALLY ANYTHING CONCERNING THE BEE-OH-WHY.
THE BOY? URK THE BOY? ACK WHO IS THIS GAH BOY?
SEE WHAT I MEAN?
PERHAPS WE SHOULD STEP OUTSIDE AND DISCUSS THIS WHILE YOUR HUSBAND GETS SOME REST.
WHAT'S WRONG WITH ME? WHY CAN'T I REMEMBER WHO I AM? THAT LADY SAYS I'M HER HUSBAND, BUT HOW DO I KNOW SHE'S TELLING THE TRUTH?
I NEED SOME HARD FACTS FROM A RELIABLE SOURCE OF INFORMATION THAT'S NOT GOING TO JERK ME AROUND. LIKE THAT IMPULSE BUYING NETWORK ON T.V.
HEY, WHAT'S THIS?
"RADIOACTIVE MAN" CLOBBERS COLOSSUS

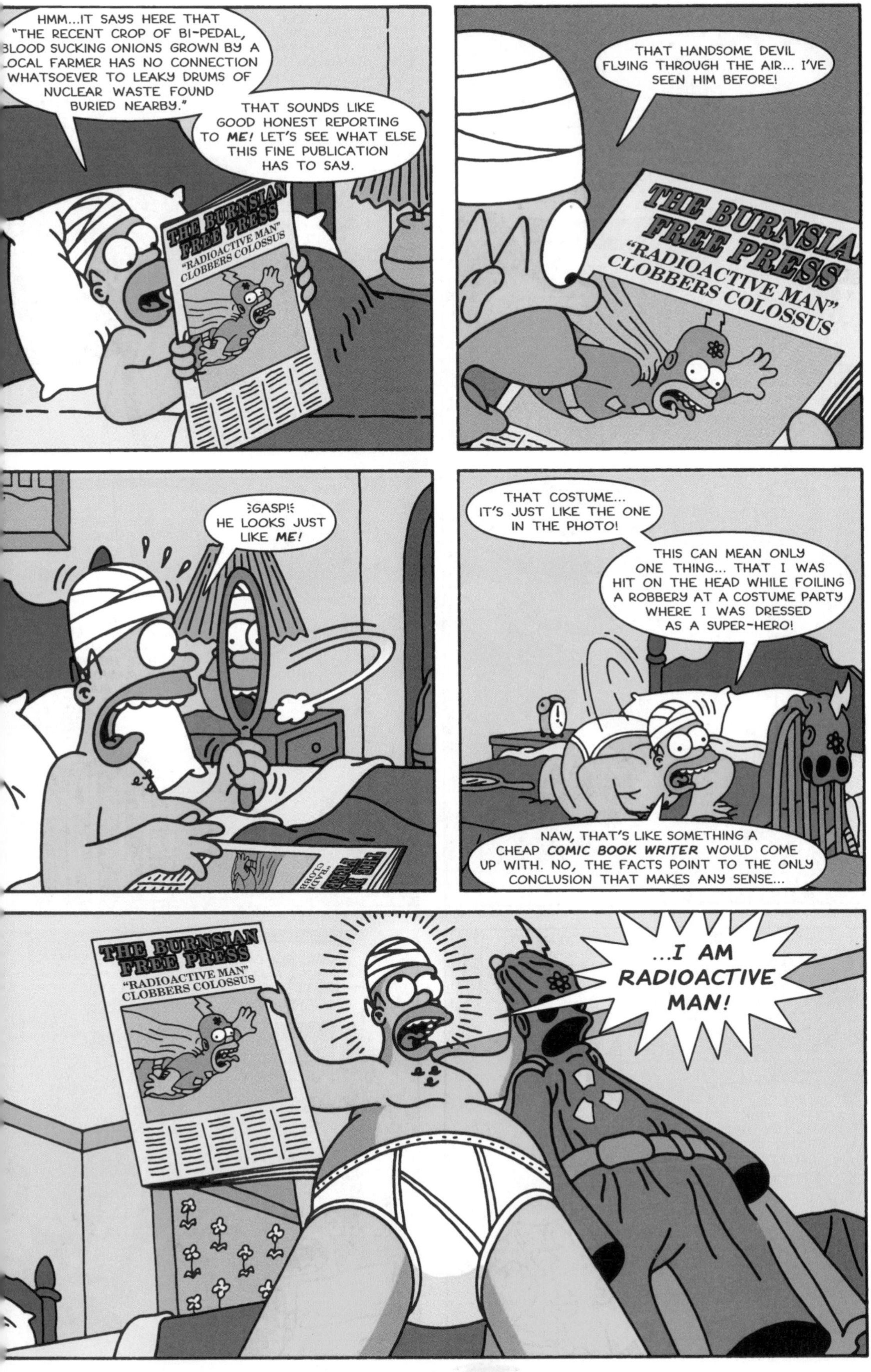

HMM...IT SAYS HERE THAT "THE RECENT CROP OF BI-PEDAL, BLOOD SUCKING ONIONS GROWN BY A LOCAL FARMER HAS NO CONNECTION WHATSOEVER TO LEAKY DRUMS OF NUCLEAR WASTE FOUND BURIED NEARBY."
THAT SOUNDS LIKE GOOD HONEST REPORTING TO *ME!* LET'S SEE WHAT ELSE THIS FINE PUBLICATION HAS TO SAY.
THE BURNSIAN FREE PRESS
"RADIOACTIVE MAN" CLOBBERS COLOSSUS
THAT HANDSOME DEVIL FLYING THROUGH THE AIR... I'VE SEEN HIM BEFORE!
THE BURNSIAN FREE PRESS
"RADIOACTIVE MAN" CLOBBERS COLOSSUS
GASP! HE LOOKS JUST LIKE *ME!*
THAT COSTUME... IT'S JUST LIKE THE ONE IN THE PHOTO!
THIS CAN MEAN ONLY ONE THING... THAT I WAS HIT ON THE HEAD WHILE FOILING A ROBBERY AT A COSTUME PARTY WHERE I WAS DRESSED AS A SUPER-HERO!
NAW, THAT'S LIKE SOMETHING A CHEAP **COMIC BOOK WRITER** WOULD COME UP WITH. NO, THE FACTS POINT TO THE ONLY CONCLUSION THAT MAKES ANY SENSE...
THE BURNSIAN FREE PRESS
"RADIOACTIVE MAN" CLOBBERS COLOSSUS
...I AM RADIOACTIVE MAN!

THIS TELEGRAM JUST ARRIVED FOR YOU MOM.

HI, DR. HIBBERT. IS OUR DAD GOING TO BE ALRIGHT?

WELL KIDS, AS I WAS JUST EXPLAINING TO YOUR MOTHER, YOUR FATHER'S *PHYSICAL* CONDITION IS FINE, BUT I'M CONCERNED ABOUT HIS *MENTAL STATE*.

WELCOME TO THE CLUB, DOC.

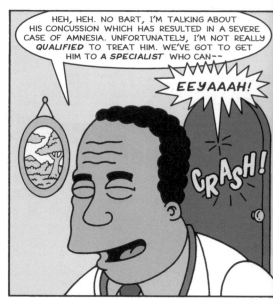

HEH, HEH. NO BART, I'M TALKING ABOUT HIS CONCUSSION WHICH HAS RESULTED IN A SEVERE CASE OF AMNESIA. UNFORTUNATELY, I'M NOT REALLY *QUALIFIED* TO TREAT HIM. WE'VE GOT TO GET HIM TO *A SPECIALIST* WHO CAN--

EEYAAAH!

CRASH!

OH, DEAR! *HOMER*--

HE'S *GONE!*

MARGE, I THINK YOU MAY HAVE A BIG PROBLEM ON YOUR HANDS. THE MASQUERADE COSTUME THAT WAS ON THAT CHAIR IS *ALSO* GONE!

IF I'M NOT MISTAKEN, HOMER SAW THAT NEWSPAPER HEADLINE AND DECIDED THAT *HE* MUST BE *RADIOACTIVE MAN!*

COOL! "MY DAD WENT NUTS AND BECAME A SUPER-HERO." IF *THIS* DOESN'T GET US ON RICKI LAKE, *NOTHING* WILL.

OH PLEASE, SHE'S STOPPED TAKING YOUR CALLS. IT'S TIME TO LET GO OF THE DREAM, BART.

I'D BETTER CALL THE POLICE AND HAVE HIM PICKED UP BEFORE HE HURTS HIMSELF!

HEH, HEH. NICE KITTY.

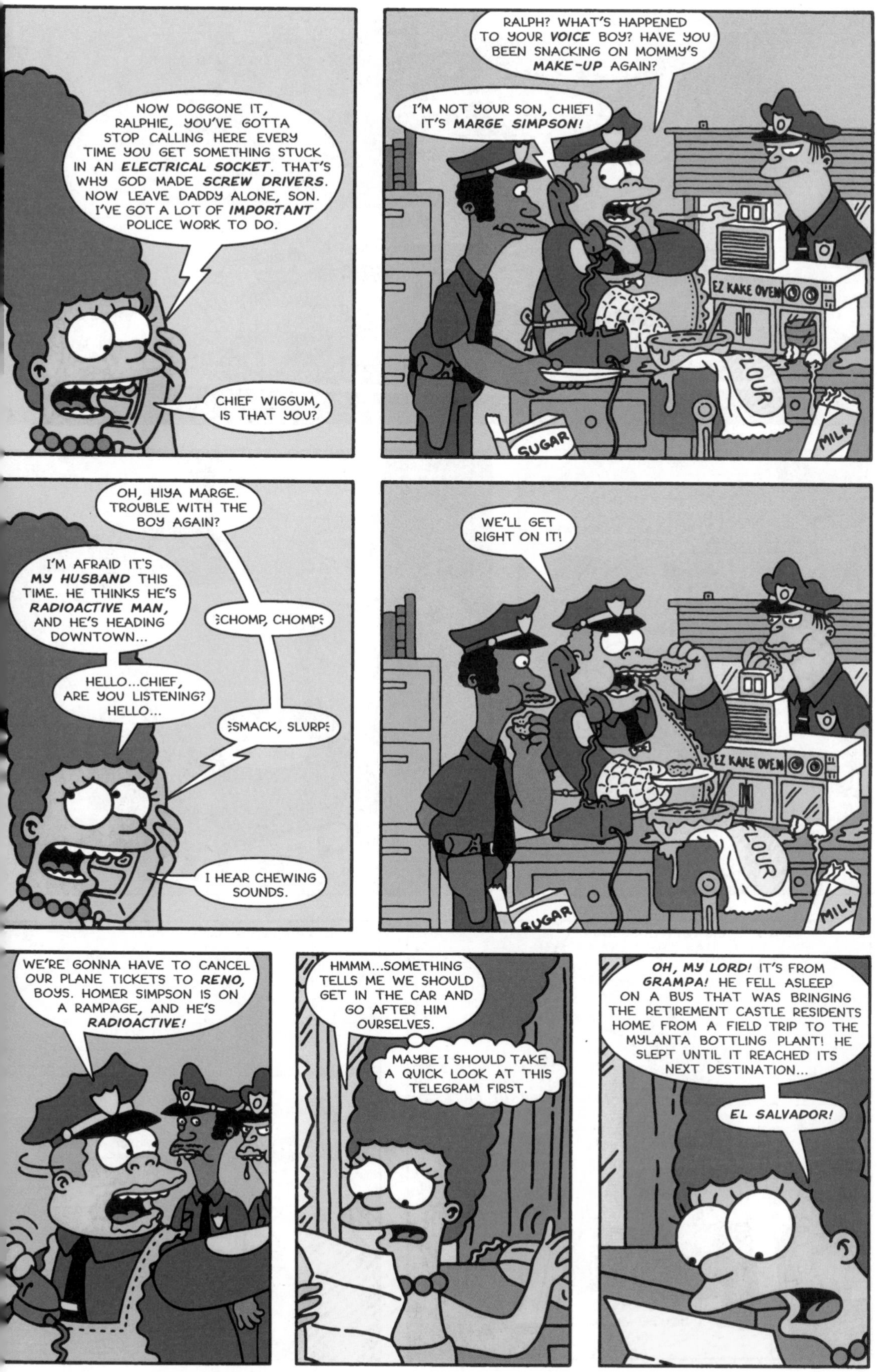
CHIEF WIGGUM, IS THAT YOU?
NOW DOGGONE IT, RALPHIE, YOU'VE GOTTA STOP CALLING HERE EVERY TIME YOU GET SOMETHING STUCK IN AN ELECTRICAL SOCKET. THAT'S WHY GOD MADE SCREW DRIVERS. NOW LEAVE DADDY ALONE, SON. I'VE GOT A LOT OF IMPORTANT POLICE WORK TO DO.
I'M NOT YOUR SON, CHIEF! IT'S MARGE SIMPSON!
RALPH? WHAT'S HAPPENED TO YOUR VOICE BOY? HAVE YOU BEEN SNACKING ON MOMMY'S MAKE-UP AGAIN?
EZ KAKE OVEN
FLOUR
SUGAR
MILK
OH, HIYA MARGE. TROUBLE WITH THE BOY AGAIN?
I'M AFRAID IT'S MY HUSBAND THIS TIME. HE THINKS HE'S RADIOACTIVE MAN, AND HE'S HEADING DOWNTOWN...
CHOMP, CHOMP
HELLO...CHIEF, ARE YOU LISTENING? HELLO...
SMACK, SLURP
I HEAR CHEWING SOUNDS.
WE'LL GET RIGHT ON IT!
EZ KAKE OVEN
FLOUR
SUGAR
MILK
WE'RE GONNA HAVE TO CANCEL OUR PLANE TICKETS TO RENO, BOYS. HOMER SIMPSON IS ON A RAMPAGE, AND HE'S RADIOACTIVE!
HMMM...SOMETHING TELLS ME WE SHOULD GET IN THE CAR AND GO AFTER HIM OURSELVES.
MAYBE I SHOULD TAKE A QUICK LOOK AT THIS TELEGRAM FIRST.
OH, MY LORD! IT'S FROM GRAMPA! HE FELL ASLEEP ON A BUS THAT WAS BRINGING THE RETIREMENT CASTLE RESIDENTS HOME FROM A FIELD TRIP TO THE MYLANTA BOTTLING PLANT! HE SLEPT UNTIL IT REACHED ITS NEXT DESTINATION...
EL SALVADOR!

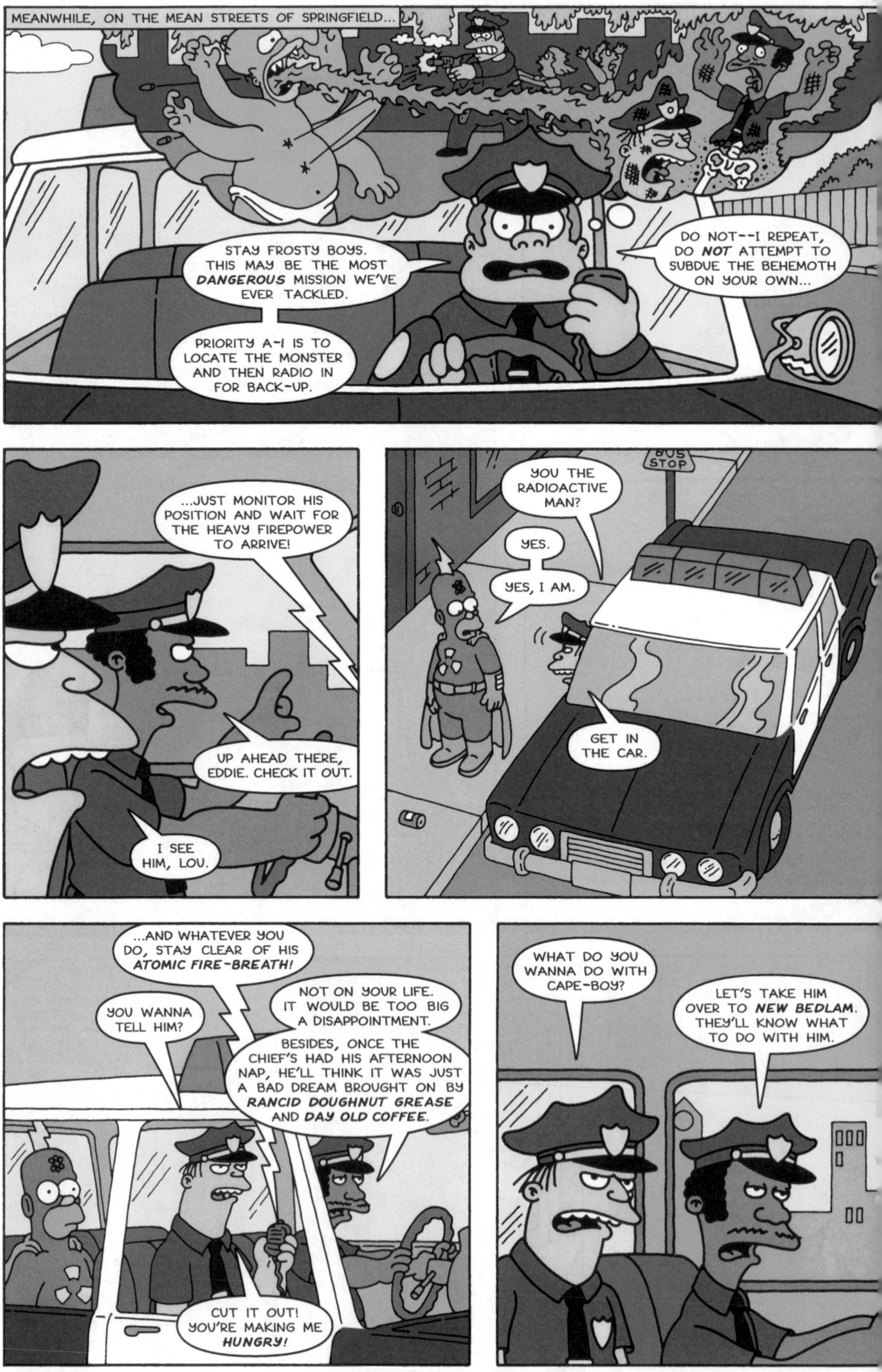
MEANWHILE, ON THE MEAN STREETS OF SPRINGFIELD...
STAY FROSTY BOYS. THIS MAY BE THE MOST DANGEROUS MISSION WE'VE EVER TACKLED.
PRIORITY A-1 IS TO LOCATE THE MONSTER AND THEN RADIO IN FOR BACK-UP.
DO NOT--I REPEAT, DO NOT ATTEMPT TO SUBDUE THE BEHEMOTH ON YOUR OWN...
...JUST MONITOR HIS POSITION AND WAIT FOR THE HEAVY FIREPOWER TO ARRIVE!
UP AHEAD THERE, EDDIE. CHECK IT OUT.
I SEE HIM, LOU.
BUS STOP
YOU THE RADIOACTIVE MAN?
YES.
YES, I AM.
GET IN THE CAR.
...AND WHATEVER YOU DO, STAY CLEAR OF HIS ATOMIC FIRE-BREATH!
YOU WANNA TELL HIM?
NOT ON YOUR LIFE. IT WOULD BE TOO BIG A DISAPPOINTMENT.
BESIDES, ONCE THE CHIEF'S HAD HIS AFTERNOON NAP, HE'LL THINK IT WAS JUST A BAD DREAM BROUGHT ON BY RANCID DOUGHNUT GREASE AND DAY OLD COFFEE.
CUT IT OUT! YOU'RE MAKING ME HUNGRY!
WHAT DO YOU WANNA DO WITH CAPE-BOY?
LET'S TAKE HIM OVER TO NEW BEDLAM. THEY'LL KNOW WHAT TO DO WITH HIM.

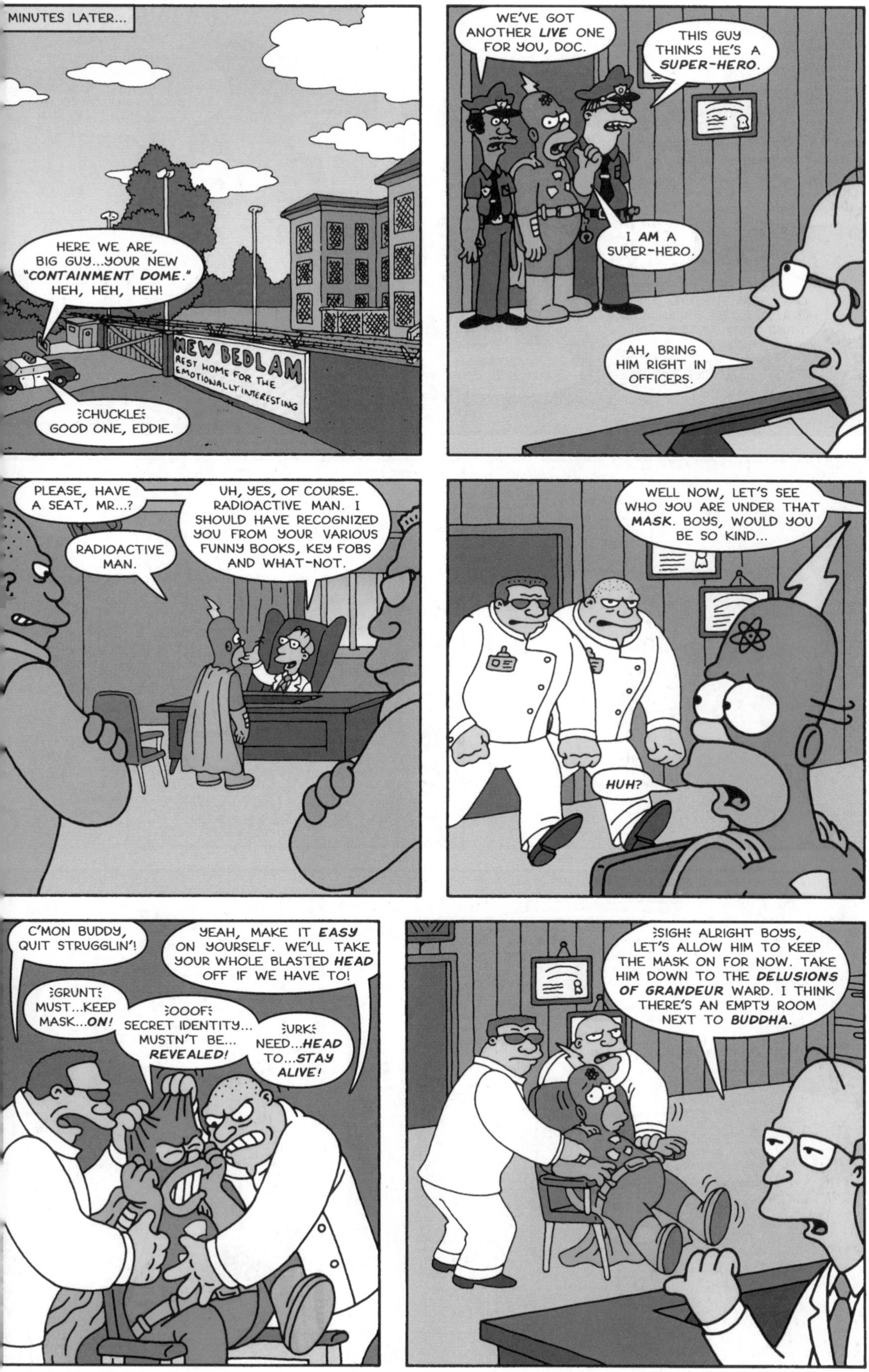
MINUTES LATER...
HERE WE ARE, BIG GUY...YOUR NEW "CONTAINMENT DOME." HEH, HEH, HEH!
NEW BEDLAM REST HOME FOR THE EMOTIONALLY INTERESTING
:CHUCKLE: GOOD ONE, EDDIE.
WE'VE GOT ANOTHER LIVE ONE FOR YOU, DOC.
THIS GUY THINKS HE'S A SUPER-HERO.
I AM A SUPER-HERO.
AH, BRING HIM RIGHT IN OFFICERS.
PLEASE, HAVE A SEAT, MR...?
RADIOACTIVE MAN.
UH, YES, OF COURSE. RADIOACTIVE MAN. I SHOULD HAVE RECOGNIZED YOU FROM YOUR VARIOUS FUNNY BOOKS, KEY FOBS AND WHAT-NOT.
WELL NOW, LET'S SEE WHO YOU ARE UNDER THAT MASK. BOYS, WOULD YOU BE SO KIND...
HUH?
C'MON BUDDY, QUIT STRUGGLIN'!
YEAH, MAKE IT EASY ON YOURSELF. WE'LL TAKE YOUR WHOLE BLASTED HEAD OFF IF WE HAVE TO!
:GRUNT: MUST...KEEP MASK...ON!
:OOOF: SECRET IDENTITY... MUSTN'T BE... REVEALED!
:URK: NEED...HEAD TO...STAY ALIVE!
:SIGH: ALRIGHT BOYS, LET'S ALLOW HIM TO KEEP THE MASK ON FOR NOW. TAKE HIM DOWN TO THE DELUSIONS OF GRANDEUR WARD. I THINK THERE'S AN EMPTY ROOM NEXT TO BUDDHA.

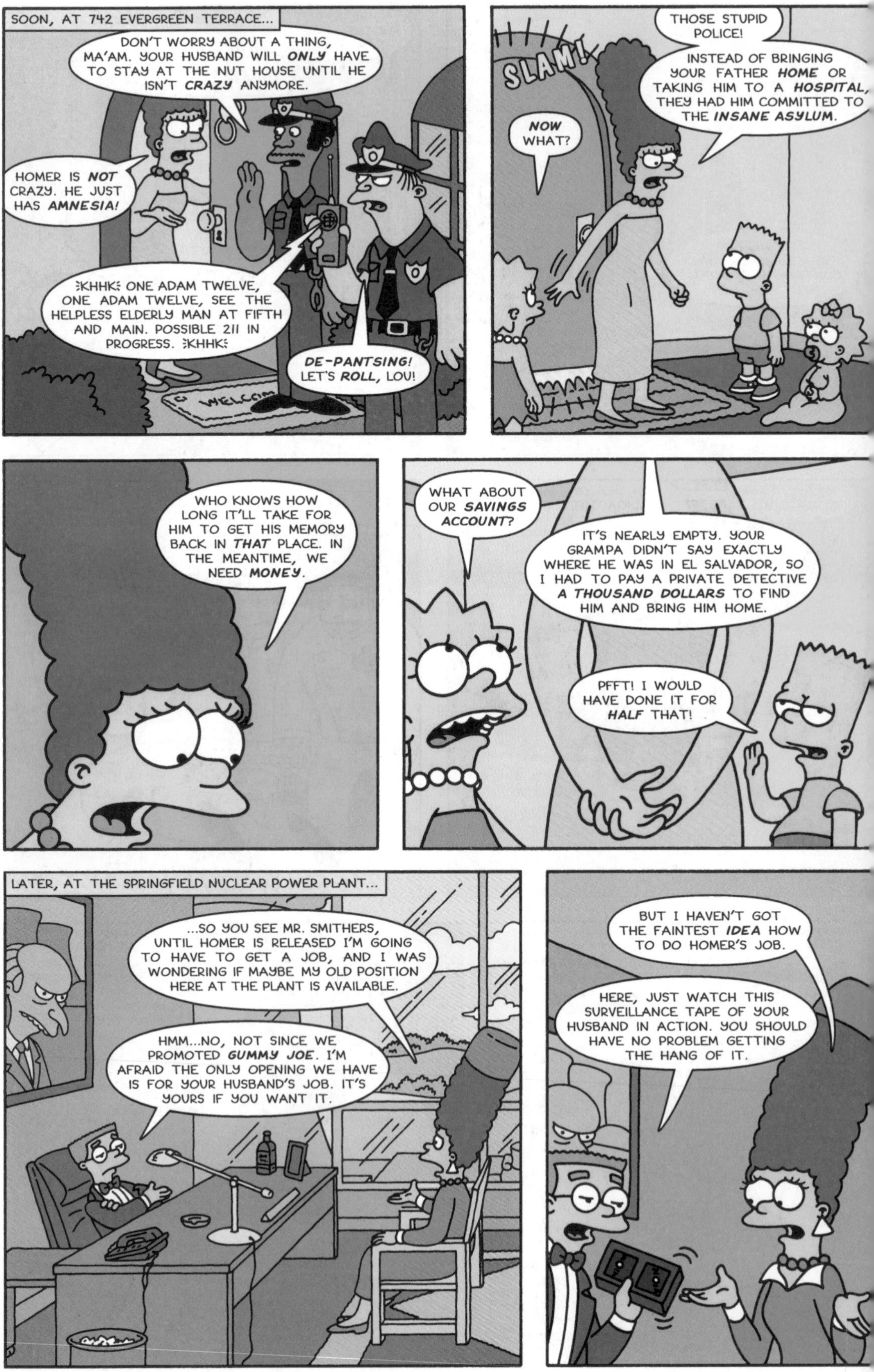
SOON, AT 742 EVERGREEN TERRACE...
DON'T WORRY ABOUT A THING, MA'AM. YOUR HUSBAND WILL ONLY HAVE TO STAY AT THE NUT HOUSE UNTIL HE ISN'T CRAZY ANYMORE.
HOMER IS NOT CRAZY. HE JUST HAS AMNESIA!
KHHK ONE ADAM TWELVE, ONE ADAM TWELVE, SEE THE HELPLESS ELDERLY MAN AT FIFTH AND MAIN. POSSIBLE 211 IN PROGRESS. KHHK
DE-PANTSING! LET'S ROLL, LOU!
SLAM!
NOW WHAT?
THOSE STUPID POLICE!
INSTEAD OF BRINGING YOUR FATHER HOME OR TAKING HIM TO A HOSPITAL, THEY HAD HIM COMMITTED TO THE INSANE ASYLUM.
WHO KNOWS HOW LONG IT'LL TAKE FOR HIM TO GET HIS MEMORY BACK IN THAT PLACE. IN THE MEANTIME, WE NEED MONEY.
WHAT ABOUT OUR SAVINGS ACCOUNT?
IT'S NEARLY EMPTY. YOUR GRAMPA DIDN'T SAY EXACTLY WHERE HE WAS IN EL SALVADOR, SO I HAD TO PAY A PRIVATE DETECTIVE A THOUSAND DOLLARS TO FIND HIM AND BRING HIM HOME.
PFFT! I WOULD HAVE DONE IT FOR HALF THAT!
LATER, AT THE SPRINGFIELD NUCLEAR POWER PLANT...
...SO YOU SEE MR. SMITHERS, UNTIL HOMER IS RELEASED I'M GOING TO HAVE TO GET A JOB, AND I WAS WONDERING IF MAYBE MY OLD POSITION HERE AT THE PLANT IS AVAILABLE.
HMM...NO, NOT SINCE WE PROMOTED GUMMY JOE. I'M AFRAID THE ONLY OPENING WE HAVE IS FOR YOUR HUSBAND'S JOB. IT'S YOURS IF YOU WANT IT.
BUT I HAVEN'T GOT THE FAINTEST IDEA HOW TO DO HOMER'S JOB.
HERE, JUST WATCH THIS SURVEILLANCE TAPE OF YOUR HUSBAND IN ACTION. YOU SHOULD HAVE NO PROBLEM GETTING THE HANG OF IT.

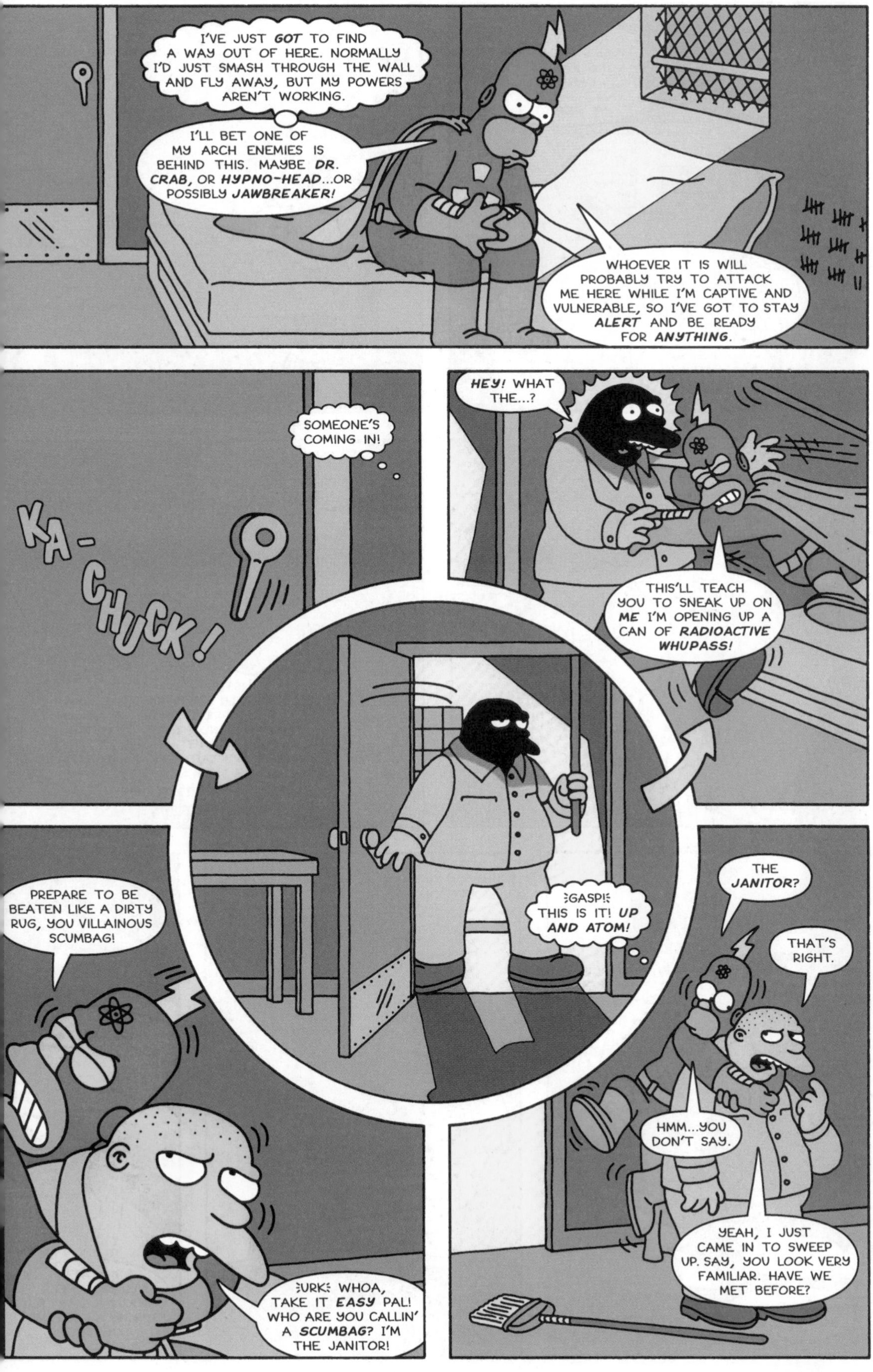
I'VE JUST GOT TO FIND A WAY OUT OF HERE. NORMALLY I'D JUST SMASH THROUGH THE WALL AND FLY AWAY, BUT MY POWERS AREN'T WORKING.
I'LL BET ONE OF MY ARCH ENEMIES IS BEHIND THIS. MAYBE DR. CRAB, OR HYPNO-HEAD...OR POSSIBLY JAWBREAKER!
WHOEVER IT IS WILL PROBABLY TRY TO ATTACK ME HERE WHILE I'M CAPTIVE AND VULNERABLE, SO I'VE GOT TO STAY ALERT AND BE READY FOR ANYTHING.
SOMEONE'S COMING IN!
KA-CHUCK!
:GASP!: THIS IS IT! UP AND ATOM!
HEY! WHAT THE...?
THIS'LL TEACH YOU TO SNEAK UP ON ME I'M OPENING UP A CAN OF RADIOACTIVE WHUPASS!
PREPARE TO BE BEATEN LIKE A DIRTY RUG, YOU VILLAINOUS SCUMBAG!
:URK: WHOA, TAKE IT EASY PAL! WHO ARE YOU CALLIN' A SCUMBAG? I'M THE JANITOR!
THE JANITOR?
THAT'S RIGHT.
HMM...YOU DON'T SAY.
YEAH, I JUST CAME IN TO SWEEP UP. SAY, YOU LOOK VERY FAMILIAR. HAVE WE MET BEFORE?

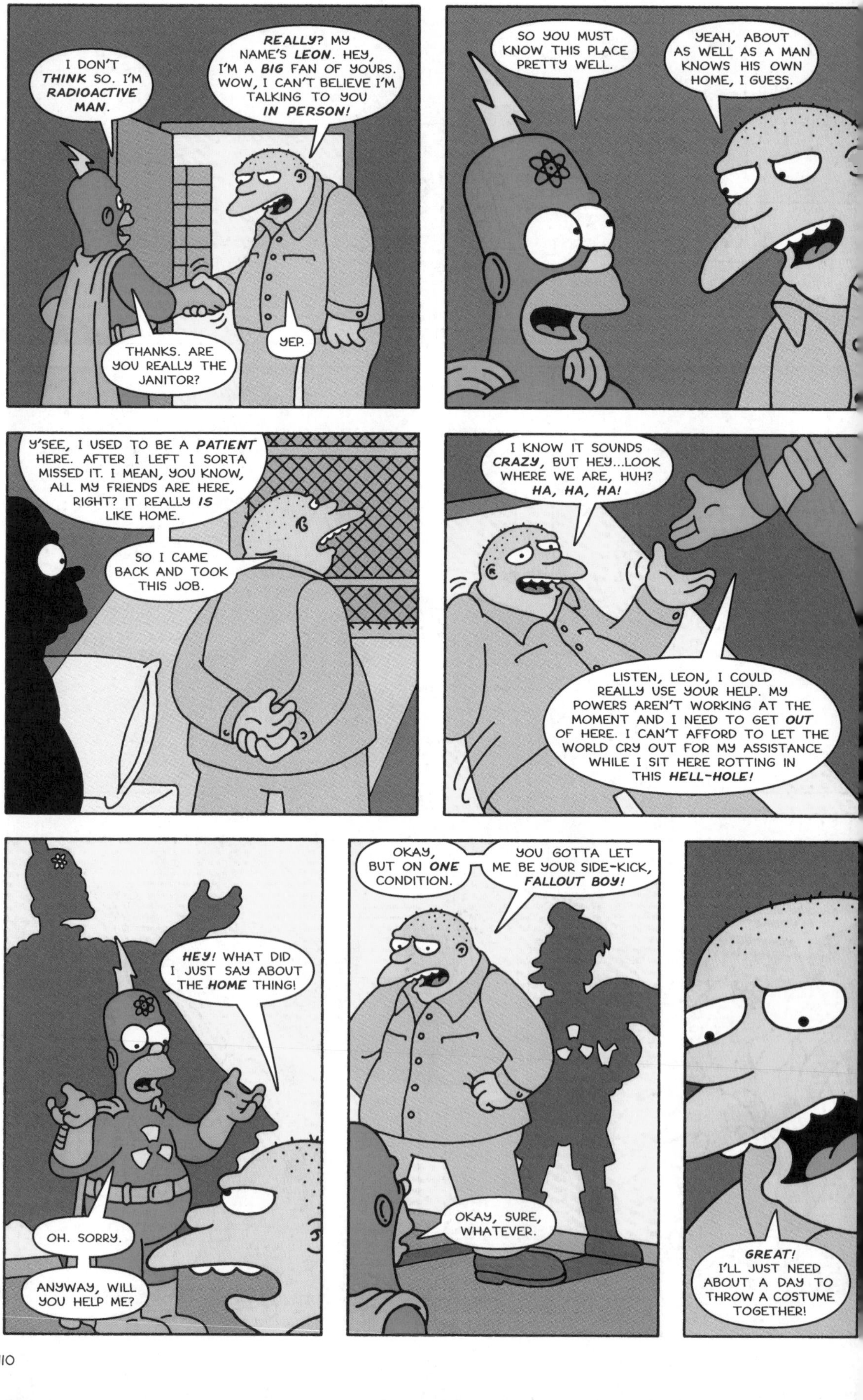
I DON'T THINK SO. I'M RADIOACTIVE MAN.
REALLY? MY NAME'S LEON. HEY, I'M A BIG FAN OF YOURS. WOW, I CAN'T BELIEVE I'M TALKING TO YOU IN PERSON!
THANKS. ARE YOU REALLY THE JANITOR?
YEP.
SO YOU MUST KNOW THIS PLACE PRETTY WELL.
YEAH, ABOUT AS WELL AS A MAN KNOWS HIS OWN HOME, I GUESS.
Y'SEE, I USED TO BE A PATIENT HERE. AFTER I LEFT I SORTA MISSED IT. I MEAN, YOU KNOW, ALL MY FRIENDS ARE HERE, RIGHT? IT REALLY IS LIKE HOME.
SO I CAME BACK AND TOOK THIS JOB.
I KNOW IT SOUNDS CRAZY, BUT HEY...LOOK WHERE WE ARE, HUH? HA, HA, HA!
LISTEN, LEON, I COULD REALLY USE YOUR HELP. MY POWERS AREN'T WORKING AT THE MOMENT AND I NEED TO GET OUT OF HERE. I CAN'T AFFORD TO LET THE WORLD CRY OUT FOR MY ASSISTANCE WHILE I SIT HERE ROTTING IN THIS HELL-HOLE!
HEY! WHAT DID I JUST SAY ABOUT THE HOME THING!
OH. SORRY.
ANYWAY, WILL YOU HELP ME?
OKAY, BUT ON ONE CONDITION.
YOU GOTTA LET ME BE YOUR SIDE-KICK, FALLOUT BOY!
OKAY, SURE, WHATEVER.
GREAT! I'LL JUST NEED ABOUT A DAY TO THROW A COSTUME TOGETHER!

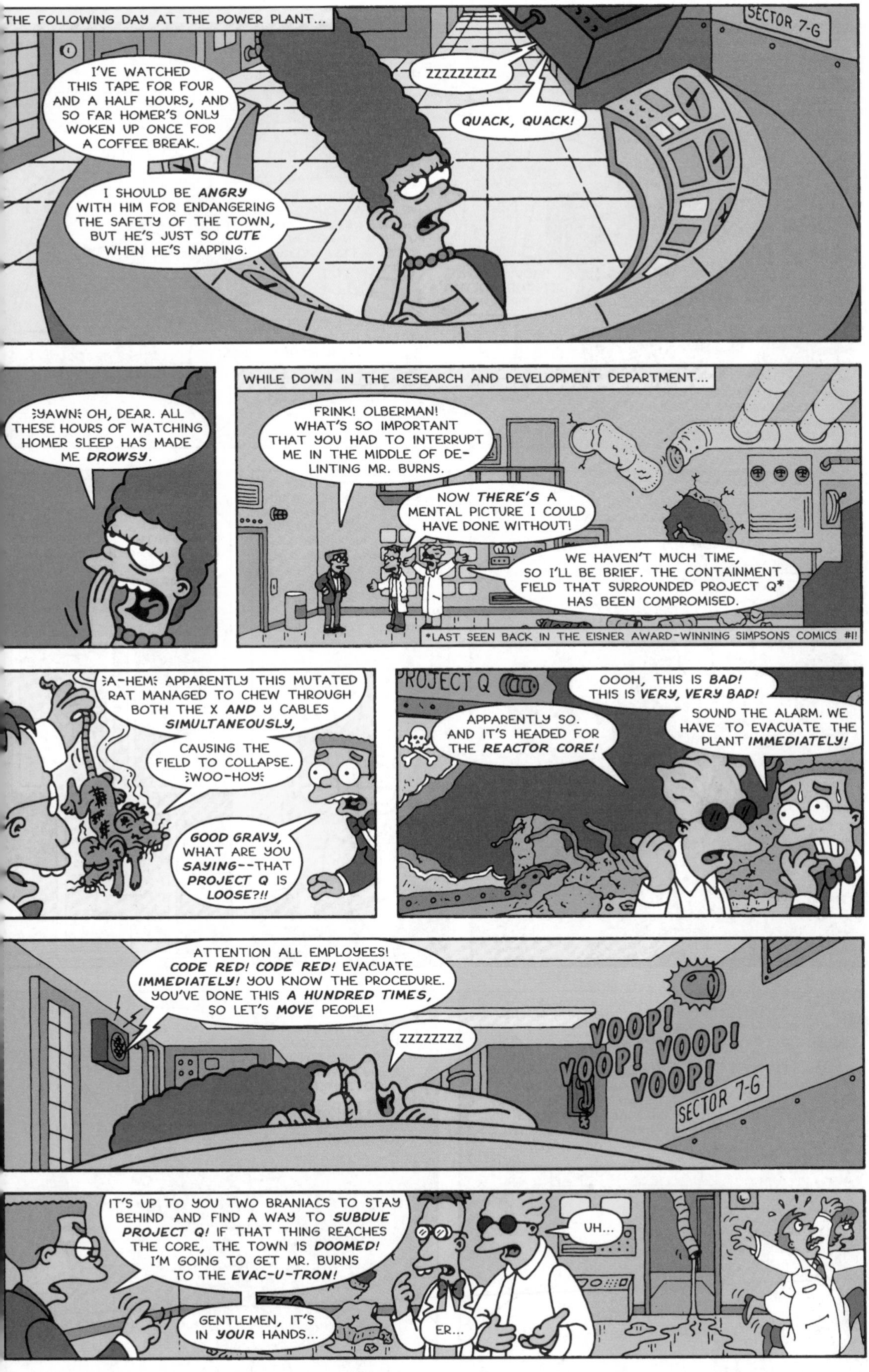
THE FOLLOWING DAY AT THE POWER PLANT...
SECTOR 7-G
I'VE WATCHED THIS TAPE FOR FOUR AND A HALF HOURS, AND SO FAR HOMER'S ONLY WOKEN UP ONCE FOR A COFFEE BREAK.
I SHOULD BE ANGRY WITH HIM FOR ENDANGERING THE SAFETY OF THE TOWN, BUT HE'S JUST SO CUTE WHEN HE'S NAPPING.
ZZZZZZZZZ
QUACK, QUACK!
YAWN OH, DEAR. ALL THESE HOURS OF WATCHING HOMER SLEEP HAS MADE ME DROWSY.
WHILE DOWN IN THE RESEARCH AND DEVELOPMENT DEPARTMENT...
FRINK! OLBERMAN! WHAT'S SO IMPORTANT THAT YOU HAD TO INTERRUPT ME IN THE MIDDLE OF DE-LINTING MR. BURNS.
NOW THERE'S A MENTAL PICTURE I COULD HAVE DONE WITHOUT!
WE HAVEN'T MUCH TIME, SO I'LL BE BRIEF. THE CONTAINMENT FIELD THAT SURROUNDED PROJECT Q* HAS BEEN COMPROMISED.
*LAST SEEN BACK IN THE EISNER AWARD-WINNING SIMPSONS COMICS #1!
A-HEM APPARENTLY THIS MUTATED RAT MANAGED TO CHEW THROUGH BOTH THE X AND Y CABLES SIMULTANEOUSLY,
CAUSING THE FIELD TO COLLAPSE. WOO-HOY
GOOD GRAVY, WHAT ARE YOU SAYING--THAT PROJECT Q IS LOOSE?!!
PROJECT Q
APPARENTLY SO. AND IT'S HEADED FOR THE REACTOR CORE!
OOOH, THIS IS BAD! THIS IS VERY, VERY BAD!
SOUND THE ALARM. WE HAVE TO EVACUATE THE PLANT IMMEDIATELY!
ATTENTION ALL EMPLOYEES! CODE RED! CODE RED! EVACUATE IMMEDIATELY! YOU KNOW THE PROCEDURE. YOU'VE DONE THIS A HUNDRED TIMES, SO LET'S MOVE PEOPLE!
ZZZZZZZZ
VOOP! VOOP! VOOP! VOOP!
SECTOR 7-G
IT'S UP TO YOU TWO BRANIACS TO STAY BEHIND AND FIND A WAY TO SUBDUE PROJECT Q! IF THAT THING REACHES THE CORE, THE TOWN IS DOOMED! I'M GOING TO GET MR. BURNS TO THE EVAC-U-TRON!
GENTLEMEN, IT'S IN YOUR HANDS...
UH...
ER...

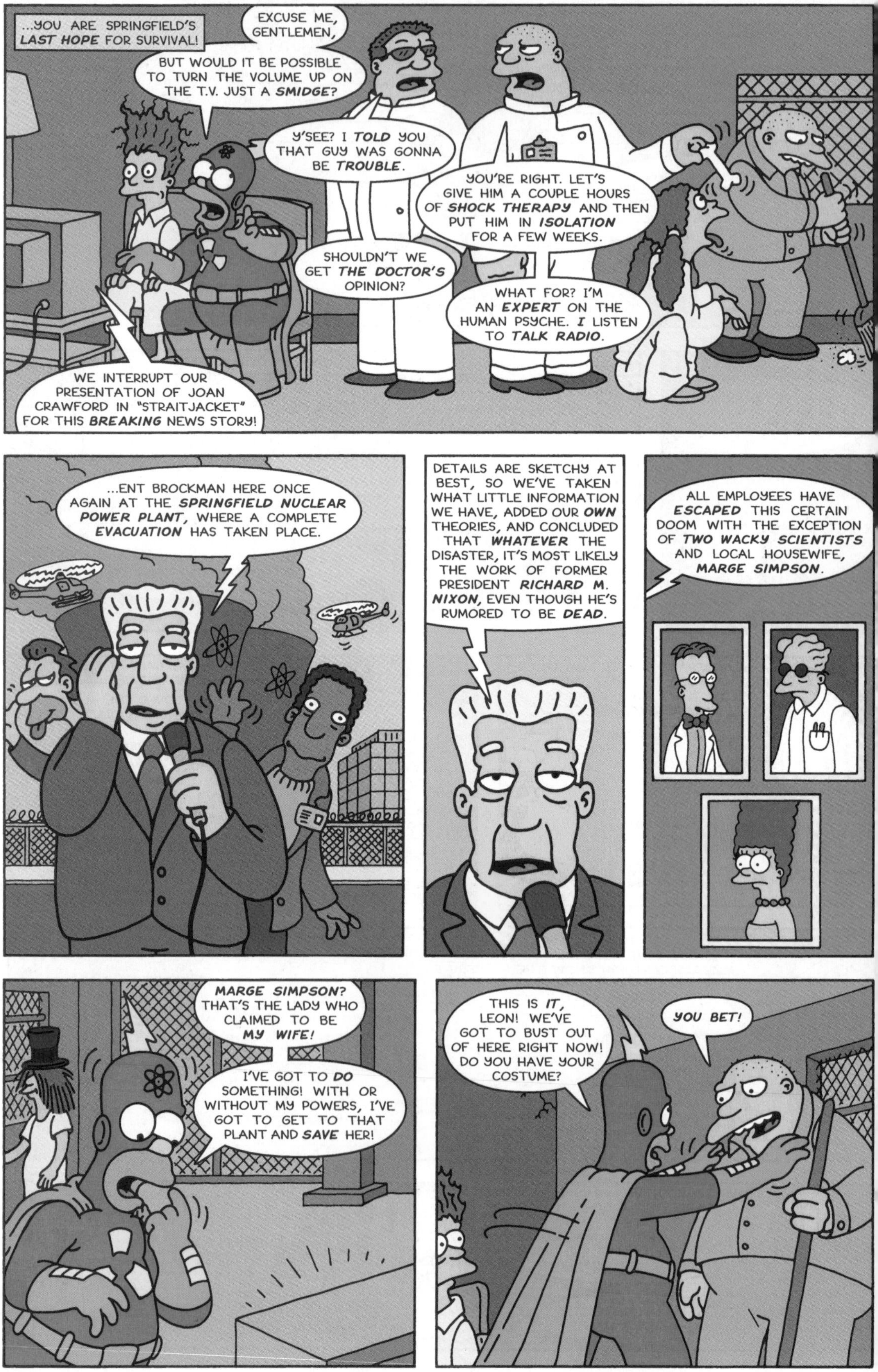
...YOU ARE SPRINGFIELD'S LAST HOPE FOR SURVIVAL!
EXCUSE ME, GENTLEMEN,
BUT WOULD IT BE POSSIBLE TO TURN THE VOLUME UP ON THE T.V. JUST A SMIDGE?
Y'SEE? I TOLD YOU THAT GUY WAS GONNA BE TROUBLE.
YOU'RE RIGHT. LET'S GIVE HIM A COUPLE HOURS OF SHOCK THERAPY AND THEN PUT HIM IN ISOLATION FOR A FEW WEEKS.
SHOULDN'T WE GET THE DOCTOR'S OPINION?
WHAT FOR? I'M AN EXPERT ON THE HUMAN PSYCHE. I LISTEN TO TALK RADIO.
WE INTERRUPT OUR PRESENTATION OF JOAN CRAWFORD IN "STRAITJACKET" FOR THIS BREAKING NEWS STORY!
...ENT BROCKMAN HERE ONCE AGAIN AT THE SPRINGFIELD NUCLEAR POWER PLANT, WHERE A COMPLETE EVACUATION HAS TAKEN PLACE.
DETAILS ARE SKETCHY AT BEST, SO WE'VE TAKEN WHAT LITTLE INFORMATION WE HAVE, ADDED OUR OWN THEORIES, AND CONCLUDED THAT WHATEVER THE DISASTER, IT'S MOST LIKELY THE WORK OF FORMER PRESIDENT RICHARD M. NIXON, EVEN THOUGH HE'S RUMORED TO BE DEAD.
ALL EMPLOYEES HAVE ESCAPED THIS CERTAIN DOOM WITH THE EXCEPTION OF TWO WACKY SCIENTISTS AND LOCAL HOUSEWIFE, MARGE SIMPSON.
MARGE SIMPSON? THAT'S THE LADY WHO CLAIMED TO BE MY WIFE!
I'VE GOT TO DO SOMETHING! WITH OR WITHOUT MY POWERS, I'VE GOT TO GET TO THAT PLANT AND SAVE HER!
THIS IS IT, LEON! WE'VE GOT TO BUST OUT OF HERE RIGHT NOW! DO YOU HAVE YOUR COSTUME?
YOU BET!

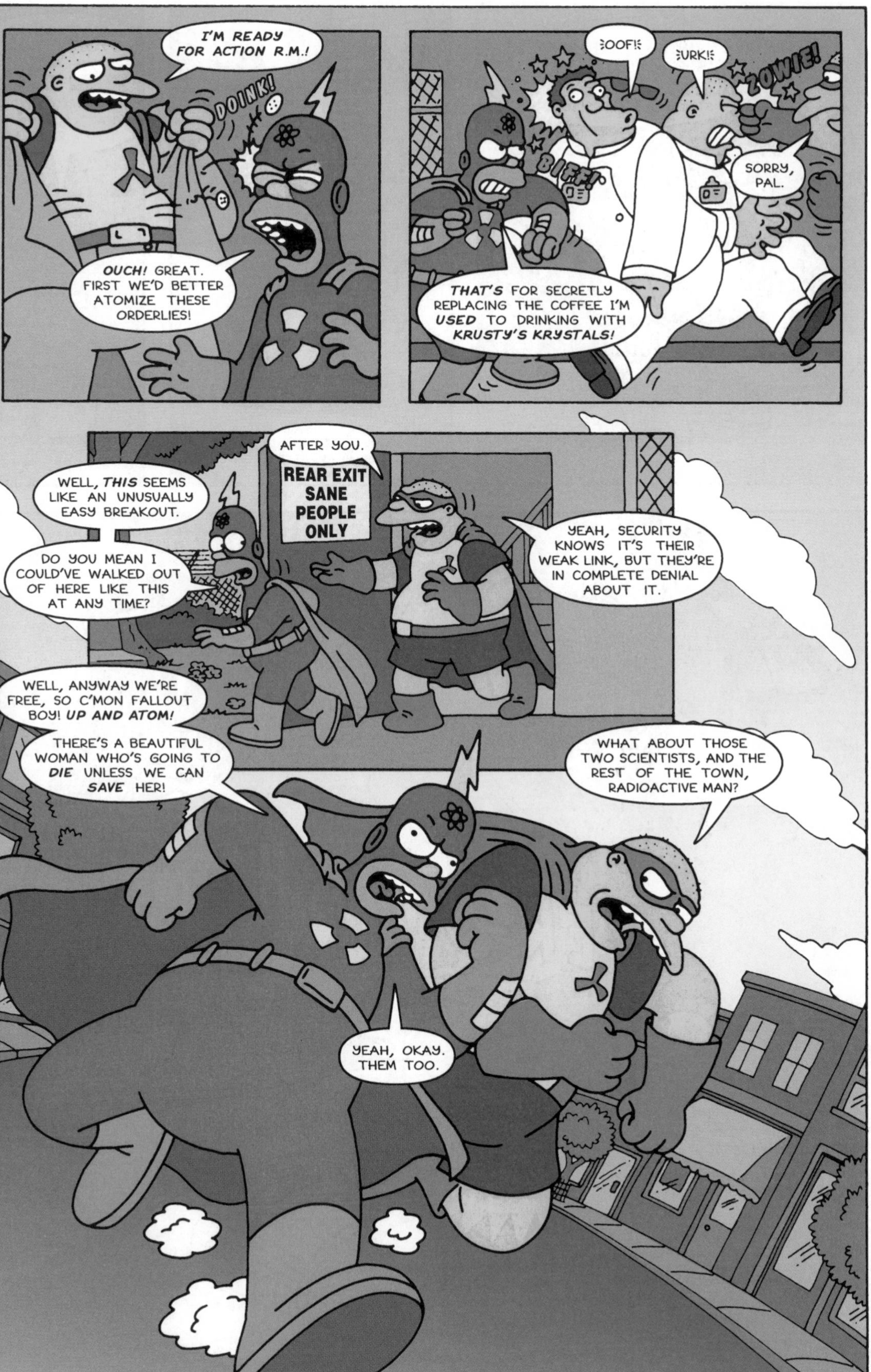

I'M READY FOR ACTION R.M.!
DOINK!
OUCH! GREAT. FIRST WE'D BETTER ATOMIZE THESE ORDERLIES!
OOF!
URK!
ZOWIE!
BIFF!
SORRY, PAL.
THAT'S FOR SECRETLY REPLACING THE COFFEE I'M USED TO DRINKING WITH KRUSTY'S KRYSTALS!
AFTER YOU.
REAR EXIT SANE PEOPLE ONLY
WELL, THIS SEEMS LIKE AN UNUSUALLY EASY BREAKOUT.
DO YOU MEAN I COULD'VE WALKED OUT OF HERE LIKE THIS AT ANY TIME?
YEAH, SECURITY KNOWS IT'S THEIR WEAK LINK, BUT THEY'RE IN COMPLETE DENIAL ABOUT IT.
WELL, ANYWAY WE'RE FREE, SO C'MON FALLOUT BOY! UP AND ATOM!
THERE'S A BEAUTIFUL WOMAN WHO'S GOING TO DIE UNLESS WE CAN SAVE HER!
WHAT ABOUT THOSE TWO SCIENTISTS, AND THE REST OF THE TOWN, RADIOACTIVE MAN?
YEAH, OKAY. THEM TOO.

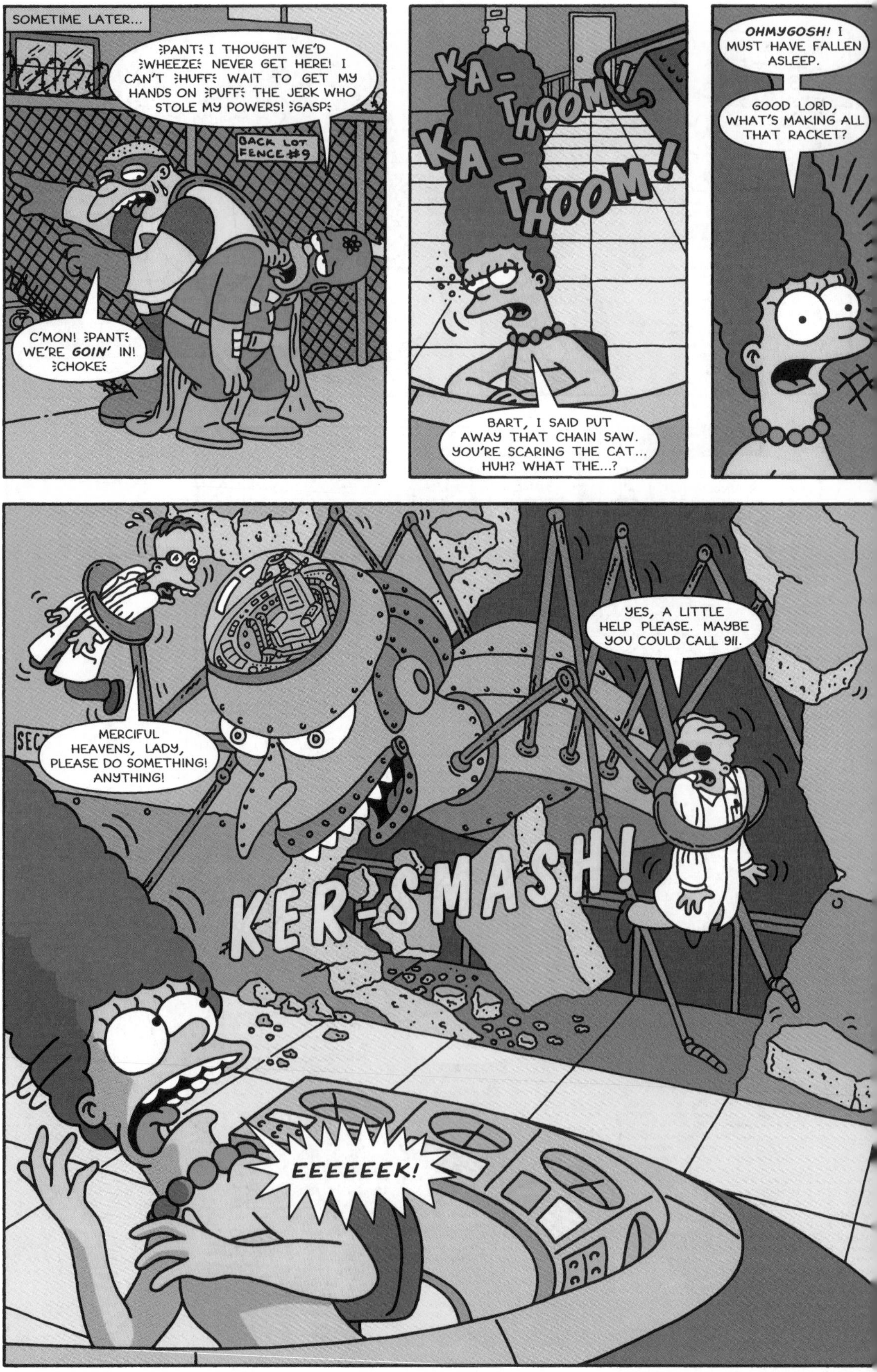
SOMETIME LATER...
⁝PANT⁝ I THOUGHT WE'D ⁝WHEEZE⁝ NEVER GET HERE! I CAN'T ⁝HUFF⁝ WAIT TO GET MY HANDS ON ⁝PUFF⁝ THE JERK WHO STOLE MY POWERS! ⁝GASP⁝
BACK LOT FENCE #9
C'MON! ⁝PANT⁝ WE'RE ***GOIN'*** IN! ⁝CHOKE⁝
KA-THOOM!!
KA-THOOM!
BART, I SAID PUT AWAY THAT CHAIN SAW. YOU'RE SCARING THE CAT... HUH? WHAT THE...?
OHMYGOSH! I MUST HAVE FALLEN ASLEEP.
GOOD LORD, WHAT'S MAKING ALL THAT RACKET?
MERCIFUL HEAVENS, LADY, PLEASE DO SOMETHING! ANYTHING!
YES, A LITTLE HELP PLEASE. MAYBE YOU COULD CALL 911.
KER-SMASH!
EEEEEEK!

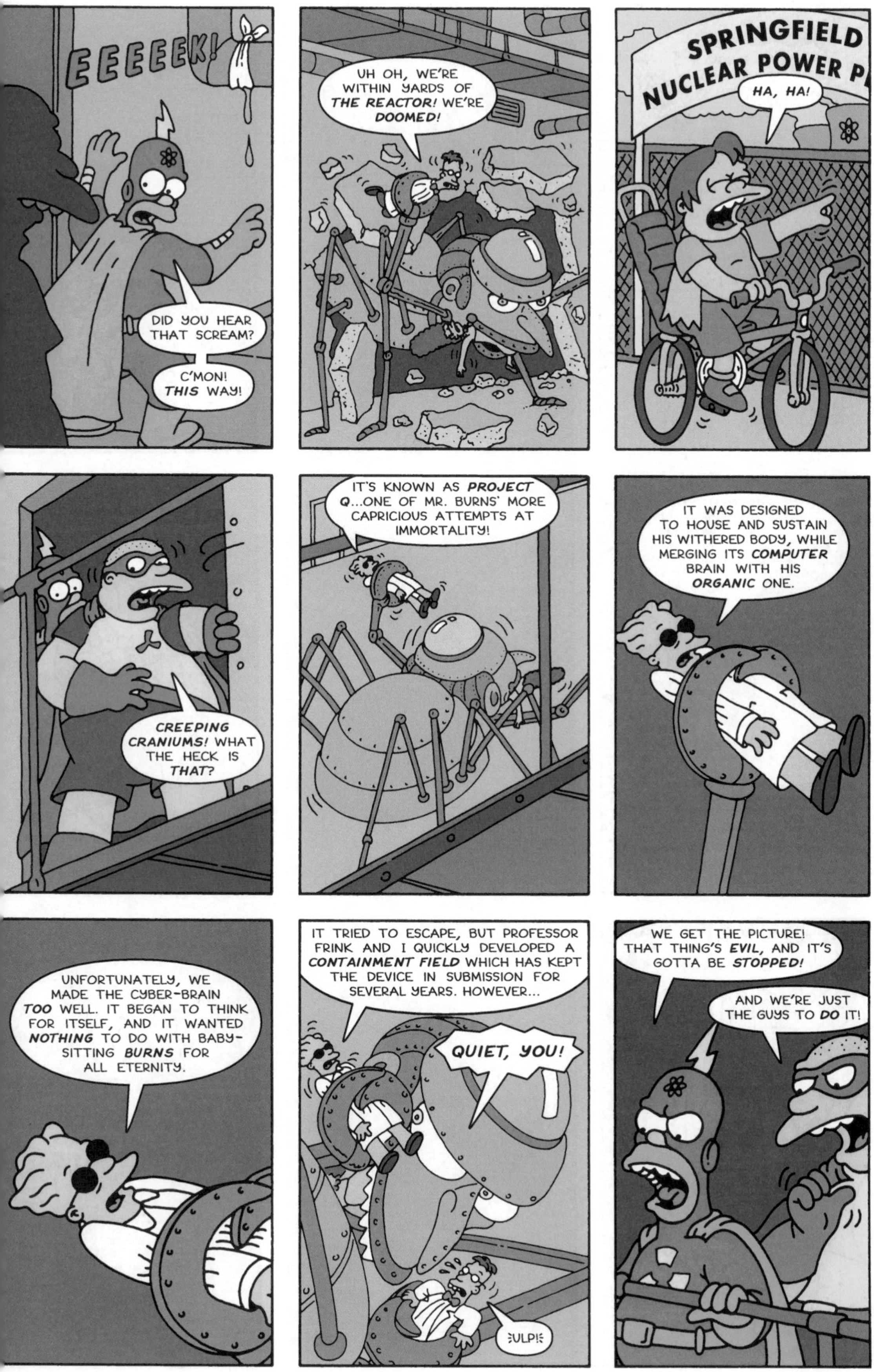
EEEEEK!
DID YOU HEAR THAT SCREAM?
C'MON! THIS WAY!
UH OH, WE'RE WITHIN YARDS OF THE REACTOR! WE'RE DOOMED!
SPRINGFIELD NUCLEAR POWER P
HA, HA!
CREEPING CRANIUMS! WHAT THE HECK IS THAT?
IT'S KNOWN AS PROJECT Q...ONE OF MR. BURNS' MORE CAPRICIOUS ATTEMPTS AT IMMORTALITY!
IT WAS DESIGNED TO HOUSE AND SUSTAIN HIS WITHERED BODY, WHILE MERGING ITS COMPUTER BRAIN WITH HIS ORGANIC ONE.
UNFORTUNATELY, WE MADE THE CYBER-BRAIN TOO WELL. IT BEGAN TO THINK FOR ITSELF, AND IT WANTED NOTHING TO DO WITH BABY-SITTING BURNS FOR ALL ETERNITY.
IT TRIED TO ESCAPE, BUT PROFESSOR FRINK AND I QUICKLY DEVELOPED A CONTAINMENT FIELD WHICH HAS KEPT THE DEVICE IN SUBMISSION FOR SEVERAL YEARS. HOWEVER...
QUIET, YOU!
ULP!
WE GET THE PICTURE! THAT THING'S EVIL, AND IT'S GOTTA BE STOPPED!
AND WE'RE JUST THE GUYS TO DO IT!

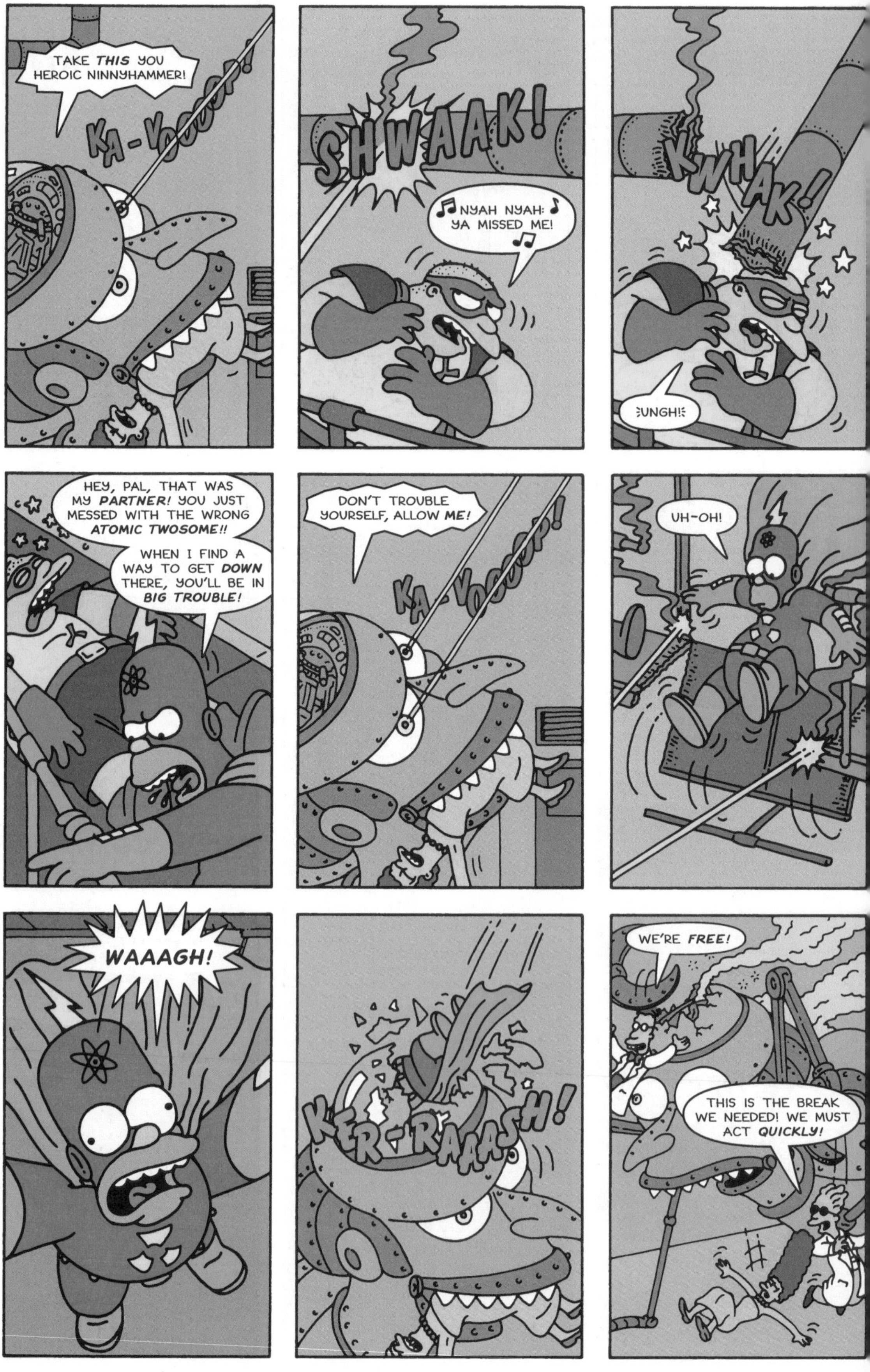
TAKE THIS YOU HEROIC NINNYHAMMER!
KA-VOOOOP!
SHWAAAK!
NYAH NYAH: YA MISSED ME!
KWHAK!
UNGH!
HEY, PAL, THAT WAS MY PARTNER! YOU JUST MESSED WITH THE WRONG ATOMIC TWOSOME!!
WHEN I FIND A WAY TO GET DOWN THERE, YOU'LL BE IN BIG TROUBLE!
DON'T TROUBLE YOURSELF, ALLOW ME!
KA-VOOOOP!
UH-OH!
WAAAGH!
KER-RAAASH!
WE'RE FREE!
THIS IS THE BREAK WE NEEDED! WE MUST ACT QUICKLY!

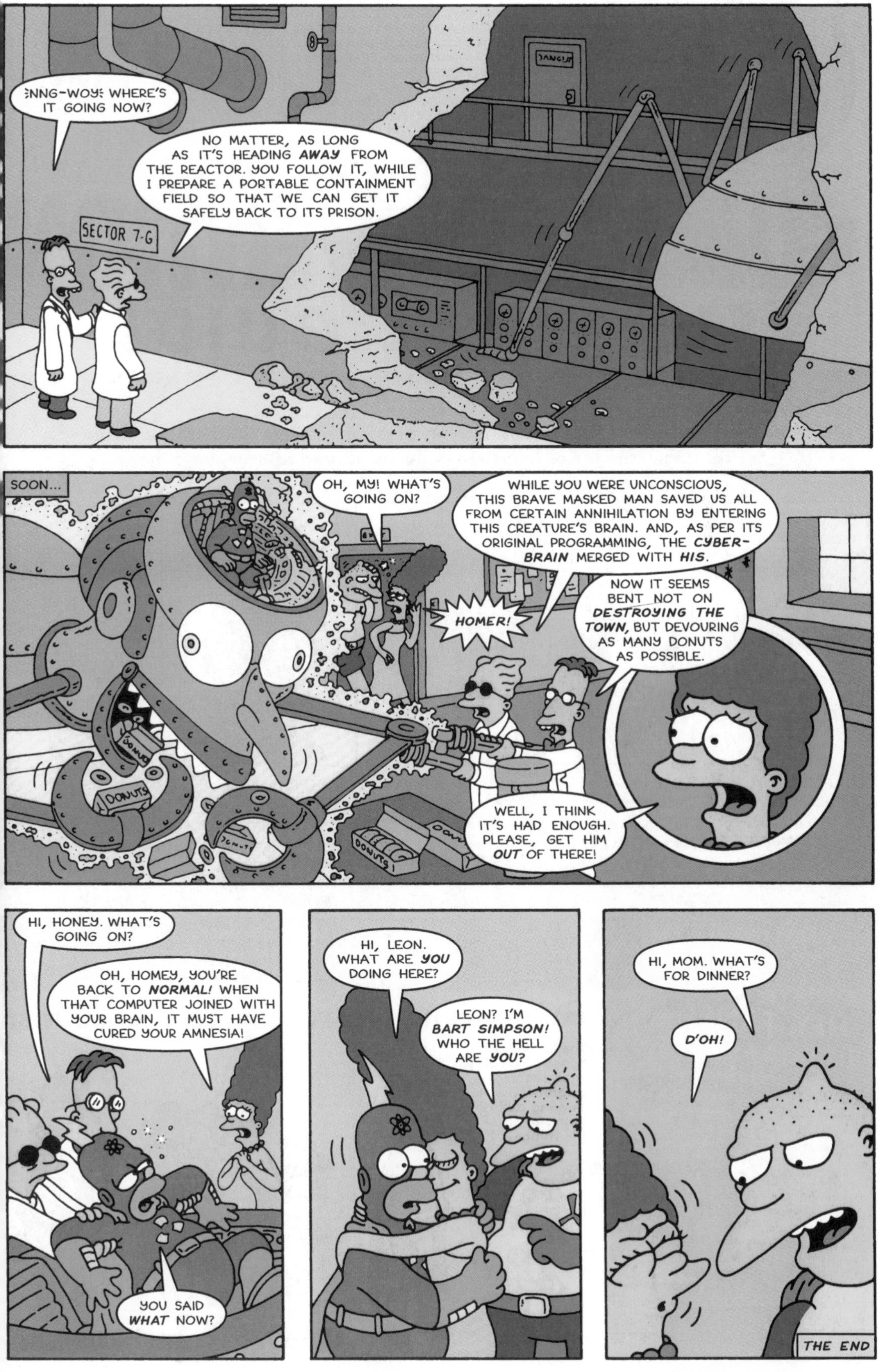

NNG-WOY! WHERE'S IT GOING NOW?
NO MATTER, AS LONG AS IT'S HEADING AWAY FROM THE REACTOR. YOU FOLLOW IT, WHILE I PREPARE A PORTABLE CONTAINMENT FIELD SO THAT WE CAN GET IT SAFELY BACK TO ITS PRISON.
SECTOR 7-G
DANGER
SOON...
OH, MY! WHAT'S GOING ON?
WHILE YOU WERE UNCONSCIOUS, THIS BRAVE MASKED MAN SAVED US ALL FROM CERTAIN ANNIHILATION BY ENTERING THIS CREATURE'S BRAIN. AND, AS PER ITS ORIGINAL PROGRAMMING, THE CYBER-BRAIN MERGED WITH HIS.
HOMER!
NOW IT SEEMS BENT NOT ON DESTROYING THE TOWN, BUT DEVOURING AS MANY DONUTS AS POSSIBLE.
DONUTS
WELL, I THINK IT'S HAD ENOUGH. PLEASE, GET HIM OUT OF THERE!
HI, HONEY. WHAT'S GOING ON?
OH, HOMEY, YOU'RE BACK TO NORMAL! WHEN THAT COMPUTER JOINED WITH YOUR BRAIN, IT MUST HAVE CURED YOUR AMNESIA!
YOU SAID WHAT NOW?
HI, LEON. WHAT ARE YOU DOING HERE?
LEON? I'M BART SIMPSON! WHO THE HELL ARE YOU?
HI, MOM. WHAT'S FOR DINNER?
D'OH!
THE END

YO, FELLOW COMICS FANS -- BART SIMPSON HERE! HAVE YOU NOTICED LATELY HOW COMIC BOOKS ARE FULL OF NOTHING BUT GRIM AND GRITTY STORIES ABOUT NEGATIVE ROLE-MODELS ENGAGED IN VIOLENT ANTI-SOCIAL BEHAVIOR, USUALLY RESULTING IN GRAPHIC PORTRAYALS OF DEATH AND/OR DISMEMBERMENT? PRETTY COOL, ISN'T IT? BUT AS MOST MEMBERS OF GENERATION X KNOW, COOL CAN BE VERY DEPRESSING. THEREFORE, I DECIDED IT WAS MY DUTY TO SHARE WITH YOU MY INSIGHTS ON HOW TO MAKE THIS HOBBY MORE FUN. MY FIRST TIP -- BUY LOTS OF BONGO COMICS! SECONDLY -- ATTEND YOUR LOCAL COMIC BOOK CONVENTION. BUT BEFORE YOU GO, BE SURE TO READ THIS --

THE OFFICIAL BONGO COMICS
COMIC CONVENTION
SURVIVAL GUIDE

THE MANY TYPES OF FANS

Meeting your fellow fans is half the fun of a convention. Study these profiles of common categories to better understand and interact with them.

THE ZOMBIE	THE GNARLY DUDE	THE SCI-FI FAN	THE ROLE-PLAYER	THE SPECULATOR
 CAPT. SQUID STINKS -- I JUST BUY IT TO KEEP MY COLLECTION COMPLETE.	WHOA! AWESOME CHAIN-MAIL BIKINI!	ACTUALLY, I PREFER THE TERM "S-F."	MY NAME IS LEWIS, BUT YOU CAN CALL ME "DUNGEON MASTER KELZOR."	READ COMICS?! I'M TOO BUSY MEMORIZING THE LATEST PRICE GUIDE UPDATE.

COLLECTION INCLUDES:
Recently completed set of **Millie the Model**.
WHAT'S ON HIS MIND:
Should I rent another apartment just to store my comics?

COLLECTION INCLUDES:
Dog-eared sword-and-sorcery comics, beer-stained undergrounds.
WHAT'S ON HIS MIND:
When Conan cuts some dude's head off with an axe, why don't they show more blood?

COLLECTION INCLUDES:
A Q-Tip once used by Leonard Nimoy.
WHAT'S ON HIS MIND:
Just what are the theoretical underpinnings of warp drive?

COLLECTION INCLUDES:
An overflowing shelf of fantasy paperbacks, **Dr. Strange** comics.
WHAT'S ON HIS MIND:
Does wearing this cloak make me look like an even bigger nerd than I really am?

COLLECTION INCLUDES:
Ten copies of the hot new die-cut, gold foil **Green Manta #1** - still poly-bagged.
WHAT'S ON HIS MIND:
Should I buy ten more copies?

HEY, FANS!

CHECK OUT THESE PROVOCATIVE PANEL TOPICS:

Lionel Hutz, Attorney at Law explains "How To Sue Your Mom For Throwing Out All Your Old Comics"

• Who's Stronger, Radioactive Man, Radiation Dude or the new amalgamated character, Radioactive Duck of the New Fantastic Sub-Atomic Free-Masons?

• Cover Enhancements: Now that they've been exposed as worthless, gimmicky marketing come-ons, should recycling be attempted, or should they just go out with the garbage? (free holo-foil comic to first 250 attendees!)

DON'T MISS THE EVER-POPULAR COSTUME CONTEST

Where fans get a chance to display their creativity, originality, and sewing ability, among other things.*

*Note to would-be entrants: skin-tight spandex probably won't look as good on you as it does on your favorite character.

PROS AND CONS:

WHILE YOU'RE AT THE CONVENTION, YOU'LL WANT TO MEET THE MANY PROFESSIONALS IN ATTENDANCE. HERE ARE SOME CLUES TO HELP YOU SPOT THEM.

THE ROOKIE
HAS DONE UNCREDITED BACKGROUND INKS ON THREE BOOKS YOU'VE NEVER HEARD OF

HEAD FILLED WITH DREAMS OF FAME, FORTUNE AND MUSCULAR GUYS IN SKINTIGHT SUITS

BUTTERFLIES IN STOMACH CAUSED BY PROSPECT OF MEETING HIS IDOLS

REAMS OF DISORGANIZED SAMPLES BROUGHT IN HOPES OF FINDING WORK

CALLUSES CAUSED BY PRACTICING SIGNING HIS NAME IN CASE SOMEONE ASKS FOR HIS AUTOGRAPH

THE OLD PRO
HAS MET 2,361 CONSECUTIVE DEADLINES

HEAD FILLED WITH RESENTMENT OVER INFLATED EARNINGS OF TODAY'S STARS

HEART WARMED BY MEMORIES OF "THE GOOD OLD DAYS"

PAGES OF ORIGINAL ART, WON AFTER YEARS OF BITTER STRUGGLE WITH PUBLISHER

ULCER CAUSED BY 2,361 CONSECUTIVE DEADLINES

THE STAR
HIS METEORIC RISE HAS AMAZED US ALL

PRETENDING TO HIDE BEHIND EXPENSIVE SUNGLASSES, BUT WILL BE HURT IF YOU DON'T RECOGNIZE HIM

OFFICIAL LICENSED EARRING

OFFICIAL LICENSED T-SHIRT

OFFICIAL LICENSED UNDERWEAR

THIS MONTH'S ROYALTIES

THE STAR'S ENTOURAGE (NOT SHOWN):
- MANAGER
- INVESTMENT ADVISER
- BODYGUARDS
- PERSONAL TRAINER
- PUBLICIST
- DRIVER
- FOOD TASTER
- THE GUYS WHO ACTUALLY DO THE WRITING AND DRAWING NOW THAT THE STAR NO LONGER HAS TIME IN HIS BUSY SCHEDULE

DO YOU KNOW THE 4 BASIC CONVENTION FOOD GROUPS? CHIPS • COLA • FRENCH FRIES • PIZZA **BE SURE TO GET AT LEAST TWO SERVINGS FROM EACH GROUP DAILY**

SO YOU WANT TO BE A CARTOONIST?

Many would-be artists bring samples of their work to conventions with the hopes of getting a valuable critique from one of the attending pros. Unfortunately, these seasoned veterans often speak in industry jargon, making their comments hard to understand. In hopes of clarifying this situation, we present translations of some commonly used phrases.

WHEN HE SAYS: **HE MEANS:**

YOU NEED TO WORK ON YOUR STORYTELLING. — HOW LONG TILL WE BREAK FOR LUNCH?

PAY ATTENTION TO THE SPOTTING OF BLACKS. — WHERE'S THE MEN'S ROOM?

YOU'VE JUMPED THE LINE AND VIOLATED THE 180 DEGREE RULE. — WHEN IS THE DISTRIBUTOR'S COCKTAIL PARTY?

INTERESTING ANATOMY. — CHECK THE BABE IN THE VAMPIRELLA COSTUME!

DON'T FORGET ABOUT
SHOPPING!

This useful economic model can help you judge the moment you'll get the best bargain.

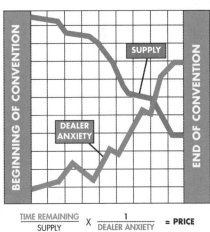

SUPPLY

DEALER ANXIETY

BEGINNING OF CONVENTION

END OF CONVENTION

$$\frac{\text{TIME REMAINING}}{\text{SUPPLY}} \times \frac{1}{\text{DEALER ANXIETY}} = \text{PRICE}$$

WARNING TO FEMALE FANS!

MALE CONVENTION ATTENDEES OUTNUMBER FEMALES BY APPROXIMATELY 99 TO 1. MOST ARE SINGLE, ADOLESCENT AND DEVOID OF SOCIAL SKILLS. YOU MAY WISH TO LEARN THE LOCATIONS OF THE NEAREST EMERGENCY EXIT.

CONVENTION PREPARATION CHECKLIST
REMEMBER THESE ESSENTIALS:

- ☐ WANT LIST
- ☐ CASH
- ☐ CHECKS
- ☐ CREDIT CARDS
- ☐ AUTOGRAPH BOOK
- ☐ TAKE SHOWER!!!

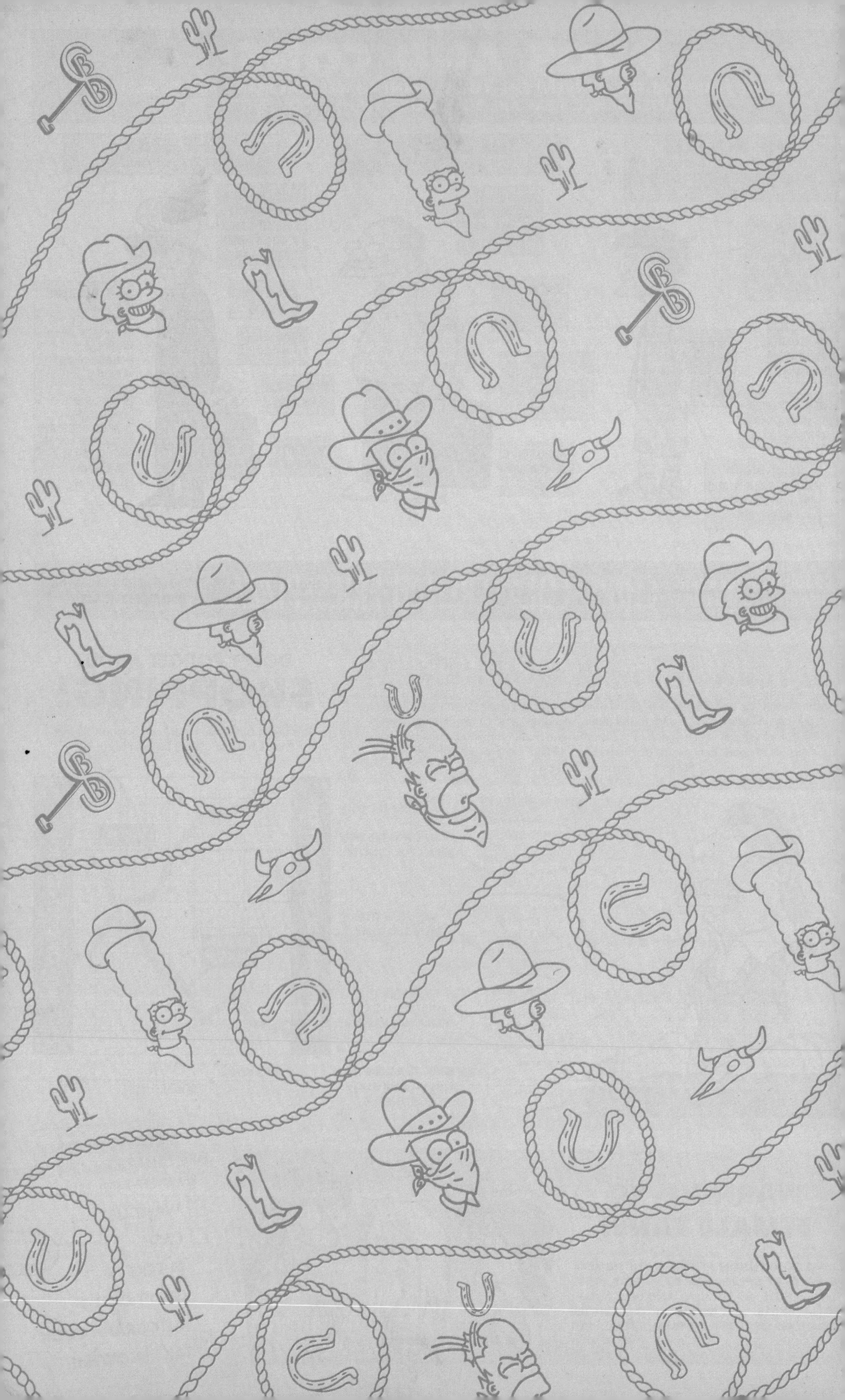